Nuggets of Truth

When It's Your Time to Speak

Linton Thomas

DEDICATION

I dedicate this book to my mother, Pearl Coke, and beloved children, Linton Mark Anthony Thomas and Abigail Renee Thomas, who have been precious blessings from God to me and my spouse, Michelle.

ACKNOWLEDGEMENTS

This book is the product of countless hours of hard work, dedication, and support from so many people who have been instrumental in my life and journey.

First and foremost, I want to express my most profound appreciation to my mother, Pearl Coke, the matriarch of our family. You have been the rock of our family, and your unwavering support and love have been a constant source of strength and inspiration to me.

I extend my heartfelt thanks to the United Brethren denomination for your unwavering support and encouragement throughout my ministry journey. I want to express my profound appreciation to the First Church of the United Brethren, Bronx, New York, members for their support, encouragement, and faithfulness. To my colleagues in ministry, thank you for your wisdom, guidance, and partnership in advancing the kingdom of God. Your friendship and fellowship have been a blessing beyond measure. I am proud to present this collection of dynamic and inspirational sermons from my tenure as a Senior Pastor. May they serve as a source of encouragement and edification to all who read them.

To my beloved wife, Michelle, and our two children, Abigail and Mark Anthony, I am grateful for your love, support, and patience during the long hours spent writing this book. Your unwavering support and encouragement have been a constant source of inspiration and motivation for me.

FOREWORD

Nuggets of Truth, a book of anointed sermons and speeches, aims to share spiritual insights and teachings, inspire and uplift readers, document a legacy, and provide a valuable resource for others. The book allows the author to share a unique perspective on spiritual and moral issues with a broader audience.

Nuggets of Truth will inspire, stimulate hope, and encourage readers to think critically. It hopes to extend the reach of preaching beyond the confines of a particular congregation or community and give readers the same sense of inspiration and uplift they would experience in live sermons. The book documents a legacy and will leave a lasting impact on future generations of preachers. It ensures that authentic teachings and insights are preserved and passed on to future generations, and it will continue to inspire and guide those who seek after God.

Nuggets of Truth is a compendium for speakers, preachers, teachers, and scholars seeking inspiration, guidance, or insight on a particular topic or theme. It delves into the depths of life's purpose and boundless possibilities. It offers a wealth of resources to extract and employ in crafting additional sermons and speeches, nurturing the growth of spiritual and intellectual endeavors.

Table of Content

Preface

Some ponder the effectiveness of preaching, while others bear witness to its profound ability to revolutionize lives. The inundation of the pulpit with unqualified preachers has nearly suffocated homiletics, the noble art and scientific discipline of preaching. Doubts arise regarding whether a converted, consecrated, and divinely appointed individual, molded in the very likeness of God, possesses the power to impart transformative change upon their surroundings. From a biblical perspective, this current epoch hurtles towards its ultimate purpose, the culmination of time itself. We have traversed numerous junctures, yet there lie unparalleled apocalyptic occurrences yet to unfold. Thus, the sacred emissaries of God bear the weighty responsibility of delivering his sacred word to the nations, skillfully deciphering and "redeeming" the signs of the times!

Hermeneutics and homiletics are two related disciplines that play vital roles in preaching. Once a hermeneutical groundwork is established, homiletics, the art, and science of preaching, come into play. Homiletics builds upon the insights gained through hermeneutics and focuses on effectively communicating the interpreted biblical truths to the audience. It encompasses the skills, methods, and principles of sermon construction, delivery, and engagement with listeners. Symbiotically, the relationship between hermeneutics and homiletics is the intellectual foundation that informs and shapes preaching content. Homiletics provides practical tools and techniques to communicate the interpreted message effectively.

Christianity must adopt new forms and styles of communicating the Gospel without violating the authenticity of the word of God. Becoming fishers of men in the 21st century requires adaptability, empathy, and a deep understanding of the ever-changing cultural and social dynamics. But most importantly, the world yearns for Christians the be authentic witnesses. Living out one's faith with sincerity and integrity can be a powerful example to others, and the positive impact of our beliefs can attract and inspire those around us. Our lives are our best sermons.

The 21st Century is chaotic; it needs people who speak peace and tranquility. Environmental, climatic, and spiritual darkness was apparent in Genesis. Still, God brought order to the earth through the power of the spoken word: "And God said, "Let there be light," and there was light" (Gen 1:3). In a world shrouded in darkness, the creative power of God's spoken words emerges triumphant. Today, as the echoes of the God of Genesis resound, we are entrusted with the sacred role of being His divine messengers and oracles.

Verbal Abuse Masked as Preaching

Preaching transcends manipulation and verbal abuse. Its essence lies in inviting people to God out of genuine love and embracing the transformative Good News of Salvation rather than instilling fear of damnation. However, not all that claims to be preaching is inherently beneficial. Exemplary preaching arises from cultivated expertise, skillfully presenting knowledge suited to the audience. Even impromptu or unrehearsed preaching draws upon the preacher's prior knowledge, preparation, and the inspiration of the Holy Spirit. An emblematic instance is Dr. Martin Luther King Jr.'s "I Have a Dream" speech delivered on August 28, 1963, during the March on Washington for Jobs and Freedom. It was not a spontaneous act but a meticulously prepared masterpiece.

Some preachers have learned to speak for an hour without saying anything significant. Ignorance, irritability, and inefficacy are not admirable principles of preaching. Have you ever been bored to death through a preacher's endless repetitions, circumlocutions, or garrulous rantings? I am a witness! But no one goes to church to be bored to death.

A preacher of the 21st Century must be succinct, sharp, and sanctified on the one hand and radical on the other. People often forget that some of the most prominent messengers of the Bible were unconventional radicals. The prophet Isaiah walked half-naked to message Egyptians and Ethiopians that their doom was impending, but Jeremiah was a friend of kings. He was educated, polished, and respectful. It is true that the radically of the prophet or preacher is proportional to his distance from the aristocracy.

Toxic Preaching and Toxic Theology

When a preacher has received a particular message from God, he should arrange it so his audience can receive it. A master chef who knows the importance of taste and presentation, a preacher should know how to prepare and present his message to his audience in a palatable way. A ranter might know how to prepare a sermon, but he might present it with monotony, violence, bombast, or abuse, defeating its purpose. Are you a preacher or a ranter? If preachers were accountable to the courts, many could be criminally charged with verbal abuse. Toxic, offensive preaching has many features. It could be passive or raucous, guttural or incoherent, appealing yet judgmental, eloquent or bitter, yet it always ends with pointing the finger. It is preaching from the perspective of the second person. Good preaching employs the third person, embracing people and calling them to a relationship with Christ. To identify with the people, preaching employs the first person: I or we. Here the preacher can address an issue or theme in a nutshell, give a panoramic view, or be specific and direct. Like the third-person omniscient narrator, the preacher is a credible narrator of truth or phenomena; he can bring God's word in a particular situation and "declare thus says the Lord."

Toxic preaching is bad; toxic theology is worse. Do you notice how some preachers like to repeat their cacophony of ignorance? Some preachers have rejected exegesis, empirical science, and evidenced-based data to cling to falsehood and traditions without Scriptural basis. Toxic theology is the theology of the backbench that openly insults, corrects, or rebukes others without presenting to them the compassion of Christ. Toxic theology justifies the abuse of children, the subjugation of women, and the servitude of black people. Theology that supports and upholds systems of government, such as capitalism and colonialism, is rooted in ignorance. The "Old-Time Religion" is just that. The religion of our oppressors silences, subjugates, and sentences people to the thralldom of servitude. Every 21st preacher must stand in the order of the prophet Jeremiah who lived at the close of his age. Like Jeremiah, 21st-century preachers must preach to a society on the precipice of imminent judgment. Like ours, its religious, political, economic, and social leaders were corrupt, and the "times of the Gentiles" were at hand. Suppose our age is the final stage of history. In that case, we must follow Jeremiah's preaching models: speaking truth to power and rebuking a populace that worships the gods of idolatry, apostasy, and capitalism.

Speak now or forever; hold your peace! Speak confidently, courageously, concisely, circumspectly, constructively, cheerfully, convincingly, candidly, and speak with clarity. People babble constantly, but there are critical moments when silence is not an option. To remain silent is to lose an opportunity to make a difference for eternity. To open your mouth and speak at the right time and place is to be the voice of God. Some events call for a word, a phrase, a sentence, or a speech! Consider those moments, and do not allow them to pass; they will never return. Have you ever forgotten to say, "I love you," and you never could repeat it because the person died unexpectedly?

Our words can heal or hurt. Hurting people hurt others. People can find the capacity to tell the truth in a tone that brings life, not death. So, when speaking for Christ, be ready to make history. Speak the truth in love! The truth will either set people free or free you from people who do not like the truth! Remember to speak confidently, courageously, concisely, circumspectively, constructively, cheerfully, convincingly, candidly, and clearly.

To speak confidently requires preparation. People will always have an adrenaline rush when they must speak. Adrenaline is a helpful boost; it triggers momentum. People must prepare well to have mastery of the material they wish to present. Writing down your thoughts logically and systematically, rephrasing sentences, and verbally presenting your speech to yourself first are not signs of weakness; they are excellent steps in preparing and delivering what you want to say.

Speak courageously. To speak courageously requires boldness. No audience, friendly or unfriendly, should intimidate you! When it is your time to speak, you are the person for the hour! It is your moment to shine! Seize the moment. Even if you do not believe what you are saying wholeheartedly, speak it confidently so that others will not know that you do not believe it. Be sincere. Once, I led an infamous debating team in the arguments in favor of capital punishment. None of my team members believed in capital punishment, but our arguments were forceful, and we won! To speak courageously, you must use tact and wit. You might have to stand in front of an audience of hypocrites whose support you need. Are you going to embarrass the hypocrites, or will you show through illustrations and the use of the Bible that they are the definition of hypocrisy? You do not have to tell a man that he is a hypocrite! Just define it; he will get the message!

To speak concisely is to be brief. Get up! Speak up and shut up! The most memorable speeches are short. They carry potent alliterations, repetition, and illustrations that capture people's imagination. Jesus's parables are short. The apostle Paul was a very learned man, but he was long-winded. This distinguished bilingual Pharisee, a member of the Jewish supreme court, the Sanhedrin, and author of over a third of the New Testament, preached until Eutychus fell through a window and died (Acts 20:9). Paul embraced the man, and resurrection ensued. How many people have died literally and figuratively during a sermon? Some preachers are verbally, mentally, and psychologically abusive! The people who are supposed to be the bearers of light and life can bring darkness and death! "Death and life are in the power of the tongue, and those who love it will eat its fruit" (Pro. 18:21).

Preachers are powerful. Speak circumspectly that is, discreetly and prudently. Words are not meant to be thrown around haphazardly. We must weigh our words. We must choose our words wisely. Remember, there are a few things that, once released; cannot return: "Four things come not back: the spoken word, the sped arrow, the past life, and the neglected opportunity."— Aiki Flinthart, The Yu Dragon

So, like Jeremiah the prophet, speak constructively. Your words are creative instruments. Construct lives with your words. Speak cheerfully! Smile. Speak convincingly; you are called to persuade people. Speak conscientiously and consider the other sides of an argument. People can use their phones to fact-check you as you are speaking! Speak candidly—truth matters. Speak with clarity "because he taught as one who had authority, and not as their teachers of the law" (Matt. 7:29). Do not speak contemptuously, circuitously, carelessly, critically, or calumniously.

The contemptuous preacher shows respect for his audience. It is easier to catch flies with honey than with vinegar! The circuitous preacher must consider one's attention span. He should stand up, speak up, and sit down! Monotony kills. Please do not send your audience to sleep; they might never wake up! If the sermon is cryptic, who will understand it? Be clear, and repeat your points for emphasis. People want to know what you are saying. Avoid the calumnious, slanderous sermon. People's businesses or weaknesses are no fodder for the speaker to exploit. But "Preach the word; be prepared in and out of season; correct, rebuke and encourage—with great patience and careful instruction" (2 Tim.4:2).

Don't Imitate another Person

Preachers come in many shapes, sizes, and genders. Their backgrounds and life experiences often shape them. The prophet Isaiah was a preacher to the Jewish Court and government. He spoke in the lingua franca of his day and knew how to present the word of God to the aristocracy without compromise. Amos was a shepherd, herdsman, and farmer shaped by the wilderness of Tekoa. He was not a "professional" prophet or speaker, but he presented God's words in a series of oracles and down-to-earth methods that were easily understood. Paul was a bi-lingual Pharisee, a former Jewish Supreme Court of Appeals (Sanhedrin) member, and an educator par excellence. God used him to write over one-third of the New Testament.

Considering how God used the Apostle Paul, one can argue that a seminary education is good, but one does not have to attend a seminar to be a good preacher. I have benefited from my seminary experience, but God used me to preach long before that experience. Nonetheless, preachers and those who wish to preach should seek to hone, improve, or perfect their skills. Sometimes a pastor may ask a church member to preach a sermon. This might be a mark of honor, but this honor could amount to disaster unless that individual is prepared. I have seen first-time preachers palpitating, breathing erratically, and fainting! I have seen others with temporary amnesia, dementia, and nervousness in the pulpit. Do we allow untrained people to perform surgery? No. Yet, we ask untrained and unprepared Christians to preach God's authoritative, infallible, and inerrant word. One of my attorney friends told me how he lost his grandmother. She was the oldest member of her congregation, and as such, her pastor asked her to prepare and deliver a sermon to the young people of their congregation. She died a few hours before she was to speak that Sunday night. From all accounts, this aged woman was thrilled with the honor of being asked to preach but overwhelmed by the fear of making a fool of herself. Was this pastor responsible for the death of his member?

Character Matters

The preacher is assumed to be a person of good character. If he is known otherwise, his character diminishes his message. Congregants assume that the preacher lives a Godly life. He is a sinner saved by the grace of God, but he keeps himself from the practice and patterns of sin. He must be known as a mighty man of spiritual courage, not a wimp or a pimp. Too often, preachers are known for their spirituality in public life and their decadence in their private lives. Despite constant temptations, a preacher must find God's presence, understand God's mind, and present the word of God to the people. Preaching is an essential aspect of ministry, but it is not the only thing that matters. A preacher should be fiscally responsible and honest in the administration of the resources of his congregation. The preacher should be accountable to someone.

Sermon Types

Sermons are speeches delivered during religious services, and they can take many different forms depending on the purpose of the sermon and the intended audience.

Expository sermons center around a specific passage or text in religious scriptures, such as the Bible. The preacher's approach involves analyzing the chosen text, delving into its significance and context, and extracting valuable lessons or applications for the audience. On the other hand, topical sermons concentrate on a particular subject or theme, such as love, forgiveness, or salvation. In such sermons, the preacher often draws upon a range of scriptural passages and additional sources to thoroughly explore the chosen topic, providing comprehensive guidance and advice to the audience.

Narrative sermons serve to illustrate specific points or moral lessons by utilizing stories and examples. The preacher may draw upon parables or other narrative accounts from religious texts and incorporate real-life examples, all aimed at helping the audience comprehend and apply the intended lesson. On the other hand, persuasive sermons are designed to convince the audience of a particular viewpoint or inspire them to take action. These sermons may concentrate on social or political issues, encourage the audience to adopt specific lifestyles or embrace certain moral principles, to motivate and influence their beliefs and behaviors.

Evangelistic sermons enable preachers to spread the Gospel of Jesus Christ to people worldwide. These sermons are commonly employed in outreach initiatives and missionary endeavors, crafted to be persuasive and compelling to encourage individuals to embrace the faith. It is important to note that while there may be various types of sermons, they are not the source of inspiration; instead, the word of God holds that role.

Sermon Poem

Sermons are words woven in a powerful display.
S.E.R.M.O.N, an acronym profound,
Each letter, a gem, with truths unbound.

S stands for Salvation, the need of the soul,
A message of hope that our souls are restored.
It speaks of redemption, of grace divine,
Guiding us to the light, where love will shine.

E is for Engagement, a vital thread,
For Eutychus' tale we must not dread.
In lively discourse, the attention we seek,
Lest slumber befall and our spirit grows weak.

R resonates with Relevance, a key,
Addressing the needs of humanity.
The sermon must speak to our struggles and pain,
Offering solace and wisdom to regain.

M brings forth Motivation, a driving force,
Provoking us to change our course.
With earnest conviction, it stirs our souls,
Prompting the question, "What shall be our goals?"

O signifies Order, a structure so grand,
For clarity guides us to understand.
With logical flow, the message takes flight,
Enlightening minds, dispelling the night.

N represents Nurture, a tender embrace,
Where growth and transformation find their place.
The sermon should nourish our spirits and minds,
Fostering growth, love, and virtues that bind.

A sermon carries salvation, engagement, and relevance!
It motivates, inspires, and orders our steps,
It nurtures our souls, igniting fire.
Embrace its message, let its wisdom unfold,
And let your spirits soar, and its truth behold.

How to Preach a Good Sermon

When preparing a sermon, consider if it would engage
you as a listener. Aim to inspire and uplift, echoing the
words of Isaiah 52:7. Relate to your audience,
acknowledging their diverse levels of knowledge. Adjust

your tone accordingly, speaking appropriately to intellectuals or Sunday school children. Remember that you are a vessel for God's message, not a display of personal attire. Focus on capturing attention rather than ensuring a complete understanding. Keep the sermon concise, respecting the limited attention spans of many. Avoid excessive academic language that may alienate or impress only a few. Instead, use relatable illustrations to explain concepts. Keep the illustrations simple and straightforward, utilizing visuals if available. Cater to different learning styles and invite a public response to the sermon's message.

How to Preach a Bad Sermon

Start with one scripture, then quote a few more!
Toss in some scholars, then leave them feeling bored!
Use illustrations that no one understands!
Use abstruse concepts; leave them grasping to understand!

Throw in some pictures, not tied to your point!
Let your sermon meander, disjointed and aimless!
Preach for too long; they'll be checking their watches
Lecture academically, don't let your message take off!
Use humor excessively, be a clown and a jester!
Ramble on pointlessly. Let your message fester!
Finally, wrap up with a check for comprehension!
Leave them wondering what just happened.

Here is a recipe for disaster!
Follow these steps, and you'll become a sermon caster!
But if you want to preach a sermon, that's great!
Now, Speak to the heart, inspire, and captivate.

Get Started

The tools for a remarkable sermon include scriptural knowledge, hermeneutical skill, thorough preparation, clear objectives, relevance to the audience, engaging delivery, illustrative examples, practical application, authenticity, and reliance on prayer for spiritual guidance

Enhancing the quality of a sermon requires the skillful application of crucial tools. Firstly, a preacher must possess a strong foundation in scripture, understanding its context, themes, and theological insights. Deep engagement with the text enables a faithful interpretation. Hermeneutics, the skill of biblical interpretation, is essential for uncovering the intended meaning and ensuring a relevant presentation. Diligent preparation, including prayerful study and reflection, provides the groundwork for a powerful sermon. Establishing a clear objective guides its development and delivery. Connecting the biblical message to the audience's lives enhances its relevance and applicability.

A sermon or speech must be engaging, incorporate relevant illustrations and stories, and encourage practical application to facilitate understanding and engagement. Authenticity connects with the audience, while prayer invites the guidance and empowerment of the Holy Spirit, ensuring a message that touches hearts profoundly.

Chapter One: Preface
Fanning the Flame

"Fanning the flame" means to put oxygen into a fire. There are dark, cold spots in Christendom today; therefore, preachers who are some of the loudest voices on earth must echo the Gospel with constancy and conviction; God's power is to bring salvation. The fire of the Holy Spirit is in the church, but it has been made dormant. A lack of consecration and a preoccupation with politics and capitalism stifle God's fire in the church. Until God releases an unparalleled outpouring of his Spirit in the telos or end of the age, we must continue to pour oxygen or life-giving messages into a world that's getting hopeless and desperate.

Rampant religious deceptions have led many to question their faith. Chief amongst those deceptions is the historicity of Jesus. A plethora of biblical and non-biblical data shows that Jesus Christ was not an English-speaking patriotic European who was passive to political aggression and condemned sinners. Instead, he was a Jewish Middle Eastern man of color who befriended the most vulnerable of society. He liberated the oppressed, spoke truth to power, lived a non-violent life, became the victim of political and religious zealots, and died to redeem humanity of its iniquity. Truthfully, if some Europeans were to meet Jesus in the flesh, they would not like him! They would seek to enslave or kill him!

Jesus was a radical, and he changed the status quo. Preachers should differentiate the colonizers' view of Jesus from the historical Jesus. The historical Christ was not tied to any country or political party. For over five centuries, Jesus has been whitewashed to foster the lie of white supremacy, but the truth is he loved everyone – the aged, children, the rich and poor, the outcast, and the blessed. Heaven is a multi-racial concept; it will be the abode of people of all races.

Jesus lived a simple yet powerful life as a healer, exorcist, and miracle worker. Most of all, he was the prince of peace. Christians who espouse violence against others in the name of Jesus do not have a relationship with the historical Jesus. Jesus is not a white man, and the concept of whiteness did not exist when he was here on earth. And he would not support the oppression, suppression, or genocide of one race by another. White supremacy is an insult to the concept of the image of God in all people.

To fan the flame of the Gospel, preachers must preach the truth. People love Jesus, but they hate the baggage of religion. They want to serve God without extrabiblical trappings that have no connection to their faith.

Like the prophets of the Bible, they must address present realities while presenting God's plan. Now is the time to preach "The Full Gospel.

Chapter One: Sermon 1-25

Sermon #1: The Imprimatur of Love

Love is written, spoken, and shared in every language, but its definition and contours are elusive. What is love? It is not easily defined, categorized, or explained. The Bible is definitive and states, "God is love." God's love is unconditional, yet some feel that it is not. In his famous song, "The Love of God," Frederick Lehman writes:

Could we, with ink the ocean fill,
And were the skies of parchment made.
Were every stalk on earth a quill,
And everyone a scribe by trade.
To write the love of God above,
Would drain the ocean dry.
Nor could the scroll contain the whole,
Though stretched from sky to sky.

First, there is Agape Love! The Greek word Agape love refers to unconditional love, and God's love for humanity despite its sins and shortcoming is a primary example. In the context of intimacy, it is love that is nonjudgmental. It is not showing kindness to someone for a reason or a season. It's love that is permanent and lasting. People often do this because of performance, beauty, ethnicity, family, relationship, or nationality. However, unconditional love is love despite all conditions. Agape love is what we need to destroy racism, sexism, ableism, and capitalism. A parent does not love a child only when he is right or does well. A child must be loved even when he is wrong! Love loves humanity even when we are in a mess.

Second, there is Philia! The Greek word philia refers to friendly love. It is the word from which we get philanthropy, the demonstration of goodwill and kindness to all humanity. We love Philadelphia. It's the city of brotherly love. And the Bible urges us to "let brotherly love continue" (Heb. 13:1). Christian nationalism, a pseudo-Christian doctrine that emphasizes one nation above all others and promotes one race above others, insults Christianity. Christian nationalism does not embody philia. It does not advocate love for all humanity. All philanthropists carry the DNA of philia. Let it continue from nation to nation, coast to coast, person to person! The world needs brotherly love. If a man or woman faints, philia should drive those around him to call for an ambulance. It's the least they can do to show their humanity.

Third, there is Storge! Although this type of love is not mentioned explicitly in the Bible, it is a Greek culture and literature feature. It is familial love or love for family. Sometimes blood is "thicker than water," and sometimes, blood is less than water. We should love our families and care for those under our preview without seeking repayment or acknowledgment. When storge is abused, incest ensues. Like prostitution, incest has been a blight on many families. Incest is a shameful, illegal scourge that has distorted the concept of love.

Fourth there is Eros! Eros is sexual, passionate, intimate love. The context of marriage is the best place for eros. Nothing is wrong with sex, and it is good and should be embraced and celebrated! But eros, sexual love comes from giving oneself to another, and it is reciprocal love where both people give themselves to each other. This type of love has proven benefits. It strengthens the immune system, helps the body fight sickness, induces sleep, lowers blood pressure, and fosters heart health. Psychologically, it calms the nerves and reduces stress. But eros was never meant to be abused or used maliciously.

Fifth, there is Unrequited Love! People cannot buy love. They will stay for the money, but their hearts are with others. Not everyone will love you the same way that you love them! Your love for someone may not be reciprocated. The person that you love may not want to love you! It's the reality of life. People must read the signs of unrequited love and learn to walk away, crawl, or run from abusive "love-like" situations. A mixed message is a message that one does not choose to be direct with you! That someone is indecisive, uninterested, or simply cold and callous. Read the signs. Like Romeo of Shakespearean fame, you must admit that your "Rosaline" has no interest in you, and it's time to find your Juliet, even if she throws you into an unimaginable ocean of emotion!

People do not have to love you back! Parents, pastors, and others who serve people know that sometimes the people who will hurt you the most are those for whom you have shared the most extraordinary love! Some people who ate Jesus' bread and fish and received healing from his ministry were among those who called for his crucifixion! After the Jews rejected him, the apostle Paul was sent to the Gentiles, but God had to deliver him from them too!

Sixth, there is Environmental Love! We should love the earth. It was specifically prepared for humanity. Not everyone can afford to go to another planet, even if it's habitable. And just in case we become confused, we should question the flora and fauna of the earth about our obligations to the planet:

> But ask the animals, and they will teach you,
> Or the birds in the sky, and they will tell you,
> Or speak to the earth, and it will teach you,
> Or let the fish in the sea inform you.
> Which of all these does not know
> That the hand of the LORD has done this?
> In his hand is the life of every creature,
> And the breath of all humanity. (Job 12:7-10)

We are stewards of the earth and are called to multiply, replenish, and subdue it! Additionally, Job admonished us to get an object lesson from the environment about the purpose of life. We are asked to question animals and birds and speak to the earth about the intent of God for his creation! People should not destroy the planet to hasten the coming apocalypse!

Climate change is not a hoax. It's a reality! Just ask farmers that have had to sell off their cows because they cannot find adequate water, look at the rising levels of the seas that threaten low-lying islands, or look at the melting of historic glaciers. Please speak to the earth; it's listening! The floating flotillas of garbage in the oceans cannot be a good thing! The Bible teaches that planet Earth will end, and a new heaven and new earth will emerge, but it does not teach us to destroy the planet. That's God's prerogative.

Seventh, there is Self-Care!
Don't be ashamed or cynical about loving yourself. It's not selfishness, and it's brilliant. Treat yourself the way you would like to treat others. Pamper yourself and take good care of yourself. One of my friends was so adept at caring for her grandmother that she forgot to care for herself, developed breast cancer, and died prematurely. Her grandmother lived her whole life, but my friend died young because she did not understand the imperative of self-care. We know our bodies are temporal and will die eventually, but we do not have to expedite our demise!

There is only one solution to empowered and weaponized hatred; it is love: "But he that hateth his brother is in darkness, and walketh in darkness, and knoweth not whither he goeth, because that darkness hath blinded his eyes." (1 John 2:11). Love of every kind is demonstrable. Show it! Don't walk in darkness!

References
Lehman, F. M. (1917). The Love of God

.

Sermon #2: Symbols of Love

First, Spending Time. A profound symbol of love is spending time with someone. To spend time with some is to show an explicit act of love. It is the most valued expression of it. Time is limited. Time is fleeting. Time is unstorable. Time is money. To spend time with someone is to value that person highly. There are many lonely people in the world. Some live in a crowd, but they are still lonely. How often do we visit our elders and give them the gift of time? One of the precursors of longevity is the ability to interact with others. Social isolation can lead to death! Loneliness can kill: "Social isolation and loneliness are widespread, with some countries reporting that up to one in three older people feel lonely. Much research shows that social isolation and loneliness seriously impact older people's physical and mental health, quality of life, and longevity. The effect of social isolation and loneliness on mortality is comparable to that of other well-established risk factors such as smoking, obesity, and physical inactivity" (WHO, 2022). With COVID-19, many feel like they are experiencing parallel pandemics of poverty, hatred, and a lack of love. Families and friends have experienced a separation hereto unknown to them. And one of the ways back to normalcy is to reconnect with families and friends. Healing from the psychological effects of a confluence of pandemics can begin with the gift of time. It takes time to build character, develop leadership, and execute a plan, but most importantly, it takes time to love.

Second, Showing Acts of Kindness. Gifts are graphic symbols of kindness. Verbalizing the phrase "I love you!" can be a positive, affirmative, and heart-warming experience for the speaker and recipient of the love. Some people wait a lifetime to hear such an affirmation from a parent, sibling, spouse, or friend. People cry when they hear those words, and some cry when they don't hear them! Loneliness and a lack of kindness have become mental health crises worldwide. But showing acts of kindness is more love than saying, "I love." The proof of love is in the pudding of kindness. Explicit gifts of food, shelter, care, and emotional support are profound examples of the expression of love. Mother Theresa's work in India, The Salvation Army, SOS villages, The Red Cross, and Global Giving are institutions that demonstrate practical love. They do not have to verbalize the phrase "I love you." They practice it.

Acts of kindness can be as simple as helping a physically or visually challenged person cross a busy street, returning a lost wallet, or writing a letter for an illiterate person. It requires minimal effort. One must go above and beyond the call of duty to assist someone. One must forgive a traitor, excuse a fault, or let go of a loss to help others to advance. Black people in America must rise above decades of institutionalized racism and forgive the descendants of enslavers to "emancipate themselves" to rise to another level of success. Forgiveness is an act of kindness. In the parable of the Prodigal Son, a father had to forgive his son even though he squandered his inheritance and returned to him financially, emotionally, mentally, and spiritually broken. Acts of kindness must emanate from all of us, especially our families. Sometimes, strangers are kinder to us than our immediate families.

Founded in 1997, The World Kindness Movement, a not-for-profit, non-religious, and non-political organization, seeks to spread acts of kindness internationally. Using innovation, infrastructure, and partnership, the organization finds profound ways to express love to help the hungry, sick, needy, and on the verge of death. It is the kind of work Jesus would do and the kind of work Christians are called to do.

Third, Serving. Serving someone is a symbol of your love for that person. To serve is to love. Acts of service to others are acts of love. Words are meaningless if matched with practical, explicit acts of charity. The most loving people in the world are those who serve humbly. Consider the love an educator, pastor, nurse, doctor, or helper gives after working for thirty or forty years! There are unsung heroes everywhere—every great leader of worth serves. Jesus was a servant of servants. Ghandi was a servant leader. When people do things for families or friends, they bring the love of Christ to them.

Some politicians are revered, and others are seen as messiahs. But many politicians and ruling class members do not serve; they take. If they wanted people to be educated, they would provide free education for them. If they wanted people to be healthy, they would implement laws to make healthcare free for all. If they wanted everyone to vote, they would make it easy. They would advocate for a living wage for workers if they wanted people to have an excellent living way. They won't allow people to pollute the world if they love it. People must speak about love through action. And as Marcus Aurelius once said: Perform every act in life as though it were your last."

Fourth, Speaking. Written words are good, and spoken words are better! The act of talking to some is a symbol of love. We are encouraged to "speak the truth in love." Verbal communication is a powerful tool for communicating care. If a man writes a poem and sends it to his lover, the recipient will be impressed with the effort, wisdom, and imagery conveyed, but if he stands next to her and recites it, she is moved by his intonations, inflections, and gestures. To speak is to give life to words. So, words can captivate, create, or deflate! A real sign of love is using words to illuminate, elevate, and elaborate. When someone is in desperation, he is fortunate to find someone to comfort, encourage, and edify him: "One who has unreliable friends soon comes to ruin, but there is a friend who sticks closer than a brother" (Pro. 18:24). Not only words can hurt, abuse, and destroy someone, but they can also build up others. The creative power of words can transform an impossible situation into a feat of great success. Motivational speakers use encouragement to inspire others to transcend their greatest dreams. There's nothing better than a word in season, for the right time, and at the right place.

How should people verbalize love? How can they express words that are full of meaning and value? Not everyone is articulate. Some can hardly put a few sentences together. The expression's essence is expressing love, syntax, and grammatical correctness. It is sincerity that counts. A verbose professor is equipped with all the oratory skills, but they cannot convey candor better than a man or woman who is truly in love or a parent who loves a child. So let love be spoken freely in every language and come "straight from the heart." Even the verbally challenged must find ways to express their feelings. People need to hear that they are loved, appreciated, and celebrated. I had the privilege to honor a distinguished deacon who had served for many decades in one of the churches I pastored in Jamaica. This man was a pillar in the local congregation and community but was never recognized or celebrated. We changed that and honored him.

Consequently, I think we added another ten years to his life. Go, tell someone that you love them. They need to hear it!

Positive words are powerful words, touching not just one's body but also his soul and spirit. People should learn positive and affirming words. It is too easy to be pessimistic. Teachers, parents, pastors, and influencers must understand the transforming power of their works. No longer can a parent or teacher call a young impressionable child "dumb," "loser," or a "mistake." Preachers must understand that "even sinners in the hands of an angry God" must hear the love of God, the message of repentance, and the call to reconciliation. Words of love expressed by anyone are a sign of love.

Fifth, Giving Attention. What does it mean to give attention to someone else? Giving someone your undivided attention is a subtle but substantial symbol of love. It is an act that gives space, priority, prominence, and pride of place to another. 21st-century people like to hear themselves, fend for themselves, and take care of themselves. They are often paid to give attention to others. To pay attention to someone without the motive of money is a sign of love. Some too many people are lonely and scared even when they are standing in a crowd. They only take some people and will give attention to others when taking a picture or video of someone's demise. They will make a video of a crime or accident, but they will not help. Ours is an age of indifference and apathy.

How many times have you been told to "pay attention?" People need us to listen to them! Have you ever seen a presenter become ballistic and verbally abusive when trying to make a point, and people ignore them? A promising sign of love is to give one's attention to another. The art of listening is a skill that must be restored. People like to talk, interrupt, speak over others, and answer questions that were not asked of them. Many parents regret not paying attention to their children's struggles and needs. If a child or senior citizen reports abuse, pay attention to it!

To give attention to someone is to love that person. Many older people live and die in nursing homes without the care and attention of their families. A strategic aspect of my pastoral ministry was nursing home visitations. The residents would wait with anticipation for our monthly visits. We dropped everything and gave attention to them through speech, reading, singing, and treating them as a family! Our yearly Christmas gifts we well received. And, if we did not carry enough skills, we would have to return to bless everyone again!

When people give attention to God, they spend time with him, read his word, and communicate with him. They put aside special times to worship or give worth to him in moments of thanksgiving, adoration, and acknowledgment. People should be encouraged and not forced or compelled to spend time with God. Everyone must consider if they have an eternal soul, and if so, why are we here? What is the purpose of their existence? And to whom do they show allegiance?

So, give attention to your studies, career, or endeavor, but most importantly, give attention to others. People matter, and life is invaluable. When we try to understand the needs and thoughts of others, we develop empathy. We can walk in the proverbial shoes of others and see their journey and conditions, and we become a source of solace and release.

Sixth, Touch. A loving, nonsexual touch can soothe, calm, or invigorate the body to release oxytocin, the "love hormone." Touching someone is a symbol and signal of love, which satisfies the need for physicality and connection. It is a therapeutic way to connect to the vulnerable - the elderly, visually challenged, and infants. Unwanted touch is deemed physical or sexual abuse, but touch that is legal, legitimate, and nonsexual is healing to the body. It conveys trust and safety. To hold someone's hand or embrace him fulfills a physical and emotional need. A baby needs the touch of its parents to foster physical bonding, security, and warmth. And the hands of a master masseur bring healing and rejuvenation.

We all want to be embraced, kissed, and touched. The Bible implores people to greet each other with a kiss and welcome to show love in the faith community. Jesus touched those who were sick, diseased, and destitute. Once, a woman with hypermenorrhea touched Jesus, and a miracle happened: she was cured! (Mark 5:21-24). Nurses are the "hands of God" because they bring healing through touch therapy. Michelangelo was right, "to touch is to give life." Even in an age of infectious diseases and physical and sexual bases, touch therapy is a need. Stephen Gaskin has said, "Touch is the first language we speak," but people will always need that language throughout their lives. The absence of physicality or relationship often signals death.

Seventh, Forgive. To forgive is to love. Forgiveness is a crucial symbol of love. Hatred is characteristic of every age. With the rise of racial tensions in America and the world, hatred has been monetarized. News outlets have become popular and lucrative due to their dissemination of hate. How can a daughter forgive her incestuous? How can the indigenous people of America forgive the white enslavers for the genocides they have committed amongst them? How can black people forgive America for slavery and systemic racism? Forgiveness is a challenging but necessary proposition, and Jesus knew its importance. By forgiving his accusers and those crucifying him, he has taught us a sacred lesson: forgiving rather than hating is better. Forgiveness is also the key to healing and deliverance. Forgiveness is not forgetting hurt, accepting evil, or compromising one's values. It is an act of self-healing.

Forgiveness is not cheap and requires genuine remorse, empathy, and honesty from those seeking it. While the seventy times seven model of forgiveness promotes empathy and understanding, it should not be used as an excuse for abuse. Turning the other cheek is about nonviolence, not allowing oneself to be repeatedly harmed. Unforgiveness hinders our forgiveness from God, darkens the heart, and hampers our prayers. The passage encourages us to consider the alternative of forgiveness. It highlights that the capacity to forgive demonstrates that we are children of the light, not under the dominion of Satan. Love is not limited to empty words but should be demonstrated through sincere and truthful actions.

What is your favorite symbol of love? Is it a tangible gift, such as flowers, or an intangible gift, such as forgiveness? Which symbol of love is the greatest? Is it spending time with someone or sending them "I love you" cards? Love is practical: "Let us not love with words or speech but with actions and in truth (1 John. 3:18). Love is truthful. A liar cannot love sincerely.

References

WHO. (n.d.). Social isolation and loneliness. Retrieved from https://www.who.int/teams/social-determinants-of-health/demographic-change-and-healthy-ageing/social-isolation-and-loneliness

Bing. (n.d.). Stephen Gaskin Quotes. Retrieved from https://www.bing.com/search?q=Stephen+Gaskin+Quotes&FORM=HDRSC1

Sermon #3: Ways to Accomplish Your Goals

To possess the land means to inherit what God has promised. The Israelites were to possess Canaan land, and Christians were to inherit heaven. However, en route to heaven, we must possess the kingdom he has destined for us. The text Genesis 15:18-20 suggests that possessing the "land "means accomplishing a goal.

First, people can possess the land of their dreams *prophetically.* To possess or inherit the land, people must understand its prophecies. Prophecy matters. To accomplish a goal requires understanding what God has declared concerning your situation. In this case, to Joshua, God said: "Arise, go over this Jordan, you and all these people, to the land which I am giving to them — the children of Israel. Every place that the sole of your foot will tread upon I have given you." (Jos. 1:3-4). God promised Israel a place that would become their permanent abode, but he also promised peace (Jos. 21:43-45). For example, if a house, career, spouse, or investment does not bring peace, it might not fall under God's purview for you! For "The blessing of the LORD enriches, and He adds no sorrow to it (Prov. 10:22). So, ask yourself, what is God's promise to me in any given situation?

Second, we can possess the land of our *dreams positionally. Christians must know their position in Christ.*

They are a member of the Joshua Generation, chosen to lead, serve, and show forth and enter your destiny: "But ye are a chosen generation, a royal priesthood, a holy nation, a peculiar people; that ye should shew forth the praises of him who hath called you out of darkness into his marvelous light (1Pet. 2:9).

Third, people can possess the land of their dreams *systematically*. Rome was not built in a day, so important things or significant accomplishments took time and effort. First, preparation or building capacity for growth must be established. Conquest is a timely business. Moses was prepared for leadership in Egypt and in the backside of the desert. The apostle Paul spent four years before his first missionary journey, and Jesus got his training and preparation in the wilderness. The journey to your promised land of dreams is not linear and is often a labyrinth. Timely efforts are required to achieve our goals. Every step is part of a system of progress to reach the goal. It is like the "Pilgrim's Progress" that charts the hazardous journey of the believer to a place of bliss.

Fourth, people can possess the land of their dreams *strategically.* People must understand their primal enemies, the flesh, the world, and the devil. Napoleon conquered the world but could not conquer himself. His pride precipitated his demise. The world that is an enemy of the believer is not the universe. It is the cosmos, a corrupt system of affairs. "Do not love the world or the things in the world. If anyone loves the world, the love of the Father is not in him. For all that is in the world -- the lust of the flesh, the lust of the eyes, and the pride of life -- is not of the Father but is of the world. And the world is passing away, and the lust of it, but he who does the will of God abides forever" (Rom 7:2, 1 John 2:15-17).

Fifth, people can possess the land of their dreams *militarily*. Through warfare, people can accomplish their goals in life. Understand the place and people for conquest. It is a place of blessing. Metaphorically, it flows with milk and honey. It is prosperous, but some enemies will resist you: "So I have come down to rescue them from the hand of the Egyptians and to bring them up out of that land into a good and spacious land, a land flowing with milk and honey—the home of the Canaanites, Hittites, Amorites, Perizzites, Hivites and Jebusites" (Ex. 3:8).

> Understand your phobias and be courageous. The fear of the unknown can be intimidating, the fear of enemies can be discouraging, and the fear of revolt among your people can be crippling. Steady persistence in adhering to a course of action, belief, or purpose is essential for success.

Sixth, people can possess the land of their dreams *comprehensively*. Sometimes discouragement, lack of interest, sickness, or procrastination cause people to stop pursuing their goals. People should complete their courses, degree, and certification. All the chapters of the book must be written. The Israelites became complacent, and "When Joshua was old and well advanced in years, the LORD said to him, 'You are very old, and there are still vast areas of land to be taken over (Jos. 13:1, NIV). Canaanites were still in the land! The job was incomplete!

Seventh, people can possess the land of their dreams *faithfully.* People must believe that they can faithfully execute the office, opportunity, or order placed on them. Backed by God's promises, presence, and provisions, a Christian can find the courage to do exploits and accomplish his purpose in life. As was a command of Joshua: "Be strong and very courageous. Be careful to obey all the law my servant Moses gave you; do not turn from it to the right or the left so that you may be successful wherever you go. Keep this Book of the Law always on your lips; meditate on it day and night so that you may be careful to do everything written in it. Then you will be prosperous. Have I not commanded you? Be strong and courageous. Do not be afraid; do not be discouraged, for the Lord your God will be with you wherever you go" (Joshua 1:7-9, NIV).

To accomplish your goals in life is to "possess the land." The experience of the Israelites shows that people can achieve their goals prophetically, positionally, systematically, systematically, strategically, militarily, comprehensively, and faithfully. What are you waiting for?

Sermon #4: Natures of the Enemy

Joshua said, "Hereby you shall know that the living God is among you and that he will without fail drive the Canaanites, and the Hittites, and the Hivites, and the Perizzites, and the Girgashites, and the Amorites, and the Jebusites out from before you (Josh 3:10).

Moses was a great and exemplary leader. He was meek and obedient. Through him, God delivered the people of Israel from Egyptian bondage. After his death, his assistant was called by God to lead Israel into the Promised Land. But the land was occupied by seven nations. Moses wrote, "When the Lord your God brings you into the land you are entering to possess and drives out before you many nations— the Hittites, Girgashites, Amorites, Canaanites, Perizzites, Hivites and Jebusites, seven nations larger and stronger than you " (Deut. 7:1). Israel was being led into a physical Promised Land. Still, the Christian is being led into a spiritual Promised Land. These nations are historical as well as symbolic. What do they represent? How do they speak to the Christian experience?

Canaanites. The name means zealots or fanatics. They represented the extreme of life: intellectual as seen in their arts, sciences, and religions. They had a fertility cult in which EL was the chief God, and El is noted for murdering his father, son, and daughter. Shulman was their God of health, and Koshar was their God of arts and crafts. This polytheistic society was very immoral with temple prostitution—Anat, Astarte, Asherah: feminine goddesses of sex and war. This was an advanced society that was about to decay. God had given the command to drive them out. To Christians, they represent secular humanism, that is, the idea that we can come to enlightenment without God; we do not need God to advance society. Their culture exemplifies those whose possessions become their "God."

Hittites – The name represents aggression. This was an aggressive tribe that had its kings. They were known for their giants, chariots, horses, and covetousness. "They were big, tough, and scary." The fear and dread of them were with all other nations. When the Syrian army attacked Jerusalem, they fled when "the Lord caused the Syrian to hear the sounds of chariots and horses and a great army, so that they said to one another, 'Look, the king of Israel has hired the Hittite and Egyptian kings to attack us!'" 2 Kings 7:6. They held to the equality of women and men; enacted enlightened laws; had brilliant military strategies; and are reported to be the first to ride on horsebacks. The Hittites, like the Canaanites, spoke beyond themselves. The Hittites represent the giants Christians will face in their quest for the spiritual Promised Land. Some of those giants include doubt, fear, complacency, pride, and indiscipline. Hittites are tough problematic sins. They must be driven out and conquered to possess the land. Joshua conquered the

Hittites. You can conquer your Hittites too (Jos 9:1,2; 10; 11; 12; 24:11).

Hivites. Unlike the Hittites, the Hivites were impulsive, unwarlike, and warmhearted. The Gibeonites were Hevites. Yet, history shows that they were deceitful and false. Some of our enemies are our warmhearted friends who show us a little love, but later, they turn around and deceive us. These are our "friend-enemies." Yet Esau intermarries with them (Gen 26:34; 36:2).

Perizzites. The name means "'to drag away violently." They are like hawks that look for unsuspecting chickens. They dwelt in cities without walls. They were doomed to destruction, Deut. 20:17. But they are not all destroyed; Israelites intermarry with them: Jud 3:5-7; Ezr 9:1,2. They represent Satan himself, anyone, or anything that pulls us away from God. They are Perizzites. Israel intermarries with them. How can one put a snake in his bosom and not hurt?

Girgashites. The name means to draw away, to entice. They were utterly immoral and corrupt, and their land was given to Abraham and his descendants (Gen. 15:21). The Girgashites represent the world and its temptations. Our lust and enticement quickly draw us away. What happens to us when we are drawn away?

Amorites. The name means 'high ones.' They were tall, and some were giants. They were a very prominent group of people. In the Psalms, we meet Sihon and Og. They were Amorite kings. They have offered young to Molech. They were proud, believed in child sacrifice, and offered their young children to the God Molech. The wickedness of the Amorites was profound. The Amorites represent the proud, arrogant, and misguided religious people we will encounter to get to our Promised Land.

JEBUSITES. The people whose chief city was Jebus. They were warlike and idolatrous. At one stage, they controlled Jerusalem. David took Jerusalem distinctively from the Jebusites (2 Sam 5:6). **Similarly,** there are groups of religious people who are not Christian who can enter a church and turn it upside down. Giant obstacles stand in the way of our accomplishments. To get to our promised lands, we must learn from the seven nations of Canaan.

The Canaanites represent intellectuals who despise God and make their possessions their "gods." Who or what is your God? The Hittites represent the brutal, problematic sin we must deal with to advance, including doubt, fear, and complacency. The Hivites represent those who are cunning and deceitful. They are those who befriend us to use or take advantage of us. We must watch out for them. The Perizzites represent those who want to "drag you away" from your commitment. They include Satan and our unsaved friends who influence us negatively. Who is trying to pull you away? The Girgashites represent temptations that come to us through our desires. They represent **enticement.** The Amorites represent the "high ones." They are the proud and arrogant people who we must overcome to reach the Promised Land. Finally, the Jebusites represent those who seek to corrupt our lives.

They want to take over Jerusalem, and they want to replace God in your life. The elimination of tribes of people seems brutal. Was it an act of God or genocide? Did they have a chance to escape?

Reference

Unknown. (n.d.). The seven lost tribes of Israel. Seed of Abraham Ministries. Retrieved from http://www.seedofabraham.net/7tribes.html

Sermon #5: Spirits

A spirit can be a disposition or a demon. Angels and demons exist! Man created in the image of God has untold powers of creativity and perception. Humans are powerful; scientists attempt to infuse human intelligence in machines to develop artificial intelligence (AI).

The Right Spirits

First, The Spirit of God is a spirit that creates paradigms. The only two things that do not change are God and transformation itself. God is consistent, constant, and complete, and he initiates change at every level: cosmic, terrestrial, or ephemeral. *The Spirit of God* is a creating spirit; he moves through darkness and creates light and meaning. He is an omniscient spirit known as the Spirit of Knowledge (Gen. 1:2; Gen. 41:38**).**

Second, The Spirit of Promise or the Promised Spirit is the Holy Spirit. Before his descent on the Day of Pentecost, many Old Testament prophecies heralded his coming. One of his essential purposes is to put a seal or mark on all believers: "When you believed, you were marked in him with a seal, the promised Holy Spirit, 14 who is a deposit guaranteeing our inheritance until the redemption of those who are God's possession—to the praise of his glory" (Ephesians 1:13-14). Are you sealed? *Thirds, He is the Spirit of Wisdom, understanding, counsel, and reverence.* It speaks of God's all-knowing, all-encompassing power in every area of life – wisdom, knowledge.

Fourth, Spirit of Prophecy. The Spirit of Prophecy is not solely about Ellen G White and her writings, "For it is the Spirit of prophecy who bears testimony to Jesus" (Rev. 19:10). Who are the oracles of God in our time? Who declares the divine will of God to humanity? Who claims, "This is what the Lord says?" Many pulpits are extensions of political platforms. Preachers often herald the talking points of political ideologies rather than the mind of God! Some Christians have the gift of prophecy, while others don't. But the Spirit of prophecy is not limited to a few. It is a discernment of the will of God given to the remnant church in the last days. Some aspects of Christianity have verged so far away from biblical truth it takes the Spirit of prophecy to uncover the truth.

Fifth, The Spirit of Glory is the Spirit of God; he rests, tarries, and stays with Christians persecuted for the name of Christ. When the Spirit of Glory rests on someone, that person is comforted and sustained during the trial. If you are being insulted, harassed, or persecuted for the name of Christ, you are blessed because the Spirit of Glory is with you! (1 Peter 4:14).

Sixth, The Spirit of humility is the attitude or disposition that is the primary prerequisite for elevation at all levels. God specializes in the elevation of those who are humble: "For those who exalt themselves will be humbled, and those who humble themselves will be exalted" (Matthew 23:12; Isaiah 57:15**).** If the Spirit of humility is the avenue for elevation, then the Spirit of pride is the path for demotion and destruction: "Before a downfall the heart is haughty, but humility comes before honor" (Proverbs 18:12). Hubris works with karma, and proud peacocks lose their feathers! Lucifer lost his place, Napoleon lost his empire, and Donald Trump lost his presidency not because of their humility but because of their pride.

Sixth, The Spirit of grace is the dispenser of favors. When one encounters this Spirit, he is given unparalleled access, opportunities, privileges, and advancement, irrespective of race, credentials, or creed. But some insult the Spirit of grace: "How much more severely do you think someone deserves to be punished who has trampled the Son of God underfoot, who has treated as an unholy thing the blood of the covenant that sanctified them, and who has insulted the Spirit of grace? (Hebrews 10:29**).** But abandonment is expected. People reject the love of God in the face of all that Jesus has done for them; some affluent parents have abandoned their children, and despite their parents' wealth and inheritance, some children have left their aged parents. In each case, these people are devoid of the Spirit of grace.

Seventh, The Spirit of Meekness. When someone has the disposition of humility, he is not a walk-over doormat. He is a strong character who exhibits the fruit of the Holy Spirit. In full knowledge of his position in Christ, credentials, and experience, the meek are cognizant of fallen human nature and attitudes and can deflect criticism, defer gratification, and determine the best path forward. It is for this reason; they will inherit the earth! Meekness is not weakness; it is inner strength. The Holy Spirit cultivates the Spirit of meekness.

Eight, The Spirit of Patience. Patience is a virtue acquired through struggle and a spirit better than the Spirit of pride (Ecc.7:8). Patience is not acquired instantaneously. It is tolerance and endurance acquired from the crucible struggles. Moses struggled with Pharaoh for the deliverance of his people, David. Joshua "fits" the battle of Jericho, and Jesus became obedient to procure salvation for his humanity. Patience is learned; it is acquired. If you ask God to give you patience, prepare for the struggles.

Ninth, The *Spirit of Truth.* The Holy Spirit is the Spirit of truth who testifies that Jesus is the way, the truth, and the life (John 14:6). In an age of misinformation, that is, falsehood intended to deceive and disinformation, that is, organized propaganda designed to mislead, people need the Spirit of truth to counteract conspiracies and delusions. Still, the world cannot receive him because they do not know him for proceeds from the Father (John 14:17). Conversely, Christians should know him, and if they don't, they are not Christians: But when he, the Spirit of truth, comes, he will guide you into all the truth. He will not speak on his own; he will speak only what he hears and tell you what is yet to come (John 16:13). How is it that millions of Americans cannot discern the efficacy of the COVID-19 vaccines?

Tenth, A New Spirit. Organ transplantation is a big business in America. Some organs are transplanted while the donors are still living, while others are transplanted after the donors die. People are waiting for everything from a new cornea, heart, lung, kidney, skin, and bones! Sometimes, a person needs not a new physical organ, although that might be necessary, but a new spirit, a heart. This heart is not the physical organ but the center of one's thoughts, being reason and consciousness. It is the place from which our obedience or rebellion emanates. When we become sinful and rebellious to the point of backsliding or rejecting God, we need a new attitude to re-emerge. Israel had lost the will to live, dream, and fight again! So, Go said, "I will give you a new heart and put a new spirit in you; I will remove from you your heart of stone and give you a heart of flesh (Ez. 36:26). Do you need a new spirit?

Sermon #6: More Spirits

The population of the world is racing towards eight billion people. How many angels are in the world? How many demons are in the world? The spirit world might be much more populated than the real world!

First, there is the spirit of jealousy. Since the dawn of history, jealousy and its consequences have dominated human consciousness. Blood has been shed through jealousy and rage. Biblically, "Wrath is cruel, anger is overwhelming, but who can stand before jealousy?" (Proverbs 27:4 ESV). This green-eyed monster, not an actual demon, although one can be possessed with a spirit of jealousy, is an insatiable desire to have what others possess and an overwhelming feeling of covetousness. Some jealousies have no basis in reality; others are pathological, morbid, and delusional. Through jealousy, Adam and Eve disobeyed because they wanted his knowledge of good and evil; Cain killed Able because God accepted Cain's gift, not his; Joseph's brothers sold him into slavery because of his coat. Rachel envied Leah because she was childless, and the Corinthians Christians became jealous of each other because of their gifts and favorite leaders! (Gen. 3:1-5; Gen. 4:5; Gen. 45:4-11; Gen. 30:1; 1 Cor. 3:3-4). People always want what others have, even if they have better.

Second, there is the spirit of slumber. Why is the nation of Israel, God's chosen people, still in a time of spiritual stupor? Why haven't they embraced the Gospel of Jesus Christ? According to the apostle Paul, of them "At present there is a remnant chosen by grace" (Rom. 11:8). Truth be told, not only is Israel in a time of spiritual slum, but the rest of the world is also! Capitalism and its pursuits have kept the world in a daze! People are working nine to five in an unending cycle of quasi-slavery, subjugation, and dismay! Many have no idea of the claim of God in their lives. The Jews are in slumber to spiritual realities, and black people are the sleeping giants in the world. We must pray for the "New Awakening!"

Third, there is the crushed spirit. There is a direct connection between a person's spirit or center of consciousness and his physical being! "A man's Spirit will endure sickness, but a crushed spirit who can bear (Prov. 18:14, RSV). Negative words can break a person's Spirit; they can kill! He who has the will to live will live, even if he has a debilitating sickness, but when a patient's Spirit is crushed, he's almost dead! Without pneuma, soma does not exist! Emotional abuse and verbal abuse destroyed the Spirit and caused depression. The church needs mental health counselors in the 21st Century. A prayer of deliverance, affirmation of the word of God, and empathy are good, but sometimes, people with clinical depression need to be referred to a professional. Too many pastors and church people have committed suicide or are living in despair.

Fourth, there is a spirit of dizziness. "The LORD has poured into them a spirit of dizziness; they make Egypt stagger in all that she does, as a drunkard staggers around in his vomit (Isa. 19:14). The context of this verse is important. God sends the Egyptian leaders into a drunken stupor before bringing judgment on Egypt. God attacks the idols, stirs civil unrest, sends drought and famine, and refutes the counsel of the magicians and elites. He attacks Pharoah (Isa. 19:1-13). Many nations have a spirit of dizziness; they are haphazard and inconsistent in government, and their countries are in shambles. God always warns the city before he destroys it!

Fifth, there is a sorrowful spirit. Some married women, like Hannah, want to have children but cannot have a child of their own (1 Sam. 1:15). They are often ridiculed, misunderstood, and sidelined. Mother's Day and other days of celebration are painful. Additionally, some are single and whose eggs are dying, but they cannot find a husband. Many of these women have become mad with God and men and feel unloved, unhappy, and unappreciated. Hannah's antidote was prayer and persistence. Conversely, some married women do not want to have children; that's their choice, and they deserve our respect too.

Sixth, there is a spirit of prostitution. In one of the most extraordinary acts of prophetic symbolism, God asked the prophet Hosea to remarry his unfaithful wife as a sign of his intent to do the same to Israel, a nation that had become idolatrous: "My people consult a wooden idol, and a diviner's rod speaks to them. A spirit of

64

prostitution leads them astray; they are unfaithful to their God" (Hos. 4:12). When the Spirit of prostitution is operating in a country, people replace the almighty with other gods, which may include, but are not limited to capitalism, materialism, fame, careers, and pleasures.

Seventh, there is the spirit of the Anti-Christ. The Spirit of the antichrist is false, forward, and fraudulent; it is untrue, contrary, and deceptive. It is a prominent spirit of the end times. Vigilance is necessary: Test every spirit, "Every Spirit that acknowledges that Jesus Christ has come in the flesh is from God, but every Spirit that does not acknowledge Jesus is not from God. The Spirit of the antichrist denies the doctrine of the incarnation, the cornerstone of the Gospel - that through Jesus' birth from the Virgin Mary, he, the only begotten Son of God, took on human nature and became the Godman. Humanity is lost without God, and Jesus is the revelation of God to humanity. As such, he alone can offer salvation. Doctrines that deny the incarnation and promote personality cults and idolatry are not of God.

What spirits are around? The world of unseen spirits is as accurate as the natural, observable world. An assortment of demonic and dispositional spirits operate to foster or thwart the plan of God. Sometimes, after an encounter, we feel that we have just met someone or are occasionally different. Yes, spirits are operating in and through people, and they are in the church and the world. Be warned.

Sermon #7: Deadly Viruses

Proverbs 20:19 highlights the importance of developing spiritual virtues to counteract negative attitudes and behaviors. These virtues include love to combat hatred, hope to combat despair, kindness to combat callousness, freedom to combat dependence, diligence to combat laziness, humility to combat pride, gratitude to combat ungratefulness, chastity to combat immorality, and justice to combat partiality. However, the passage also acknowledges that people often overlook the existence of spiritual viruses within the church. These viruses represent toxic and unspiritual behaviors in specific church cultures. Recognizing and addressing these sinful habits that hinder embracing spiritual virtues is important.

As for viruses themselves, they are microscopic organisms that multiply within living cells and consist of genetic material enveloped in a protein coat. Examples of significant viruses include Marburg and Ebola, which cause severe illnesses such as hemorrhagic fever. Rabies and HIV are other viruses that impact human health, with rabies affecting the brain and HIV remaining incurable. Smallpox, once a major threat, has been eradicated through vaccines. Seasonal flu viruses and the SARS-CoV-2 virus, responsible for the global COVID-19 pandemic, continue to affect the world. Church viruses, on the other hand, are non-productive and unspiritual behaviors that arise from a failure to embrace spiritual virtues within specific church cultures.

Church viruses are toxic, non-productive, and unspiritual behaviors characteristic of specific church cultures. They are sinful habits that result from the inability to embrace spiritual virtues.

First, there is a virus of gossip. Some people did not know the art and science of gossip until they became church members. It has been said that loose lips sink ships, but church gossip kills, literally. Calumny is a special kind of church gossip, "making false and defamatory statements about someone to damage their reputation" (Online Dictionary). It is deliberate slander. Have you ever seen an anonymous letter sent to the leadership of a church from a so-called credible or concerned member who was unwilling to put his name or reputation back its authenticity? I've seen many. To gain power, look holier-than-thou, curry favor, or assassinate the character of a perceived opponent, some church people will infect the church with the dangerous and deadly virus of gossip. Gossips are not prepared to go to a sinning brother or sister; call for two or three more if he refuses to listen or take it to the church's leadership as the scripture enjoins (Matt. 18:15-17). They are willing to assassinate a character with "true Christian love!" They are ready to kill emotionally! Slander-mongering and malicious gossip create a culture of spiritual fear and terror. James, the brother of Jesus, makes it clear, "If anyone thinks he is religious and does not bridle his tongue but deceives his heart, this person's religion is worthless" (Jam. 1:26, NIV). Why do you think much of the misinformation about vaccines is coming from people who claim to be Christians? What they have practiced in the church, they bring to the world!

Second, there is a virus of hypocrisy. Some people have erroneously said that the church is full of hypocrites! That's not true; the statement is an unbounded generalization! But it is safe to say that hypocrisy is a definite feature of church culture. There is hypocrisy in leadership. Many who lead on a Sunday are devils during the week; members who condemn and judge others live the same lifestyle they condemn. Some members have learned to wear a holiness mask to appear spiritual "before others." For some, testimonies are practiced lies; giving is not an act of worship and a show of affluence; for some, worship of the Lord is the worship of self. The church is the pillar and ground of truth, but in some local church cultures, hypocrisy is a lifestyle.

> "And when you pray, you must not be like the hypocrites. They love to stand and pray in the synagogues and street corners so that others may see them. Truly, I say to you, they have received their reward" (Matt. 6:5).

Third, there is a virus of unknown origin. Sometimes, a spiritual virus of an unknown origin appears in one's life, but when it comes, it stays for a very long time! Like an infectious disease, it comes, and in a short time, it overwhelms your home, office, or school. Nothing remains the same. It could be an accusation with legal ramifications, such as sexual harassment from a stranger. Maybe someone helps someone who was at the point of death, and now, in a move of ingratitude, the rescued sues the rescuer! Or someone enters your world and claims to be your son or daughter. A trial erupts without warning, reason, or perceived purpose. Do you know someone who has never smoked but has developed lung cancer? Have you ever seen a strong man in the prime of his youth struck down in an accident? Sometimes trials do not result from one's lifestyle, sexual inclinations, or proclivities! Some life events occur "suddenly." But it is then that we understand that God is with us, and he will rebuke the wind (Matt. 8:23-27).

Vaccines Vs. The Blood of Jesus

Like the vaccines for natural viruses, Jesus's blood is safe; it does not cause sickness or death; protects and continues to protect; efficacious in neutralizing; priceless; stable and easy to administer; and has no side effects. Viruses are physical and spiritual. Not all biological viruses have a vaccine or cure, but the blood of Jesus is enough for all spiritual viruses. We take physical vaccines for physical viruses; we must apply the blood of Jesus for all spiritual viruses! Spiritual viruses are contagious and deadly as biological viruses.

Reference

Karki, G. (2019, December 5). Vaccine: Characteristics and types of vaccine. Molecular Biology 0. Retrieved from https://www.onlinebiologynotes.com/vaccine-characteristics-and-types-of-vaccine/

National Institute of Allergy and Infectious Diseases. (2021, September 7). Vaccines. Retrieved from https://www.niaid.nih.gov/research/vaccine-types

Bing Dictionary. (2021, September 7). Retrieved from https://www.bing.com/search?q=calumny+definition&form=WNSGPH&qs=LS&cvid=93593ff5501d4f72b4809439bf353af2&pq=calumny&cc=US&setlang=en-US&nclid=4C63F2CFABDADB8F29EAE6C5A833979F&ts=1631056552086&wsso=Moderate

Harding, A., & Lanese, N. (2020, March 4). The deadliest viruses in history. Retrieved from https://www.livescience.com/deadliest-viruses.html

Sermon # 8: A Time to Dance

Dancing is controversial in some religious settings but has always been an integral part of Israel's culture, deeply rooted in their celebrations, victories, and expressions of joy. It is a powerful and uplifting way to connect with God, express our love and adoration, and unite with our fellow believers in celebration. It should be approached with reverence, guided by righteousness, and used as a tool to glorify God and inspire others to join in the worship and celebration of His goodness.

First, dance for deliverance and victory. In our lives, there are moments when God delivers us from trials and triumphs over our enemies. Just as Miriam and the women danced after crossing the Red Sea, we, too, can dance to celebrate God's deliverance. Dancing is a joyful expression of gratitude for God's victories.

Second, dance for restoration and affirmation. When God restores us and brings healing to our brokenness, we can dance in celebration. As mentioned in Jeremiah 31:4 and 13, the restoration of Israel called for dancing. Like David, who danced before the Ark of the Lord, we can affirm our trust in God's faithfulness through dancing.

Third, dance to praise God. The Psalms encourage us to praise God through dancing. In Psalm 149:3, we are called to praise His name in the dance, accompanied by the timbrel and harp. Dancing becomes an act of worship, a physical expression of our love and adoration for God.

Fourth, dance for Joy and happiness. Dancing is also appropriate during times of joy and happiness. Ecclesiastes 3:4 reminds us that there is a time to dance, emphasizing the importance of embracing moments of joy in our lives. We can dance in celebration of God's goodness and blessings.

Fifth, dance is an act of defiance. The account of the golden calf in Exodus 32 serves as a reminder that dancing can be misused when it becomes associated with idol worship and rebellion against God. We must guard our hearts and ensure our dancing is rooted in righteousness.

Dancing holds a special place in our spiritual journey. It reflects our joy, serves as an act of worship, and celebrates restoration and affirmation. We can express our gratitude, praise God, and rejoice in His victories through dancing. Let us embrace dancing as a wholesome and righteous expression of our love for God and our fellow brothers and sisters in Christ. As we dance, may it be an overflow of our hearts filled with joy, faith, and gratitude. Dancing can bring glory to God and inspire others to celebrate His goodness.

Sermon#9:Overcoming Your Goliath

Goliath, a gigantic nemesis, terrorized the Israelites with fear! He lives in infamy as an arch-enemy or obstruction to progress. In life's journey, people must confront and defeat their goliaths to enjoy the richness of God's provisions. Goliath could be a physical, spiritual, or emotional person or entity. David's defeat of Goliath is a template for success. What stood in the way of Israel's success?

How not to kill Goliath? How not to overcome your obstacles! *First, Fear.* The giant of *fear* must go to defeat Goliath! It was not Goliath's stature that was the main obstacle to defeating him; it was the fear he commanded. Fear paralyzes, and the fear of Goliath cripples the army of Israel. He defied or challenged the armies of the Israelites. Difficulties can challenge peoples' beliefs about the power of God, and fear can stop them from stepping out! However, "Love has in it no element of fear, but perfect love drives away fear because fear involves pain, and if a man gives way to fear, there is something imperfect in his love" (1 John 4:18).

Second, Doubt. Doubt makes you feel helpless. The giant of *doubt* must go! Unbelief is limiting God! David did not feel helpless. He was energized to confront his enemy! He drew from his experience in destroying wild animals and was a warrior. And he knows God for himself. Be warned:

doubt can prevent us from enjoying God's promises: "So we see that they were not able to enter, because of their unbelief" (Heb. 3:19).

Third, She was murmuring or complaining. Murmuring must go. Murmuring in the face of an enemy is unproductive. Talk to God. Too many see the problem, but sometimes no one wants to do what it takes to solve it!

Fourth, Lethargy. Complacency or utter laziness can keep us from overcoming our goliaths. The Israelites had won many battles before and knew what God could do, and they had to prove that God was with them, but it is easy to be "at ease in Zion."

Fifth, Comparisons. The Israelites were comparing themselves to Goliath instead of comparing Goliath with God. Don't compare yourself with others. To some people, the sons of Anak are giants, and to others, they are grasshoppers. The battle is not ours. It's God's.

Sixth, Discouragement. Goliath's ancestors were no match for Joshua, who drove them out of the land of Canaan. But now, there he stood to exact revenge. Goliath stalked Israel to crush their spirits. "On hearing the Philistine's words, Saul and all the Israelites were dismayed and terrified (1 Sam. 17:11, NIV). A discouraged person is no match for a legendary enemy. One must speak the word of faith in the face of this enemy, "You come against me with sword and spear and javelin, but I come against you in the name of the LORD

Almighty, the God of the armies of Israel, whom you have defied (Sam 17:45, NIV).

Seventh, Loneliness. Presents were Saul and his army, Goliath and his army, and David. When David took on the task of defeating Goliath, he became the titular leader of Israel's army. The gravity of leadership brings loneliness, but those who fight goliaths must know that God will never leave nor forsake his children.

How to Defeat Goliath

First, know your God: He is the 'living" God! He's omnipresent, omniscient, and immutable: every present, all-knowing, and unchanging! In this encounter, David's faith was focused on God alone. He knew what God had done and what he could do. He was armed with the knowledge of his past victories and testimonies of the mighty acts of God. Focus on God when if you encounter Goliath!

Second, Know your enemy. He is an "uncircumcised philistine" with no right, authority, or permission to hurt God's people. His size, stature, and sword do not matter, and he's your enemy, not your friend.

Third, Preparation. Make mental, spiritual, physical, and logistical preparation to fight. Please do not underestimate your enemy, and prepare to defeat him. David knew the powers of serenity, mediation, and supplication.

Fourth, Positioning. You are a child of God in God's army, and you are positioned in his kingdom: "far above all rule and authority, power and dominion, and every name that is invoked, not only in the present age but also in the one to come" (Eph 1:21, NIV).

Fifth, Permission. It was King Saul's job to fight Goliath, but he was afraid. He handed his responsibility to David and said, "May the Lord be with you! Kingdom people must know that permission has been given to fight the enemy." Jesus said, "I have given you authority to trample on snakes and scorpions and to overcome all the power of the enemy. Nothing will harm you" (Lk, 10:19, NIV).
Sixth, Prayer. Pray, and pray again. The Psalms of David are full of his prayers to God.

Seventh, Pounce. Attack with God's word (1 Sam. "David triumphed over the Philistine with a sling and 17:50). Finally, he obtained what he had sought – divine favor.
21st Century Goliaths include poverty, social injustice, depression, eating disorders, drug addiction, mental health issues, physical sickness, pornography, church abuse, alienation, distraction, and despair! People need spiritual, professional, and social help to overcome these giants! Pastors must be smart enough to refer their congregants for professional help. David had one sling but many stones!

Sermon #10: Evangelism in the 21ˢᵗ Century!

"The Gospel of the kingdom will be proclaimed throughout the entire world." (Matthew 24:14)

To win the lost at all costs, Christianity has employed aggressive or coercive approaches to spread the Christian message. These methods included high-pressure persuasion, manipulation, or emotional manipulation to compel individuals to convert to Christianity. While the intention may be to save souls, the consequences of forceful evangelism can be detrimental. It can lead to a sense of resentment, alienation, or hostility from those targeted, as they may perceive such tactics as disrespectful or intrusive. Forceful evangelism can strain interfaith relations and hinder constructive dialogue between different religious communities. Additionally, it can create a negative perception of Christianity and undermine its core values of love, compassion, and respect. Instead, promoting a more gentle, respectful, and dialogical approach to evangelism can foster understanding, mutual respect, and genuine engagement with diverse belief systems.

First, 21ˢᵗ-century Evangelism must be Socially Relevant. At one of Jesus' evangelism events, the disciples asked Jesus to dismiss the crowd so that the people could find food. To the disciples, Jesus said, "You give them something to eat – In Mark 6:37, "But he answered, "You give them something to eat." They replied, "That would take more than half a year's wages! Are we to go and spend that much on bread and give it to them to eat?" Providing for the social needs of the poor is evangelism; it shows that you care! It's evangelism of love!

Second, the 21st century must be interrogative. People have questions, and we must be prepared to give an answer to each of them: "1 Peter 3:15 15 says, "But in your hearts revere Christ as LORD. Always be ready to answer everyone who asks you to explain your hope. But do this with gentleness and respect. And, if we don't know the answer to a question, we must not make up the story! Do your research! People have questions about who they are, why they are here, and where they are going!

Third, 21st-century Evangelism must be Apologetic! Acts 8: 34-38, Philip met an Ethiopian: "And the eunuch said to Philip, "About whom, I ask you, does the prophet say this, about himself or someone else?" Then Philip opened his mouth, and beginning with this Scripture, he told him the good news about Jesus. And as they were going along the road, they came to some water, and the eunuch said, "See, here is water! What prevents me from being baptized?" And he commanded the chariot to stop, and they both went down into the water, Philip and the eunuch, and he baptized him. It must be a defense of the Gospel. People need to know that the atrocities committed in the name of Jesus were done by those who hijacked the religion and that they do not represent us! We must make a case for why serving Jesus is what the world needs! We must be ready to give a reason for t hope in Christ (1 Pet. 3:15). *Fourth, 21st-century Evangelism is Experiential.* Those who are followers have Christ have had experiences with him. We must let the world know of the power of the transformational work of Christ in us! Those who have been healed and delivered need to speak – let the redeemed of the Lord say so! Nothing beats a good story!

Fifth, 21st-century Evangelism is a Lifestyle. It becomes challenging when Christians put politics or patriotism above Christ! How we live is our most incredible testimony!

Sixth, Use Culture to show Christ. The apostle Paul used a social construct, an altar to "an invisible God," to present Christ as that invisible God to the people of Athens (Acts 17). 21st-century Christians can do the same! Where was the church when women protested for equal pay for equal work? Where is the church when the police kill unarmed black men? They didn't care, or if they did, they didn't manage to show they did. All cultural events are opportunities to show the power of Christ in the world. These events are usually diverse – just as God has made the universe and its people, they express music – even heaven is abuzz with music.

Seventh, 21st-century evangelism should use Social Media: social media will carry the Gospel from a local church, tent meeting, or just a dinner table to the ends of the earth! I believe the church should develop its own media platforms soon.

Christianity, the religion that bears the name of Christ, has been hijacked, transformed, and reinvented into a 21st movement in support of the most anti-Jesus movement of all time.

Sermon # 11: A Time for Laughs

Laughter is good medicine: "A merry heart doeth good like a medicine: but a broken spirit drieth the bones." (Prov. 17:22). Medical evidence attests to the good effects of laughter. They include improved health, a sense of optimism, a release of stress, and prolonged life. Laughter is therapy. People laugh for different reasons. Multiple references to laughter are in the Bible. There is good laughter, and there is terrible laughter. People laugh, and God laughs. Even fool laughs! Why do you laugh?

The Bible gives us several perspectives on laughter.

First, God laughs with mockery (Psa. 2:4). Laughter is a rebuke. The omnipresent and omniscient One laughs at the vein, doomed plots of humanity to discredit his existence: "The One enthroned in heaven laughs. The Lord scoffs at them (Psalm 2:4). God laughs from a position of strength, stability, and knowledge. He's enthroned, but he has the world's purview in sight. No philosophy or ideology can replace humanity's need for God. A revolt against your maker is futile: "Since you disregard all my advice and do not accept my rebuke, I, in turn, will laugh when disaster strikes you. I will mock when calamity overtakes you" (Prov. 1: 25-26).

Second, People laugh in glee. Laughter is therapeutic. There is "a time to weep, and a time to laugh. A time to mourn, and a time to dance" (Ecc. 3:4). We were created for celebration, and celebration brings laughter. We laugh when we hear, see, touch, smell, or taste something wonderful. It is an automatic response. We like comedy, funny stories, and general levity. But we laugh not only when something is funny but also when we are nervous, excited, tense, tricked by someone, or simply because someone else is laughing. Human laughter is spontaneous and contagious. It is said that of all mammals, only humans have mastered the art of laughter.

Third, there is the laughter of false contentment. Laughter is false. Impending sorrow is predicted for those who "laugh now," who live in false contentment, oblivious to the world and their duty to the community. Nothing is wrong with having a comfortable life or having wealth, success, and fame! God does not envy the rich! But if this life is preparation for the next, those who are laughing now will not have the last laugh. They could encounter great disappointment and the loss of eternal life. It's like reaching one's acquired destination but being unable to enjoy the fruit of his labor because the life he has is temporal. Jeff Bezos spent billions for 12 minutes in the sky and a few seconds of weightlessness while starvation roams throughout the earth, and poor and indigenous people do not have drinking water! While people say "Peace and safety," destruction will come on them suddenly, as labor pains on a pregnant woman, and they will not escape (1 Thess. 5:3).

Fourth, there is the laughter of deliverance. Laughter is a celebration of redemption, and it is spiritual. Throughout history, people have celebrated their deliverance from tyranny. Henry J. Zelley's iconic hymn captures the essence of the Israelites' deliverance from Egypt: When Israel out of bondage came, A sea before they lay. My Lord reached down His mighty hand and rolled the sea away." The psalmist said, "Our mouths were filled with laughter, our tongues with songs of joy. Then it was said among the nations, "The LORD has done great things for them" (Psa. 126:2). Why did they laugh? They saw the mighty acts of God, marveled at his wisdom, and laughed at his timely! Sometimes our laughter is a testimony of the goodness of God!

Fifth, there is the laughter of unbelief. Those who fail to believe that God can defy nature, conventional wisdom, or tradition laugh when they are told of God's predestined plan. Disbelief can arise after much disappointment. A woman prayed for a child when she was long, and God didn't answer. Now that she's old, she is told that God is ready to answer her prayer: "Abraham and Sarah were already very old, and Sarah was past the age of childbearing. Sarah laughed as she thought, "After I am worn out, and my LORD is old, will I now have this pleasure?" Then the LORD asked Abraham, "Why did Sarah laugh and say, 'Will I really have a child, now that I am old?' Is anything too hard for the LORD? I will return it to you at the appointed time next year, and Sarah will have a son." Sarah was afraid and lied, saying, "I did not laugh." But he said, "Yes, you did laugh—the laughter of disbelief named her son Isaac which means laughter. When Jesus told the people that Lazarus was asleep, they laughed (Luke 8:52). Then the Bible says, "They laughed him to scorn, knowing that she was dead" (Luke 8:53). This is the laughter of unbelief. God can change our mourning into dancing! Don't laugh at what God says. Trust him!

Sixth, *there is the laughter of a fool*. "For as the crackling of thorns under a pot, so is the laughter of the fool" (Ecclesiastes 7:6). The laughter of a fool is not just an incoherent cacophony of sounds that does not make sense. It is, more importantly, a disorderly attitude to life. The person laughs ridiculously, but there is no rhyme or reason for his laughing! A fool is, essentially, a person who denies the existence of God. His attitude to life and destiny is a casual compendium of folly!

Seventh, there is the laughter of Salvation. Jesus said, "Blessed are you who weep now, for you will laugh" (Luke 6:21, NIV). This is laughter in celebration of victory over sin, reconciliation with God, union with Christ, and membership in the body of Christ. "If you only knew the blessing that salvation brings, you would never stay away." In salvation, God replaces emptiness and void with joy and happiness. This is the laughter Christians experience knowing they are justified, sanctified, and one day we will be glorified.

Christian can laugh and mock death: "Death, where are they sting?" They can laugh because their names are written in the Book of Life. What is the nature of your laughter? Is it medical, spiritual, emotional, or psychological?

Reference

Zelley, H. J. (1912). He rolled the sea away. Retrieved from

https://hymnary.org/text/when_israel_out_of_bondage_came

Sermon #12: Leadership Matters

"It's lonely at the top, so you better know why you are there" - John Maxwell

There are many books on leadership styles. But what does leadership entail? One thing is sure; people know a leader when they see one. A leader has the power to influence and the charisma to shed light on a situation.

First, leadership is radical; it departs from established norms. It is different, dynamic, and dignified. It is different in the following ways: Incorporating the outcasts of society and women. Jesus was a radical leader. He was revolutionary because he went against the grain of popular opinion and common thought and introduced women into his ministry. Jesus preached non-violence when his people wanted war against the Romans. He, the perfect alpha male, exhibited genuine emotions when he was broken (he wept). He ushered in a new phase, "the kingdom of God." He healed people on the Sabbath day and defied the status quo. He abandoned old Jewish irrelevant traditions. He showed mercy when others wanted blood (The woman in the act of adultery). He flogged the money changers who had corrected the sanctuary. He was unconventional in many ways – "You have heard it said... but now I say unto you." John the Baptist was a radical preacher.

It was dynamic in that it was not dead. It was lively, moving, and stirring. Jesus was a radical leader. he ushered in a new phase, "the kingdom of God." He healed people on the Sabbath day and defied the status quo. He abandoned old Jewish irrelevant traditions. He showed mercy when others wanted blood. He flogged the money changers who had corrected the sanctuary. He was unconventional in many ways. John the Baptist was a radical preacher.

Second, leadership is relational. It is the ability to create positive relationships within a group and has everything to do with working with people harmoniously. Relational leadership involves the creation of associations or groups. Relational leadership concentrates on affection, and leadership should be loving. Look at the example of Jesus, Lazarus, Mary, and Martha. Relational leadership involves affirmations: Jesus looked at Nathaniel and said, "Behold, an Israelite in whom there is no guile." What do you think this did for Nathaniel?

Third, leadership is rational, and an erratic leader is mentally unstable. The apostle Peter failed in leadership when he fellowshipped with Gentiles in Antioch but later separated himself from them when high-ranking Jews visited him from Jerusalem (Gal 2:11-14).

Fourth, leadership is reproducing. A leader should be training a subordinate, and he should always have an assistant. Elijah trained Elisha, Moses trained Joshua, and Paul the Apostle trained John Mark. Leaders reproduce themselves in others. Paul has said, "Follow me as I follow Christ."1 Cor. 11:1. Churches reflect their leaders.

Fifth, leadership is releasing (To set free from confinement, restraint, or bondage). Release people to use their gifts and talents. Train and delegate responsibilities to people and trust them to do their jobs. Give oversight and follow through.

Sixth, leadership is resilience; it recovers readily from adversity, depression, or other challenges. A leader must have the ability to bounce right back after disappointment. If something does not work, try something else. If someone is unwilling, ask another. A vital trait of a leader at any level is not only the ability to persevere but to be flexible, constantly changing to meet the needs of the times.

Seventh, Leadership is Resolute: (Firm, unyielding, determined). Don't be a quitter. Every leader will face challenges, the quagmire of doubt, and the inevitable Judas! He must be resolute to stay focused on his goal and press forward! He might face termini on his journey but has a vision of the end.
Leadership is radical, relational, rational, reproducing, releasing, resilient, and resolving. Leave your stamp, your imprimatur, on the world.

Sermon #13: Toxic Leadership

There have been meetings of only a moment, which have left impressions of life for eternity. No one can understand that mysterious thing we call 'influence' ...yet every one of us continually exerts influence, either to heal, to bless, to leave marks of beauty, or to wound, to hurt, to poison, to stain other lives - J.B. Miller

Are leaders born or made? Who are the models of outstanding leadership in our time? What are the different styles of leadership? What type of leader are you? Hubris, ignorance, and arrogance are threats to good leadership. To be a good leader, one must deal with hubris, that pride that comes before a fall. He who exalts himself shall be abased. John Maxwell once said: "A leader is great, not because of his or her power, but because of his or her ability to empower others." Ignorance can destroy a leader and a nation: "My people are destroyed from lack of knowledge" (Hosea 4:6). Arrogance is akin to pride, but the arrogant leader knows everything and is not teachable and refuses to consider the expertise of any other person!

Toxic Leadership

First, a good leader is not *repulsive. H*e is attracted. Good leaders do not repel people, and they embrace them. People should want to follow a leader. The apostle Paul said, "Follow me as I follow Christ." A leader who repels others is toxic. His selfish attitude, crude tone of voice, partiality, criticism, and disrespect are natural repellents. Repulsive leadership is leadership that scatters rather than gathers and divides instead of unites. Are you a repulsive leader?

Second, a good leader is not *reactive. H*e is proactive. Good leaders do not wait for bad things to happen, and they discern and prevent them from happening. They precipitate and stimulate good happenings!

Third, good leaders are not *reposing*; they are proposing! Whenever a body lies in repose, it is dead. Leadership must engender life and not stifle people's abilities or talents. A leader should harness the skills under his purview and give those who follow a reason to serve. I know a pastor who, in his 45 years of ministry, has never trained or appointed another minister. He has no leadership posterity! Do you know a leader whose leadership is dead?

Fourth, a good leader is not a *ranter.* He's composed. Like Jesus, the servant-leader, he's administering as one with authority, and who knows how to use it! Ranting leads to boredom! Moses learned that although eloquence is important, it is not the quintessential quality of leadership (Ex. 4:10). God assured Moses that leadership is the ability to influence, not the ability to babble or rant!

Fifth, a good leader is not *reluctant* to make decisions. He is willing to lead in the decision-making process. In Ezekiel 22: 30, God "looked for a man among them who would build up the wall and stand before me in the gap on behalf of the land so I would not have to destroy it, but I found none." God looked in the nation for one person: Man, woman, boy, girl, young or old, who would be willing to rebuild not only the city walls but also build the walls of morality, honesty, justice, and love. Lamentably, God said, "I found none." No one in aristocracy, religion, industry, or commerce was willing to lead the nation.

Sixth, a good leader is not a *rogue!* He's not a dishonest, deceitful, and unreliable person. A rogue does not know how to use power without manipulation. He empowers people and shows sympathy for the needs of others. Sadly, corrupt authoritarian leaders are in vogue! People are willing to be driven like enslaved people and treated with disrespect. A respectful and compassionate leader is not a weakling!

Seventh, a good leader is not *random* or haphazard in his approach to leadership. He is deliberate. He values the community of experts in his circle, works collaboratively, and focuses on the goal to be accomplished. While timidity is not a good leadership trait, recklessness is forbidden. A good leader is patient and calculating. People, institutions, and cultures do not change overnight. The apostle Paul refused to train John Mark, and when he returned to his family during the first missionary journey, he was distraught! (Acts 15:37-39). But when John Mark regained his courage and requested to join Paul's team, Paul's arrogance got the better of him! He refused to give the young man a second chance.

Paul failed this test of leadership. In the end, when most had abandoned him, he wrote: "Only Luke is with me. Get Mark and bring him with you, because he is helpful to me in my ministry" (2 Tim 4:11, NIV). To put people in leadership without training is dangerous! Preparation must precede promotion! Who would fly with an untrained pilot? A good leader is not often developed rapidly. It takes time to develop good leadership skills. Would-be leaders must be willing to be trained! They must hone their powers of perception and discernment, communicate a vision clearly, be goal-oriented, show compassion for people, and unleash the forces of innovation in their followers while becoming a good listener!

Leadership is not repulsive, reactive, reposing, or ranting. A leader is not a ranter, a rogue, or a random, haphazard practitioner! His leadership is exemplary, firm, and fair. "Leaders have two characteristics: first, they are going somewhere, and second, they can persuade other people to go with them" [John Maxwell].

Sermon 14: Living in the 21st Century?

Text: Genesis 5:21-24

The walk is a metaphor for a lifestyle or way of living. How should Christians live in the 21st Century? Christians should not live-in ignorance, hypocrisy, or spiritual darkness. They should live like a pilgrim whose suitcase is packed.

First, Walk Circumspectly (Eph. 5:15-16). To walk circumspectly, Christians must live wisely and not foolishly. It calls for an ethical and morally sound lifestyle in every cadre of life. The Christian must take full advantage of every opportunity to present Christ to the world with the full knowledge that he has a limited time to do so. The 21st century captures the perpetual war between good and evil, and it is about to be disrupted by the wrath of God. Christians who vote, represent, worship, do business, and practice social activism must consider this imperative: live wisely because the allotted time for humanity is running out. Lifestyle evangelism is better than a fake testimony. Like Enoch, walk with God (Gen.5:21-24).

Second, walk in Unconditional Love (Eph. 5:2). Followers of Christ should love the outcast, prostitutes, thieves, and offenders as Jesus did. They cannot follow Christ and hate refugees, for as a child, Christ was a refugee in Egypt. They cannot despise drug dealers, gay and lesbian people or fail to seek justice for the poor and oppressed. What is unconditional love – it is love without a condition! One does not have to like someone's gay lifestyle to love him if his love is unconditional. A pastor does not have to marry gay people, but he is called to love them, for as human beings, they are created in the image of God! 21st-century church people must imitate the love of Christ. If they can't, they are not Christians!

Third, walk in Truth. An apostle's most significant moment of joy was to find his spiritual "children walking in the truth, just as the Father commanded" (2 Jhn1:4, NIV). Some aspects of 21st-century Christianity have become blasphemous heresy, and as such, some Christians are not walking in the truth. The doctrines of devils have seeped in and corrupted the Christian witness. Christian nationalism and Christian supremacy have corrupted the Evangelical Church. Patriotism and love for the country have replaced love for God and neighbor. Love for all has been replaced with a passion for a particular race or culture! Cultural genocides have replaced the preaching and teaching of the Gospel. Capitalism has replaced compassion! Jesus chased the capitalist for the temple, but now Christians place the rich on a pedestal as the standard of God's blessings! Christians have become so assimilated worldwide that divorce rates in the North American Church are almost the same as in the general populace. To walk in truth is to follow Christ, not religious propaganda. Truth matters in the courts, cockpit, and surgical theater! Truth saves physical lives and eternal lives! Christians who uphold the lie of white supremacy deny that all people are created in the image of God! Whiteness is a political ideology. It has no biblical basis!

Fourth, walk in the Newness of Life (Rom 6:4). The new life is a life of resurrection! It is a unique, dynamic beginning that is full of promise! The spiritually resurrected person has conquered the powers of death and darkness and is determined to complete his new mission and purpose. Water baptism is a symbol of the death and resurrection of the Christian. How, then, is the oxymoron of a dead Christian a reality? Some are church members, but they have never been dead to sin! They are still sinners in need of salvation! The dead believer cannot walk, but the resurrected will have a particular urgency to his walk**!**

Fifth, walk not after the Flesh: "There is therefore now no condemnation to them, which are in Christ Jesus, who walk not after the flesh, but after the Spirit (Rom. 8:1, KJV). Ignoring morality and living according to one's carnal instincts is easy. Our fleshly desires are powerful, and sometimes they drive our actions. But what would happen in the world if everyone was to do what is right in his own eyes? Before converting to Christianity, my grandfather created colorful expletives and was prolific in using them! That was when he lived according to his sinful nature. But when he became a Christian, he was annoyed when his grandchildren used the expletives he created! He was now living according to a higher power – the power of the Spirit! Walking in the spirit means that someone lives his life with greater consciousness and recognition of what God requires of him at a different level! He is on earth but functions in a domain mastered by the Holy Spirit. Hence, he is not susceptible to his carnal nature (Gal. 5:16). He walks worthy of his vocation or a new purpose in Christ. He is fruitful and exemplary. In this way, a Christian becomes one who walks in light, having fellowship with others like himself, and as a blessing, Jesus' blood continues to pour on him and cleanses him from any sin that he might commit on his journey (1 John. 1:7).

Sixth, walk honestly (Rom. 13:13). Because biblical Christianity has been replaced in many areas of Christendom, some Christians are not. They are fed with wild interpretations of the Bible. The Christians of the 21st Century can drink wine, just as the Christians of the first century! Jesus made the best wine, but he was no drunkard or riotous person! A simple lifestyle is balanced, benevolent, and believable. A secret life is suspicious! Paul openly rebukes Peter for his duplicitous attitude, compelling Gentiles to embrace Jewish traditions. Living an honest life in a world where lies are celebrated and rewarded is difficult! But one's public and private life must correlate! To walk honestly is to live without hypocrisy!

Seventh, walk by Faith, not by sight (2 Cor. 5:7). "Faith is taking the first step even when you don't see the whole staircase." – Martin Luther King, Jr. The ten lepers who began to move found that they were healed. Blind

Bartimaeus refused to stop crying out! A hemorrhaging woman continued to push through the crowd. A ruler of the synagogue who fell on his knees and begged for his daughter's life is a witness of what faith can do! Faith is not the power of intention or good karma! It is a belief in God's steadfast provision, protection, and management! Faith is comforting, and it is not a wild abandonment. It is standing on the promises of God!

A walk is a way of life. Walk circumspectly with unconditional love. Walk in truth and the newness of life! Do not walk after the flesh. Walk honestly! Walk in the light!

Sermon #15: Challenges to Success

Success is not a mystery! It is living in your purpose. It is longevity, prosperity, or recognition! One can be very successful, yet one's financially poor! A group of women funded Jesus' ministry, yet he is the best success story ever!

First, laziness, the quality of being unwilling to work or use energy, is the fourth largest killer in the world: "It is linked to the development of chronic health problems like heart disease, type 2 diabetes, obesity, depression, dementia, and cancer. It can make us feel bad about ourselves, guilty and frustrated, appeased only with the ever-alluring reward of inactivity – comfort, rest, and stress-free) (Knight, 2015). A sedentary, inactive lifestyle is unbiblical, unhealthy, and nonsensical. Everyone must be engaged in meaningful pursuits. Jesus knew this well: "Why were you searching for me?" he asked. "Didn't you know I had to be in my Father's house?" (Luke 2:49, NIV). Inertia is a terrible force that keeps people in one place for too long. Lethargy is not an asset. It is a liability to success. There is no benefit to laziness. It can increase physical, physiological, and spiritual diseases! The sloth is never promoted; he's ridiculed or left behind. The characteristics of slothfulness include procrastination, indifference, carelessness, neglect, and waste. "The slothful person is shortsighted, never thinking of the future, and only interested in his desires for the moment." If someone has this multifaced malaise, hear this: "You have stayed long enough at this mountain. Break camp and advance into the hill ..." (Deut. 1:6-7, NIV).

Second, a Lack of Purpose. Humanity exists for the pleasure of its creator (Rev. 4:11). He is blessed to "Be fruitful and increase in number, fill the earth and subdue it. Rule over the fish in the sea, and the birds in the sky and over every living creature that moves on the ground" (Gen. 1:28). One's purpose includes productivity, procreation, and governance. Each person has a reason to exist. The discovery of one's God-given purpose can be elusive. There are many things that an individual can do! The global pandemic has helped many to sort their priorities and discard attitudes and behavior that are meaningless or hurtful. A job that sickens, stresses, or stifles creativity insults one's purpose, even if it gives a lucrative remuneration. A God-ordained life of purpose involves helping others, leaving indelible footprints of service, enjoyment of nature, and love.

Third, Cowardice is a lack of courage. It blocks success through self-doubt. It springs from fear, and fear is a tormentor! Who gets a reward for cowardice? Julius Caesar is famous for saying, "Cowards die many times before their deaths. The valiant never taste of death but once" (Shakespeare, ...). When they refuse to act with gusto and enthusiasm, cowards experience mental deaths repeatedly. Still, he who works with bravery never experiences those emotional pangs. Even when he dies physically, it will be calculated, not capricious! Every Olympian knows that success comes not from cowering from his task but from confidently facing it. How many times did God command Joshua to be strong and courageous? (Jos.1:6,7,9). As people face the biological, nuclear, economic, mental, and spiritual enemies of the 21st Century, they too need to put away cowardice and harness themselves in courage: "People will faint from terror, apprehensive of what is coming on the world, for the heavenly bodies will be shaken" (Lk. 21:26, NIV).

Fourth, The inability to seize the moment. The rejection of laziness, cowardice, and fear should not open the door to impulsive behavior. "Be anxious for nothing, but in everything by prayer and supplication with thanksgiving let your requests be made known to God" (Phil. 4:6). Those who succeed in war marshal their forces, manage their resources, and ask for his perfect timely: "Over time, David inquired of the LORD. "Shall I go up to one of the towns of Judah?" he asked. The LORD said, "Go up." David asked, "Where shall I go?" "To Hebron," the LORD answered" (2 Samuel 2:1). Divine purpose must meet divine timing for success to come! Haste is not a sound principle of success. Success comes with calculated strategies and effort. One must live with the disposition that he can seize every moment of opportunity. Brutus reminded Cassius, "There is a tide in the affairs of men. Which, taken at the flood, leads to fortune. Omitted, all the voyage of their life Is bound in shallows and miseries (Shakespeare). If a ship does not move out in the sea at high tide or the moment of opportunity, it could remain on the shore for a long time!

Fifth, Failure to learn from mistakes. Some of the kings of Israel were notorious for following the errors of their predecessors. They were over thirty evil kings, and less than ten were upright. Manasseh acted "more wickedly than the Amorites who preceded him" (2 Kgs 21:11). The sins of King Jeroboam inspired King Zachariah to follow suit. King Josiah removed "all the abominations seen in the land of Judah and Jerusalem, and King Jehoshaphat, who "did what was right in the eyes of the Lord," were outliers. *(2 Kings 23:24, 2 Chron. 20:32).* Not only should we learn from the mistakes of others, but we should also learn from our own mistakes. It is a process of self-analysis, action, and growth. George Santayana said: "Those who do not remember their past are condemned to repeat their mistakes. Those who do not read history are doomed to repeat it. Those who fail to learn from the mistakes of their predecessors are destined to repeat them. Those who do not know history's mistakes are doomed to repeat them". The Church should learn from ineffective or coerced evangelistic strategies such as the Crusades and the witch trials, unholy alliances with politics as were the case of Hitler and the German Church, and the tyranny of forced conversions as in the case of Constantine and Christianity. Mistakes must become the springboards to new levels of adventure. History undertakes to record the past transaction for the instruction of future ages. — Gibbons. History teaches us that religion is dangerous, but spirituality is beneficial.

As was said by Lord Acton, "All power tends to corrupt. Absolute power corrupts absolutely." Empires rise and fall due to immorality. Service to others brings the greatest fulfillment. Truth liberates! Life is challenging, but there is order in the universe. So people should live with purpose, repentance, patience, and prayer.

Sixth, Unbelief. Some people do not believe in their abilities to accomplish their goals. The sin and spiral symphony of unbelief leads to inertia and hopelessness. A student who doesn't have confidence that he can rise out of poverty via education will not do well in school. A fighter who does not believe that he can win his fight begins from a position of failure, and a person who does not believes in his capacity to be a mover of shaker in society is a dead log! But this is what unbelief does. It kills the spirit which controls the body! Many Israelites did not enter their Promised Land due to unbelief, and the peoples of subsequent generations will be denied rest if they live without it: "So we see that they were not able to enter, because of their unbelief" (Heb. 3:19, NIV). The opposite of unbelief is faith. It is the capacity to envision accomplishments before they enter our physical existence. The key to overcoming unbelief is understanding God's will for humanity, our personal lives, and our ultimate destiny! The problem is that some people do not believe in a loving, purposeful God or his plan for their lives. In whom and in what do you trust?

Seventh, Making Excuses. An excuse is a surrender; it is not a strategy for success. Eve's excuse for failing was the serpent; Adam's was the woman. Moses' excuse was a lack of eloquence; Jeremiah's was that he was inarticulate. The sluggard's excuse is "There is a lion in the road" (Prov. 26:13). What's yours? Henry Wadsworth Longfellow once said, "Heights by great men reached and kept were not obtained by sudden flight but, while their companions slept, they were toiling upward in the night." Thus, success is not achieved overnight; it requires determination and consistency!

There are many challenges to success. They include laziness, lack of purpose, courage, inability to seize the moment, failure to learn from mistakes, unbelief, and making excuses. One must overcome these challenges to get to the apotheosis of success!

Reference

Shakespeare, W. (n.d.). [Title of play]. In A. Editor (Ed.), The Norton Shakespeare (2nd ed.). W. W. Norton & Company.

George Santayana. George Santayana - Wikiquote. 9/4/2021

Wikiquote. (2021, September 4). George Santayana. https://en.wikiquote.org/wiki/George_SantayanaThe New York Times. (1880, April 18). Success. https://www.nytimes.com/1880/04/18/archives/success.html

Sermon #16: A Healthy Church

Text Acts 2:41-47

What are the characteristics of a healthy church?

First, it has an Inward Focus. It develops and edifies the members through teachings, seminars, and sermons Acts 2: 42 (Apostles' teaching). Daily fellowship Acts 2:46

Second, It has an Outward Focus and trains and involves its members in evangelism. It reaches out to the world; it is a Gospel with social concerns (Acts 2: 44-46).

Third, It has an upward Focus. It is involved in the worship of God. Acts 2:42, 44. Fellowship was vital, being together was emphasized, and joy was contagious.

Fourth, It has a lateral Focus – It emphasizes being your brothers' keeper Acts 2: 45. It has the power of influence, and people were pulled to its fellowship.

Fifth, It has a spiritual Focus – It is not a political or social club with a religious flare. It is the body of Christ to develop the spiritual man. Acts 2: 41, 46. Diverse groups attend to all small and large groups' needs, and breaking bread and prayer are emphasized (Acts 2:42).

Sixth, it has a proactive Focus: It is on the move "against the kingdom of darkness." The reactive average only engages the forces of evil when confronted. The healthy

Church has a constant engagement of defiance against evil Acts 2:41. The power of God was tremendous.

Seventh, Holistic Focus – It cares for the individual's body, soul, and spirit. Salvation has to do with the "whole man." Salvation –means redemption from the power and penalty of sin. Acts 2: 42, 44, 45. The church cared for the congregants' financial, social, practical, material, and economic needs.

The key characteristics of the early Church include the following focuses: Inward, outward, upward, lateral, spiritual, proactive, and holistic.

Sermon #17: An Abusive Church

One example of an abusive church with a charismatic leader is the People's Temple, led by Jim Jones. Jones claimed to be the reincarnation of Jesus Christ and controlled all aspects of his followers' lives, including their finances and relationships with others. He also led them to commit mass suicide in 1978. Another example is the Branch Davidians, led by David Koresh. Koresh claimed to be a prophet and messiah, controlling all aspects of his followers' lives, including their diets, clothing, and sexual relationships. This led to a standoff with law enforcement in 1993, which ended in a violent confrontation and the deaths of many of Koresh's followers.

First, Autocratic Leadership. It subscribes to an inerrancy or infallibility of the leaders or founders. A church extols the founder or pastor's writings, sayings, or pronouncements above the written Scripture. Examples: "What pastor says trumps "what the Scriptures say, and what the Book of Mormons says is more significant than what the Scriptures teach. "What the pope says is more important than the Scriptures. Abusive churches are often led by a single charismatic leader who claims to have exclusive access to divine truth. This leader controls all aspects of the group's activities, including how members dress, who they associate with, and what they believe.

Second, Isolationism. The church isolates members from their families or close friends. And as such, it becomes an exclusive club for its members. Abusive churches often discourage or forbid contact with outsiders, including family members and friends not in the group. This isolation makes it difficult for members to leave the group or seek help from outside it.

Third, Manipulation and Intimidation. Members are usually intimidated by punishment if they do not follow the dictates of the leaders. Leaders in abusive churches often use manipulative tactics to control members, such as guilt, fear, and shame. They may also use love bombing and other forms of positive reinforcement to draw members in.

Fourth, Elitism. Members feel that they are the remnant Church, the only voice of God on earth. They think that they alone are the people of God. Abusive churches often have strict beliefs that are presented as absolute truth. Members who question or deviate from these beliefs may be punished or expelled from the group.

Fifth, A Martyr Complex. They feel everyone is against them or out to get them. Suffering is emphasized, and there is little or no joy in this life, just the life to come.

Sixth, Conformity is a priority. There are specific unspoken rules, traditions, codes, or practices besides the Scriptures. They are secretive, and leaving is difficult due to the created emotional abuse and dependence. Group identity trumps personal individuality. Abusive churches use harsh and punitive forms of discipline to enforce conformity among members, including shunning, public humiliation, and physical abuse

Seventh, Situational and Replacement theologies. Rules and regulations undergo metamorphosis, and they change according to the whims and fantasies of the leader.

Abusive leadership is autocratic, isolationist, manipulative, elitist, Victim-focused, conforming, and situational.

Churches That Abuse

From Wikipedia, the free encyclopedia ....
http://en.wikipedia.org/wiki/Churches_that_Abuse

Sermon #18: The Church Needs Jesus!

Text: Matt 11:12 "From the days of John the Baptist until now, the kingdom of heaven has been subjected to violence, and violent people have been raiding it."

On a day like today, we must ask, what does the Church need? Some say that the Church has failed to be the light in the world! It can be argued that through slavery and the genocides of indigenous people, it has been one of the most brutal institutions ever! Through its institution of celibacy, priests resorted to rape, murder, and every imaginable evil.

What does the Church need? The answer is simple; the Church needs Jesus! The Church needs to rediscover Jesus, its founder. It has moved away from its roots and has embraced politics and social issues that are not a part of the teachings of the Gospel of Jesus Christ. Jesus sent his disciples to go and preach the Gospel, and he did not send them to make disciples of capitalism, socialism, or communism.

Others argue that as an institution, the Church has stood the test of times and needs a little fine-tuning, that it needs just a little adjusting to being relevant in the 21st Century!

What the Church Needs

First, Reformation. It can be said that the Church needs to be reformed; it needs improvements to become better. Christianity is a chaotic mess of structured and unstructured churches that have spun many doctrines and practices that have confused the world. A monumental reformation is said to be the way to go!

Second, Rehabilitation. The Church is a sick institution that needs rehabilitation. For the Church to be restored to its former glory, it must regain its spiritual health and reputation. *Third, Refinement.* It can be argued that all the church needs is its modus operandi refinement. That the removal of unwanted practices and doctrines is the removal of the old-time religion; hence, we must refine Christianity and make it more easily understood.

Fourth, Revamping. It can be said that what the Church needs the most is a new and improved image, for example, a name change. Some churches have become cultural centers. *Fifth, Revision.* Some contend that modifying ancient practices to adapt to the 21st Century is needed. *Sixth, Restoration.* Restoration of the Gospel of Jesus Christ with a focus on the principles of the Beatitudes, love for God and neighbor, and a message of reconciliation have eluded the Church for a long time. Some believe that nothing but a return to the 1st-century teachings of Jesus can save the Church from becoming a pariah in the world.

Seventh, Revolution. Some call for a revolution in the Church, and there is consensus that a sudden, drastic change is needed in Catholicism and Protestantism. Eight, Reclamation. There is an argument for the Church to claim or reassert its place in the world even by force. *Ninth, Refashioning or Rebranding.* Like Facebook and other commercial franchises, all the church needs rebranding. But what would be the new name? What would be its unique identity? Or it is just the same old Church with a new name. Tenth, Reorganization. Reorganize and bring the Church in a new order of theoria and praxis.

Eleventh, Repair. Some say that if a thing is not broken, one should not attempt to fix it! Christianity is the largest religion in the world, and as such, it must be doing well. Hence, repair it, and mend the broken pieces. *Twelfth, Revival.* Some have argued that the Church needs a revival, a great awakening, a rebirth, a comeback from the setback! And an Ezekiel 37 type of resurrection is required.

What was the Reformation? The Reformation was a time in the History of Europe when some people began questioning some of the Teachings of The Catholic Church and challenging the Pope's authority. It started in Germany in 1517 to protest abuses in the Church. The supporters of this desire for reform were called "Protestants."

What caused the Protestant Reformation?

Simony, nepotism, absenteeism, pluralism, and the vast wealth of the Church compared to the poverty of its members precipitated the Protestant Reformation. In addition, the lack of an organized structure and the fighting among Bishops and priests were also prevalent issues. Many priests were uneducated, and the people were ignorant of their religion. The rise of new ideas, such as the Renaissance, the emergence of the printing press, and the desire of European kings to extend their power, also added to the challenges faced by the Church.

A New Protestant Reformation
A new Protestant Reformation is needed for the following purposes:

First, A restoration of the image of Jesus Christ and the person of Christ. Jesus was never white; he was not born Caucasian and is not a descendant of the people who lived in the Caucasus of Europe. He was born as a man of color in Israel. Jesus rejected racism, and he was not as racist as some Christians are. Acts 1: 8 But you will receive power when the Holy Spirit comes on you, and you will be my witnesses in Jerusalem, and in all Judea and Samaria, and to the ends of the earth." The Gospel is universal, and heaven is diverse! Jesus was not nationalist; he did not come to promote the country of Israel. He came to preach the kingdom of God. Jesus was not wealthy, and he hated capitalism. Christianity is the greatest upholder of the slavery of capitalism but looks at what Jesus did to the money changers: Matthew 21:12-13, "Jesus entered the temple courts and drove out all who were buying and selling there. He overturned the money changers' tables and the benches of those selling doves. "It is written," he said to them, "'My house will be called a house of prayer,' but you are making it a den of robbers. Jesus was full of love, not hate!

Second, the catholic church needs to reform its doctrine of celibacy. Priests are having too much sex out of wedlock. Like the Apostle Peter, they should be allowed to marry. The sexual abuse of priests is astounding! There are graphic reports in every nation among all people. How many more boys must lose their virginity to these big older men? If the ruling class did not support and uphold them, that institution would be history.

Third, the deconstruction and reconstruction of Christianity have begun. Some are tired of the Church's hypocrisy, lies, and misinformation! What do people do when they know that the preacher is lying? They deconstruct – leave, or they reconstruct their faith! Now is the time for us to take the Gospel to top the ends of the earth! Parts of Christianity are asleep. There is a need to bring the Gospel to the Southern Hemisphere, the Middle East, and other parts of the world!

Sermon #19: Decolonize Christianity

Text: "Woe to you, scribes and Pharisees, hypocrites! You travel across sea and land to make a single proselyte, and when he becomes a proselyte, you make him twice as much a child of hell as yourselves (Matt. 23:15, ESV).

Christianity is declining in the Western World, and younger generations do not see religion's relevance, rationale, and readiness to direct their lives. One way to stimulate renewed interest in religion is to decolonize and liberate Western Christianity from the tentacles of white supremacy, male hegemony, systemic racism, and an extra-biblical focus on faith. To decolonize is to "free (a people or area) from colonial status: to relinquish control of (a subjugated people or area)."

Biblical Christianity has been enslaved and white-washed, so it has become unrecognizable in some aspects of the modern church.

Decolonize church leadership through diversity.

Church leadership can be decolonized by embracing the diversity of leadership, decentralizing administration, and allowing native people more ownership of their ministry and destinies. Female pastoral leadership is on the rise, but the heads of most denominations are still old white men who are influenced by their superiority complex. The lack of leadership diversity at the helm of most Western denominations is antithetical to the "12

Disciples Approach" to church governance established by Christ. In his leadership team, Jesus had the following: Simon (also called Peter), Andrew (Peter's brother), James (son of Zebedee), John (James' brother), Philip, Bartholomew, Thomas, Matthew (the tax collector), James (son of Alphaeus), Thaddaeus, Simon (the Zealot), Judas Iscariot (who later betrayed him). There was diversity in character traits, careers, and conceptualization of the world. Some were fishermen, Matthew was in finance, and Simon, the Zealot, was a political activist. Peter was an impetuous conservative who loved the status quo, while James and John, the "Sons of Thunder," were opportunists searching for power. Thomas was a detached, skeptical pessimist who was a matter-of-fact person. Nonetheless, they formed the best proto-typical leadership team the world has ever known.

Decolonize church, the translation of the Bible into the native language of the people.

There are nearly 450 translations of the Bible in the world. Some are word-for-word (literal translations through formal equivalence), some are thought for thought (dynamic translations or dynamic equivalence translations), and others are paraphrases or restatements of Scripture. Individuals wrote some and others by groups of people. Everyone writes for an audience with a particular purpose; hence, a translation of the Bible can be skewed to distort, misrepresent, alter, pervert, or falsify the original text deliberately or through ignorance. It is not acceptable for people of color to read translations of the Bible that were not done by a racially diverse group because, like history, everyone interprets from their perspective! In his article titled, "Why it matters if a racially diverse group translated your Bible?" Esau McCauley maintained that it is very important that people of color understand the philosophies and backgrounds of those whose translations of the Bible they read because if the translators hold harmful or injurious beliefs against others, those beliefs will be reflected in their interpretation. If a translator believes that the Bible justifies slavery, the "curse of Ham," or the superiority of one race above another, those should be disclaimers. The Bible has been used to justify every imaginable atrocity against indigenous people.

Decolonize the church through a change in church Imagery

Many of the pictures of Jesus need a little color. What are the most profound visual, auditory, tactile, olfactory, and gustatory images associated with the Christian church? How do we perceive worship in the presence of God? God is spirit, but our visual image of him is important. Jesus, God's son, is presented to us as a blue-eyed white man with all the trimmings of a Caucasian, yet Jesus never lived in the Caucus Mountains of Europe. He is presented to us as a white man, although the concept of whiteness was not even invested when he lived. Most historical images of Jesus are that of a man of color, and people have come to recognize the church's deception as it presents a white man living in Nazareth in the first century! The visual imagery of the Jesus we see and dream about is distorted. The image of Christ has been taken, bleached, white-washed, and reconfigured to perpetuate the notion of white superiority in the world. White Christianity has done a magnificent photoshop on Jesus! Thus, we must return to the Jesus of Nazareth, the Christ – a man of color, and his mother, Mary - the Black Madonna. We must see the 12 Disciples as men of color in Israel. This perspective of the context of the historical text is critical in translating the Bible.

Decolonize the church through New Forms Evangelism

Christianity has had a history of forcing people to accept Christ. Evangelism by force is unbiblical; it is not Christlike. The Crusades against Muslims did not force them to accept Christ. The inquisitions did not force people to accept Christianity. The decimation of so-called witches in the ignominious witch Trials did not stop the practice of witchcraft, and colonization and neo-colonialization, which disrupted and destroyed many indigenous cultures, did not result in the wholesale conversion of native people. We are called to use the powers of persuasion, not the power of the gun, to convince people of their need for salvation: "Therefore, since we know what it means to fear the Lord, we try to persuade men. What we are is clear to God, and I hope it is also clear to your conscience (2 Cor. 5:11, BSB).

Evangelism that involves the presentation of Christ while respecting a people's cultural and historical ethos is desirable. Evangelism without respect, love, or grace is forced evangelism! In America, white evangelicals want to "own the libs," that is, dominate, defeat, or humiliate their political and social opponents. It echoes the past, where colonizers tried to force repentance on the "heathen" or so-called "uncivilized." It never worked then, and it will never work now! The Gospel is the power of God to bring salvation. People's choices to reject Christ must be respected.

Decolonize Church Theology

Theology is the study of God, and Christian theology is how God is revealed in the Scriptures. Many Central American Christians embraced liberation theology to join the cause for social justice. Evangelical Christians have embraced the prosperity gospel to present capitalism as God's plan for everyone. To escape accountability, many 21st-century Christians embrace situational theology. Their actions and morals are based on how situations and events present themselves. We need a re-emergence of the "Old Time Religion" that has been sanitized and decolonized. How is God revealed to the 21st-century person with access to technologies, libraries, and historical and archaeological records? In an age of late-stage capitalism, a theology of resistance must be established against the one percent who controls the world's resources and pollutes the earth without respect for the working class, people experiencing poverty, and the vulnerable. A theology of preparation for hard times must be established. People need to know how to martial their forces and husband their resources. A proper eschatological theology is not just waiting for the apocalypse but preparing for it and surviving it! It's an abandonment of the theology of reticence and reluctance. A theology that sees the image of God in all humanity and seeks to protect it.

Decolonize church Attire

The church has been a major purveyor of culture. In Africa, many judges still adjudicate as they wear thick, white wigs. The kind of wigs that are worn in the United Kingdom. Why do African judges wear wigs in the hot African Sun? They are following their colonizers. Ethnic churches should begin to wear the colors and attire of their native countries in the courts of law or the courts of God. Attire must be a matter of choice, not force! A three-piece suit is best suited for cold climates, not the center of the earth.

The church has been a primary center for fashion, and some people go there to show off their new clothes and affirm their social status. Religious garbs, robes, and paraphernalia have been bequeathed to the church from enslavers.

Decolonize the church through Education

Catholics who operated residential schools in North America used them to educate and Christianize indigenous people. This educational approach that resulted in thousands of children's deaths was perpetuated worldwide. Seeing a church or religious school is traumatic to many former students, now adults in society. Christian education must change. It cannot be forced, limited, or myopic. Christianity can hold its place among all religions if taught with honesty and love.

In an age of misinformation and disinformation, can the church be a source of truth: biblical, social, and political truths? Or is the church so steep in misinformation and miseducation that it cannot decipher good from evil? An anti-intellectual church is a church that is ripe for manipulation and abuse. Another "Dark Age" is imminent if Christians do not abandon conspiracy theories and hold to the truth!

Christ is the only true liberator! Great missionaries have tried to bring the Gospel of Jesus Christ to a world without understanding him. Some have used unbiblical, inhumane, and lethal methods of conversion. A colonized world needs therapy and liberation from the trauma of many mean nuns and perverted priests. Across the globe, Christianity needs liberation from the tentacles of colonizers. Colonizers have framed our concept of God, beauty, loyalty, power, and identity in the world.

References

Merriam-Webster. (n.d.). Decolonize. In Merriam-Webster.com dictionary. Retrieved May 10, 2023, from https://www.merriam-webster.com/dictionary/decolonize

McCaulley, E. (2019, September 23). Why it matters if your Bible was translated by a racially diverse group. The Washington Post. Retrieved May 10, 2023, from https://www.washingtonpost.com/religion/2019/09/23/why-it-matters-if-your-bible-was-translated-by-racially-diverse-group/

Sermon #20: The Darkest Moments of Jesus

What was your darkest moment? Was it when you failed a medical or academic test, a loved one passed, lost a good job, or discovered that your best friend was a frenemy? Jesus was destined for glory through suffering (Isa. 53:3-5).

A Friend Denied him. Denial, an act of disowning someone, is ubiquitous. Which is more profound: A parent's denial of a child, a sibling's denial of another sibling, or the denial of a friend? Peter's denial of Jesus was comprehensive. He adamantly refused to admit his knowledge of Christ three times: Singularly before a servant, privately before a bystander, and publicly before a crowd. This intensification of denial indicates a complete repudiation of his master and friendship. Which of these denials was worse? Peter's denial was fierce because he was a member of the inner circle of Jesus's friends. They shared important moments and had unforgettable memories. In this moment of self-preservation, Peter renounced and rejected his relationship with Jesus. The denial was problematic, pitiful, yet prophetic: "Truly I tell you," Jesus said to him, "tonight before the rooster crows, you will deny me three times." (Matt. 26:34). What were the consequences of this denial on Christ and Peter: Christ felt the power of rejection, repulsion, and reproach, Peter felt the power of his frailty, fear, and fate. Peter is not the only one guilty of denying Christ: "Thousands of Christians compromise their faith in Jesus Christ by denying Him. Even some clergymen neglect or deliberately refuse to close a public prayer in the name of Jesus for fear of offending an unbeliever. They cannot endure the persecution that may follow an acknowledgment of Jesus Christ."— Billy Graham. He's correct. By moving away from biblical Christianity, a large part of the universal church has denied and disgraced Christ and put him to open shame.

Abandoned by his Prayer Group (Gethsemane)

Is the church losing its place as a citadel of communion, fellowship, and support? Overwhelmed with physical, psychological, emotional, and mental despair, Jesus' disciples abandoned him in one of the dark moments of his life. Jesus' anguish was so deep that "his sweat was as it were great drops of blood falling to the ground." The moment of death was imminent, and his agony had commenced. The specter of death surrounded him, yet no one was there to hold his hand or pray with him. But Jesus' final sting of abandonment would come not from his friends but from his father: "And about the ninth hour Jesus cried out with a loud voice, saying, "Eli, Eli, lema sabachthani?" that is, "My God, My God, why have You forsaken Me?" (Matt. 27:46). Abandonment from God or man, whether redemptive or punitive, is painful. Children abandoned in childhood become emotionally unstable adults—the abandoned needy healing.

Betrayed by a Brother (Judas)

Betrayal, a treacherous and fraudulent act of delivering someone into the hands of an enemy, is inevitable. Every significant leader of history has been betrayed, and Jesus is no exception. A group of greedy conspirators assassinated Julius Caesar, the prodigious Roman General, and his nephew, Marcus Brutus, was amongst them. Benedict Arnold was overlooked for promotion and stirred with greed, shared secrets, and joined ranks with the British against a fledging American nation!

Judas delivered Jesus to his enemies through fraud: "What will you give me if I deliver Jesus to you?" (Matt. 26:15). It was a betrayal from greed.

Mocked by his enemies

A mockery is a tool of psychological and spiritual warfare. It uses words to tear down, degrade, and denigrate someone. It's one thing to be roasted by a friend and another to be criticized by detractors and enemies. Mockery takes effort and is often calculating, confrontational, and cruel. Before his crucifixion, people mocked *Jesus' divinity.* As God, he knew everything, yet they blindfolded, mocked, and cursed as they asked him to identify his antagonist. They mocked his divinity and *royalty*: "They bowed and mocked Him, saying, "Hail, King of the Jews!" (Luke 22: 63, Matt.27:29). Further, they mocked *his capability*: "He saved others, let him save himself." Finally, they mocked his *credibility:* "for he said,

'I am the Son of God" (Matt.27:43). Satan used mockery to strike at Jesus' heart and questioned his existence, purpose, and destiny!

Exposed and violated by thieves (Robe)

Jesus was stripped of his clothes in the act of public humiliation. And, in the act of prophetic fulfillment, Roman soldiers divided his clothes into four and used a selection process to decide who would get his undergarment. It was seamless (John 19:23,24). Such behavior could have embroiled Jesus' emotions and distracted him from his purpose of dying for the redemption of humanity. But Jesus showed restraint under pressure and love in humility. His focus was constant, and his love was unconditional. What would you do if you were robbed and humiliated in public view?

Jesus was isolated from a mother, Rejected by a Father (John 19:25-27, Matthew 27:45-46). Hanging between heaven and earth, Christ, the one who was with the Father in the creation of the universe, stood alone. His mother, some of his brethren, and a large crowd were present, but they could not comfort him. He looked to heaven for solace but felt no warmth from his father. He was isolated from his mother and rejected by his father. It was a moment of profound alienation! Some question whether a righteous God could reject his son, even for a moment! But how could a holy God embrace a son carrying the world's sins? "He was despised and rejected by men, a man of sorrows and acquainted with grief, and as one from whom men hide their faces he was despised, and we esteemed him not" (Isa. 53:3).

He was crucified as a common criminal. Crucifixion is an ancient method of execution, where the condemned is tied or nailed to a large wooden cross and left to hang until dead. Roman crucifixion was a form of capital punishment reserved for individuals considered the worst criminals, and Jesus of Nazareth was executed in this way. Hebrew culture also supported that this punishment was reserved for the most odious: "Christ redeemed us from the curse of the law by becoming a curse for us, for it is written: 'Cursed is everyone who is hung on a tree'" (Galatians 3:13).

Roman crucifixion was a particularly severe execution. The cross, the instrument of execution, consisted of two beams of wood called the stipes and the patibulum. The stripes were the upright beam that remained implanted in the ground at the place of execution. The patibulum or crossbeam was carried across the shoulders of the prisoner to the execution site. This crossbeam generally weighed approximately 110 pounds. Scourging prisoners was a separate form of punishment, which consisted of flagellating the prisoner with a short, heavy whip made of leather thongs with lead balls at the end of each thong. That Jesus of Nazareth was both scourged and then crucified reveals the enormity of the price He paid for the ransom of sinners. "For even the Son of Man did not come to be served, but to serve, and to give his life as a ransom for many" (Mark 10:45).

In the darkest moments of his life, Jesus was denied, abandoned, betrayed, mocked, exposed, robbed, isolated from his mother, rejected by his father, and crucified. But having completed his mission on earth, no grave could hold his body down! "Therefore, I will divide him a portion with the many, and he shall divide the spoil with the strong because he poured out his soul to death and was numbered with the transgressors, yet he bore the sin of many and makes intercession for the transgressors (Isa. 53:12). Every dark moment is a moment for God to shine. He is the light. Jesus faced many dark moments, and so will you! "Then Jesus said to his disciples, "If any of you wants to be my follower, you must give up your way, take up your cross, and follow me" (Matt. 16:24).

Sermon #21: Making Decisions in Life

"Do not be anxious about anything, but in every situation, by prayer and petition, with thanksgiving, present your requests to God" (Phil 4:6).

Only the dead do not make decisions. Those alive determine their daily, weekly, monthly, and yearly mode of operation! The decisions we must make are varied and complex. So how people navigate life's critical decisions determines whether they live fruitfully or exist on the periphery of life! How do you make decisions?

1. People make decisions *rationally or cerebrally.* Their approach to decision-making is methodical and researched. They are not impetuous, and they assess options critically, then they decide. A biblical example of rational decision-makers is the Berean Jews: "for they received the message with great eagerness and examined the Scriptures every day to see if these teachings were true" (Acts 17:11).

2. People make decisions *irrationally or casually.* Without much thought, people often jump to profound, life-altering **Conclusion**s without traveling on the ladder of inference. Ultimately, they tend to ask, "how did I get here?" Irrational decision-making can lead to regret. Impulsive or nonchalant people actors are acting from the perspective of purpose. In a moment of irrationality, Simon Peter cut off the right ear of a high priest servant,

forgetting Christ's redemptive purpose. Many crimes, suicides, and regrettable investments are made in the heat of the moment!

3. People make decisions *culturally.* People make patterns of choices based on familial or societal traditions. Religion is a fundamental aspect of culture. Christians claim that their interpretation of the Bible governs their decision-making process. Muslims appeal to the Koran for important decisions. Hindus demand to their pantheon of gods and sacred writings in crucial moments. Abraham impregnated his maid to procure his posterity. It was a cultural practice, but it was not divinely authorized. Cultural practices can be diametrically opposed to the will of God.

4. People make decisions *ideologically.* A particular political belief and tribal instincts govern them. Capitalists make decisions based on free enterprise, competition, and greed. Socialists embrace reform, social justice, and equality for all. Pacifists are pragmatists who are pro-peace and anti-militarist. An ideology is limited. No one lives his life based solely on the doctrine of a few. Capitalism, socialism, pacifism, and all other isms were created with a particular intent. What did Jesus do to the capitalists in the temple?

5. People tend to make decisions *intuitionally or abdominally, and a*n immediate and direct apprehension directs their paths. Gut feelings control these people! Many say, "trust your intuition," but not all gut feelings are correct! What would you do if your gut feelings were incestuous, murderous, or terroristic?

6. People often make decisions based on the *fallacy of popularity.* If a famous person eats dirt, then dirt must be good! If most people believe that vaccine is harmful, then it is terrible! The majority can be wrong! The people's voice could be the voice of the devil and not the voice of God!

7. People make decisions *altruistically.* They are conscious of being their brother's keeper. They love God, man, and the universe! They are socially, ethically, and globally aware.

8. People make decisions *anally.* They have no good intentions! Meanness and disdain for others propel them, and they act in a spirit of superiority and arrogance.

9. People make decisions *comically.* They accept the journey of life with a sense of humor! They can turn even negative situations into cheerfulness and joy! They have an ironic, parodic, and satirical disposition. For some, life is not a joke; others feel it is! Humor is good medicine, but it might not be a tool for living.

10. People make decisions *intrinsically.* They do what is natural to them. Some believe that humanity is intrinsically flawed and lacks goodness in human nature. It might be natural for someone to do good in a certain situation, but another person would do the opposite in the same situation. When people make life situationally, they ignore a greater body of truth.

11. People make decisions *scientifically*. They examine and analyze scientific studies to formulate an opinion.

They look particularly at evidence-based, peer-reviewed research that carries empirical data. Some might argue that empirical data can be manipulated.

12. People make decisions *devotionally*. Christians believe that through prayers and fasting, listening to the advice of the aged and experienced, and reading the Bible for confirmation from God, they can confidently make decisions! King David made multiple inquiries of God. In his lessons from the Prayer Life of David, Tom Stuart wrote: "One of the salient features of David's prayers, as demonstrated primarily in the Psalms, is the variety of types and foci of prayer. Some psalms are petitions, complaints, laments, spiritual warfare, prophetic declarations, litanies of God's faithfulness, and hymns of praise. There are psalms focused on Israel, the nations, the enemy, the oppressed, the overcomer, the sinner, the forgiven, the past, the future, the wonder of creation, and the glory of God" (Stuart, 2014).

People should use multiple tools to make crucial decisions. If someone has an intuition, it would be in his best interest to investigate it scientifically, intrinsically, altruistically, rationally, and biblically before deciding to move forward.

References

Stuart, Tom. Lessons from the Prayer Life of David. March 3rd, 2014.

https://tomstuart.org/2014/03/03/lessons-from-the-prayer-life-of-david/

Sermon #22: Seven Challenges of Mephibosheth

2 Samuel 9:1-13 introduces Mephibosheth, a character with a funny-sounding name but a tragic story. Mephibosheth, whose name means "born to destroy the shame," is the grandson of Saul, the first king of Israel. Despite his potential to become king himself, Mephibosheth finds himself in a twisted and broken state. He is physically incapacitated, with twisted limbs and broken ankles, and lives in exile in a place called lo-debar. This situation reflects how Satan aims to silence and imprison us, leading to lost integrity, mortality, and respect. The passage raises questions for introspection, asking if we find ourselves in relationships resembling lo-debar, where communication is absent, or if we are crippled by the actions of others that have pushed us into self-imposed exile.

Seven Challenges of Mephibosheth

First, he was an orphan without a will. His parents had died unsuspectingly. This wounded man lost his birthright without uttering a word or committing a single evil deed. He was a frightened little boy of five years old when he was buried in the land of silence. At five, he was separated from his father, grandfather, and destiny. 1 Sam 31:2, 8 (the Philistines killed Saul and his sons).

Second, he was disabled and physically challenged. He was lame or disabled in both feet. It was not Mephi's Fault (2 Sam 4:4-6).

Third, he was exiled to Lo-Debar. What is the meaning of Lo-debar? In Hebrew, Lo- means "no, or not." Debar means word. The Lo-Debar is a place of no words, no communication, a place of silent exile. Mephi did not put himself into exile. He was a frightened little boy of five years old when he was buried in the land of silence.

Fourth, his self-esteem was in the gutters. Despite possessing a sound mind, Mephi, referring to himself as a "dead dog," faced physical challenges. He desired to walk, but his condition hindered him from doing so. Despite his efforts, the truth remained that he was physically disabled, unable to move or reach his destination independently. As a grown man, he relied on others to carry him to fulfill his calling and receive the kindness of the King, as he was paralyzed.

Fifth, he lost his inheritance. What was Mephi's situation? His father and grandfather had died, and his uncles had died. There was no one to inherit the posterity of Saul. When King David met Mephi, he said: "I will restore to you all the land that belonged to your grandfather Saul ..." 2 Sam 9:7. Lord, restore my inheritance.

Sixth, he didn't know his rights and privileges as royalty. "And hath made us kings and priests unto God and his Father, to him be glory and dominion forever and ever. Amen," Rev 1:6. A son of royalty was on the brink of poverty, and starvation was knocking at his door. Lord, restore my rights and privileges.

Seventh, he lived in fear of death. He was hiding. When he saw David, he thought that the king had come to kill him. His grandfather had tried to kill David. But the king had come to bless him and restore him. David said to him, "Do not fear, for I will surely show you kindness for

Jonathan your father's sake and will restore to you all the land of Saul, your grandfather, and you shall eat bread at my table continually." 2 Sam 9:7 David made a covenant with Jonathan in 1 Samuel 20, promising to show kindness to Jonathan's descendants. David's kindness was linked to his covenant.

Despite his physical challenges, Mephi was a prince vested with royal blood and deserving of a life of power and prosperity. Mephibosheth was called from "a place of no return" to a place and peace and honor! Some of Mephi's handicaps were not visible, and his legs were always under the table, but it prevented him from rising to greatness. There are hidden issues in our lives that no one sees. What is sentencing you into silence?

Sermon #23: Baptismal Imperative

Text Matt. 3:13-17

A Christian baptism is an obedience to Christ's command, submission to God, identification with Christ, and a public testimony of faith. It is an essential rite of passage for Christians, marking the beginning of a new life in Christ.

First, it is Purposeful. Water baptism does not save people but demonstrates they have decided to follow Christ. The purpose of baptism is found in Matthew 3: 15: "And Jesus answering said unto him, Suffer it to be so now: for thus it becometh us to fulfill all righteousness. Then he suffered him".

Second, it is an acceptance of Power. The power comes from the new life, and the power comes from being baptized in Jesus' death and raised through baptism to walk in the newness of life. Romans 6:4 "Therefore we are buried with him by baptism into death: that like as Christ was raised from the dead by the glory of the Father, even so, we also should walk in newness of life."

Third, it brings the Pleasure that comes with obedience; it's a fulfillment that comes with the forgiveness of sin.

Fourth, it is an act of Positioning, preparing the believer for ministry, just as Jesus was baptized before His ministry.

Fifth, Placement. People are baptized "in Christ."

Sixth, Potential. After water baptism, a believer can walk in the newness of life: Therefore, we are buried with him by baptism into death: like as Christ was raised from the dead by the glory of the Father; even so, we also should walk in newness of life" (Rom6:4). "

Seventh, Progress. Water baptism is a checkmark on one's spiritual journey.

Baptism does not save anyone, and it is an outward sign of an inner decision that one has already made to follow Christ. But there are imperatives of baptism that have several significant implications.

Sermon #24: Super Bloom

I want to share a recent fantastic phenomenon in California: the super bloom of wildflowers that has transformed the landscape into a magnificent and colorful sight. Visitors flock to the area to bask in nature's glory! The super bloom is so incredible it can be seen via satellite. This event speaks to us; is a clear reminder of God's faithfulness, provision, and predestination, even during difficult times. A fundamental DNA marker of a Christian is bloom, not gloom!

In the book of James, we read that "Every good and perfect gift is from above, coming down from the Father of the heavenly lights, who does not change like shifting shadows" (James 1:17). The super bloom is a perfect example of this. The seeds that lay dormant in the soil for decades are now blooming exponentially, bringing new life to the earth. Seeds are metaphors. The super bloom of seeds represents important concepts:

First, they represent ideas and creativity. Like a seed, an idea may start small, but it has the potential to grow into something big and transformative. Creative minds often use the seed metaphor to describe the germination of new ideas and artistic visions. A futuristic concept is ready for manifestation: "And the Lord said to me, "Write my answer on a billboard, large and clear so that anyone can read it at a glance and rush to tell the others. But these things I plan won't happen right away. The time approaches when the vision will be fulfilled slowly, steadily, and surely. If it seems slow, do not despair, for these things will surely come to pass. Just be patient! They will not be overdue a single day!" (Habakkuk 2:2-4). Second, they represent potential and possibility. Seeds represent the potential for growth and the opportunity for a better future. They are metaphors for untapped potential, hidden talents, or unfulfilled dreams. Talents, skills, and aptitudes can rise again! Like the seeds that waited for their opportunity to bloom, our dormant talents wait for their opportunities to manifest.

Third, they represent change and transformation. Just as a seed is transformed into a plant or tree, people and societies can undergo transformation and change. Seeds can metaphorize personal or societal growth, development, and progress. God's Timing and Blessings are Perfect. Just as the rain eventually came to California, so too can God's blessings rain down on us when we least expect it. We must trust God's timing, for He knows what is best for us. The super bloom did not happen overnight; it resulted from a long waiting period and hoping for rain. Similarly, God's blessings may take time to manifest, but we must remain steadfast in our faith and trust in His plan for our lives.

Fourth, they represent faith and spirituality. In many religious and spiritual traditions, seeds are metaphors for faith and belief. Just as a seed requires faith in the soil to grow, a person may require faith in a higher power to achieve personal growth and transformation. Waiting for one's super bloom can be difficult, but it's worth the wait. People should wait for their super bloom. The seeds that God has planted will answer the call of God and the universe. When it's your moment for exponential growth, the rain will break out! "But those who wait for the Lord [who expect, look for, and hope in Him] shall change and renew their strength and power; they shall lift their wings and mount up [close to God] as eagles [mount up to the sun]; they shall run and not be weary, they shall walk and not faint or become tired" (Isa. 40:31). You might be a resting or a restive seed. Still, soon you will experience the latter rain!

Fifth, they represent relationships and connections. Seeds are metaphors for the connections and relationships between people. Like a seed that requires sunlight, water, and nutrients, relationships require care, attention, and nurturing to flourish. Sixth, they represent timing and divine providence. May we have the patience to wait for the rain of extraordinary rain blessings yet to come in due time. And let us remember that which is dormant is not dead and that our talents, dreams, visions, and ideas may just be waiting for their transformation.

Seventh, they represent a cause for celebration and thanksgiving. We should be very thankful when abundance comes to us. Not everyone will celebrate our success; haters will be haters. But give thanks, anyway! Never forget - that which is dormant is not dead, and talents and dreams are just waiting for their opportunities to rise. If a man is not dead, do not call him a ghost; if a seed is dormant, it's just a host! The seeds sown in our lives for decades will bloom exponentially at the right time. God's faithfulness and provision will come to us in His perfect timing. May we continue to trust in Him and give thanks for His blessings even before they arrive!

Sermon #25: Seven Important Christmas Gifts

Text: 1 Cor. 13

The wise men brought three gifts to Jesus: gold, silver, frankincense, and myrrh. The silver and gold attest to His kingship, the frankincense attests to His divinity, and the myrrh attests to His bitter suffering, which would bring salvation and healing.

What are the other gifts for which we might be thankful?

First, let us be thankful for the gift of life. We are alive – standing on redemption ground; possibilities are endless. We are in the land of the living. Some relish their lives without thinking about life after death. We all are going to live forever. The question is, where? The gift of hope, a hope that does not put us to shame (Rom. 5:5).

Second, let us be thankful for the gift of love. There is a love that flows from God to family and friends. God accepts us just as we are. Race, gender, or ethnicity does not matter, and social, religious, or financial status is irrelevant to Him. We are loved (John 3: 16. 1 Cor. 13).

Third, let us give thanks for the gift of friendship. "A friend sticketh closer than a brother." "The greatest gift is not found in a store nor under a tree but in the hearts of true friends. -- *Cindy Lew.* "True friends are hard to find, difficult to leave, and impossible to forget" - Amanda Kunkle. In an age of betrayal, friendship is scarce, so treasure it if you have it! We must find the courage to abandon toxic friendships. Some who pretend to be friends are blood-sucking parasites. They take but never give! Narcissists cannot develop genuine friendships. They lack the capacity for empathy. But a true friend can be closer to you than a blood relative.

Fourth, let us give thanks for the gift of service. We have an opportunity to serve God and our fellowmen. Some serve voluntarily; others are employed. Some serve in the church; others serve in the secular society. But we serve. Continue. Service excellence should be our goal. Find the time to serve someone. The server is more significant than the served. Fifth, be thankful for the gift of laughter. Laughter is good medicine. Laugh at yourself, laughter at the paradox and mysteries of life. Proverbs 15:13 says, "A glad heart makes a cheerful countenance." Proverbs 17:22 says, "A cheerful heart is a good medicine, but a downcast spirit dries up the bones." God gives us this gift so that we can laugh at life's mysteries, contradictions, and complexities.

Sixth, be thankful for the gift of tears. Have you ever gone beyond sadness? Grief can create an inability to cry. People who are severely depressed lose the gift of tears. The eyes and natural values of the emotions can become dry as the forest. Be thankful when you can cry for joy and when you can cry for sadness. Everyone who can cry should cry. It is a cathartic, exhilarating experience! Men should cry. Women have perfected the art! Jesus wept for the loss of a friend, and so should you! Remember, "weeping may remain for a night, but rejoicing comes in the morning."

Finally, be thankful for the Gift of Christ. Some question the historicity and divinity of Christ, but we must be thankful for the gift of Christ, the promised Messiah.

Chapter Two: Preface Preach Truth

And there are also many other things that Jesus did, which, if they were recorded one by one, I suppose that even the world itself could not contain the books that would be written (Jhn. 21:25, AMP).

Knowledge has increased exponentially! Encyclopedias must be updated regularly to keep pace with the rise in information, yet some are rigorously opposing historical, scientific, and personal truth! Content is created every second, and discoveries render previously held beliefs false. Hebrew enslaved people didn't build the pyramids; the Egyptians did. The Great Walls of China are not the only places visible from space! And more species of biological life are discovered every day!

Archeologists continue to find artifacts that help us to piece together a more wholesome picture of the past. A more authentic portrayal of the biblical landscape is emerging, and it does not hurt the biblical text; it gives credence to it. Evidence strengthens faith. But it can turn people away when discrepancies arise. For this cause, some have abandoned the true and living God. They have left Christ, "the truth and the life," and abandoned Christianity's true history and message. Christians must be prepared to answer questions relating to the actual canon of Scripture, why the King James has 66 books, the Orthodox Bible has 74, the Catholic Bible has 72, and the

Ethiopian Bible, which is older than all others, have 81 books. With the advent of knowledge, people are asking why the original king James version of 1611 had all the Catholic books of the Bible and why they were removed. People need clarity to "rightly divide the word of truth."

In their quest for historical truth, historians and archaeologists have had to go back to artifacts and writings of ancient people to bring us a more accurate story of humanity! So, writing is critical for the survival of civilization. Much of the history fed to Western cultures are from the colonizing victors' perspective; thus, history revisions are overdue.

Only truth can give credibility to Christianity. A wind of change has come, and the rejection of the Christian faith has accelerated. Those who still believe that Jesus is Christ must seek to contend with the negative issues of our Christian past and the issues of life and death. And they must employ many methods to take the Gospel globally and not repeat the errors of the past. Missionaries must preach Christ, not capitalism. How Christians penetrate cultures with the Gospel must be transparent and honest. We cannot win the "lost" at the cost of honesty and truth! For example, due to their lack of understanding of sin and guilt, the Panare Indians of Venezuela had difficulty grappling with what Christ had done for them. Thus, Catholic missionaries created a Bible for them. It was not a translation or transliteration but a travesty of the truth. It was not faithful to the original text. It was a bible that told a story that the

Panare Indians were the ones who had crucified Christ. It was a bald-faced lie! In the newly minted Bible for the Panare Indians, scenes in the life of Jesus were reimagined, reconfigured, and restructured, and the people were sold a message, at best, was harmful to the cause of Christ. Our methods of evangelism must be creative, not clandestine! The Gospel of Christ is the power of God that brings salvation. A Gospel of lies cannot bring salvation to anyone. Chapter Two: Sermons 26-50

Chapter TWO: Sermons 26-50

Sermon #26: Seven Little Foxes

In the Song of Solomon, we find a beautiful love story between King Solomon and his bride. This poetic book uses the imagery of love and marriage to illustrate the relationship between God and His people. In chapter 2, verse 15, we find a call to action, a plea to catch the little foxes that spoil the vineyards. Today, we'll explore what this verse means and how to apply it.

I. The Vineyard and the Foxes
The Vineyard and the Foxes is a metaphorical concept that symbolizes our relationship with God. The vineyard represents this relationship, serving as a place of growth and productivity. Just like a well-tended vineyard yields abundant fruit, a strong connection with God brings blessings and fulfillment. The foxes represent the various factors that can harm or ruin our relationship with God. These can be considered negative influences, temptations, or distractions that divert our attention and devotion from God. They may appear insignificant or harmless at first glance, referred to as "little foxes." However, they can cause considerable damage and hinder our spiritual growth if ignored or allowed to persist unchecked.

II. Identifying the Little Foxes
  A. Gluttony, envy, malice, pride, lying, laziness, slander

First, Gluttony. Gluttony is the over-indulgence and over-consumption of food, drink, or intoxicants to the point of waste. Proverbs 23:20-21 warns, "Do not join those who drink too much wine or gorge themselves on meat, for drunkards and gluttons become poor, and drowsiness clothes them in rags." We should not allow our appetite for food to control us; we must control our cravings.

Second, Envy. A feeling of sadness or displeasure on hearing about the success or prosperity of another. Romans 13:13 "Let us walk honestly, as in the day; not in rioting and drunkenness, not in chambering and wantonness, not in strife and envying." James 3:16 "For where envying and strife are, there is confusion and every evil work." Examples: Cain Gen. 4:5; Joseph's brothers (Gen.37:11).

Third, Malice. The desire to injure someone.1 Peter 2:1 says, "Wherefore laying aside all malice, and all guile, and hypocrisies, and envies, and all evil speaking." Fourth, Pride. Pride is self-importance, an excessive opinion of oneself. Proverbs 16:5 "Everyone proud in heart is an abomination to the LORD: though hand joins in hand, he shall not be unpunished." Prov 29:23 A man's pride shall bring him low: but honor shall uphold the humble in spirit.

Fifth, Lying. Ephesians 4:25, "Wherefore putting away lying, speak every man truth with his neighbor: for we are members one of another." Revelation 21:8, "...and all liars shall have their part in the lake which burneth with fire and brimstone."

Sixth, Laziness. Laziness is inactivity at work, and it's a dislike for work. "Yet a little sleep, a little slumber, a little folding of the hands to sleep: So, shall thy poverty come as one that travelleth and thy want as an armed man" (Proverbs 6:10, 11).

Seventh, Slander. It encompasses murmuring, complaining, and gossiping, which is warned against in Colossians 3:8. Negative behaviors are "little foxes" that potentially slowly erode our relationship with God. To protect our connection with Him, we must be watchful and identify these harmful tendencies before they cause significant damage. Taking proactive measures such as confessing our sins, seeking forgiveness, and making positive changes in our lives is crucial. Additionally, cultivating healthy habits like prayer, reading the Bible, and serving others can help us capture and overcome these "little foxes" that threaten our spiritual well-being.

The little foxes may seem insignificant, but they can cause significant damage to our relationship with God. Let us be vigilant and catch the little foxes that spoil our vineyards. Let us confess our sins, ask for forgiveness, and change our lives. Let us develop healthy habits that will strengthen our relationship with God. And let us remember that just as Solomon and his bride found love in the vineyards, we, too, can find love and joy in our relationship with God.

Sermon #27: Seven People Who Encountered Despair

Text: "They repay me with evil for the good I do. I am sick with despair" Psalms 35:12. Despair is a terrible negative emotion that can drive an individual to the brink. Despair can overcome a person or a church, or a nation.

Elijah. He had just called down fire from heaven and killed the prophets of Baal. He had been waging war against sin and corruption. His despair was not a result of sin but his opposition to sin.1 Kings 19:4 "But he went a day's journey into the wilderness, and came and sat down under a juniper tree: and he requested for himself that he might die; and said, It is enough; now, O LORD, take away my life; for I am not better than my fathers."

David. He had committed adultery and murder, and he lost a child. His house was in an uproar. "He lifted me out of the pit of despair, the mud, and the mire. He set my feet on solid ground and steadied me as I walked along" Psalms 40:2. A song for the ascent to Jerusalem. From the depths of despair, O LORD, I call for your help" Psalms 130:1. It takes the hand of God to take one from distress.

Samson. He disobeyed God and married the wrong woman, so in his physical and spiritual blindness, he prayed" "And Samson called unto the LORD, and said, O Lord God, remember me, I pray thee, and strengthen me, I pray thee, only this once, O God, that I may be at once avenged of the Philistines for my two eyes"(Jud. 16: 28). His despair was a result of disobedience.

Cain. Genesis 4:13,14 say, "And Cain said unto the LORD, my punishment is greater than I can bear. Behold, thou hast driven me out this day from the face of the earth; and from thy face shall I be hidden; and I shall be a fugitive and a vagabond in the earth, and it shall come to pass, that every one that findeth me shall slay me." His despair was a result of jealousy, anger, and murder.

Ahithophel. Ahithophel, a counselor of King David, experienced the devastating effects of despair. His loss of hope became apparent when his advice was disregarded, leading him to believe his cause was doomed. Overwhelmed by sadness and helplessness, Ahithophel felt incapable of altering the situation. Despair impaired his judgment, leading him to make regrettable decisions, such as joining Absalom's rebellion against David. Consumed by despair and with no expectation for a better future, Ahithophel resorted to self-destructive behavior, taking his own life due to his shattered hopes and failed plans.

Judas Iscariot. Judas Iscariot's decision to take his own life was driven by his overwhelming despair, which stemmed from his profound guilt and remorse for betraying Jesus. The weight of his actions became unbearable, leading him to cast down the thirty pieces of silver, a symbol of his betrayal, in the temple before hanging himself. Judas's suicide was a tragic outcome of his deep anguish and despair over his role in the betrayal of Christ.

Israel. In Joel 1: 12, the prophet describes a situation in Israel where various trees, including the vine, fig tree, pomegranate tree, palm tree, and the apple tree, have withered. This imagery represents the land's desolation and lack of vitality and explains that this devastation has occurred because joy has faded away from the people of Israel. It suggests that the nation of Israel has fallen into deep despair and sorrow because God has chosen to withhold His blessings from them.

To overcome despair, seeking support and assistance, prioritizing self-care, engaging in mindfulness practices, reframing negative thoughts, and discovering personal meaning and purpose are beneficial. It is essential to recognize that each person's journey is unique, and what may be effective for one individual might not work for another. The key lies in being open to various strategies and persistently experimenting until finding the best approaches.

Sermon #28: Seven Styles of Christian Worship

Worship experiences can vary from church to church, generation to generation, and coast to coast. They range from lifeless stoic experiences to animated experiences of all kinds. But each experience is sacred to the adherents and should be respected. Some churches have had to create contemporary worship experiences for younger worshipers and maintain the purity of the fixed worship styles for veterans and boomers.

The different styles of Christian worship serve different purposes, including connecting believers to the historical traditions of the church, creating a sense of relevance and meaning in contemporary contexts, emphasizing the work of the Holy Spirit, sharing the gospel, and inviting people into a personal relationship with Jesus Christ, and creating a sense of unity and inclusivity among believers from different backgrounds and traditions.

First, there is traditional worship. Traditional worship styles, such as liturgical worship, focus on formal and structured expressions of faith. Ancient hymns, creeds, and rituals often characterize these styles. The purpose of traditional worship is to connect believers to the historical traditions and practices of the church and to emphasize the continuity of the Christian faith across time. Catholics, Anglicans, and Methodists exemplify this style of worship.

Second, there is contemporary worship. Contemporary worship styles often involve more modern music, informal language, and casual dress. A greater emphasis on personal experience and emotional expression often characterizes these styles. The purpose of contemporary worship is to connect believers to God in a way that feels relevant and meaningful to them in their current context.

Third, there is charismatic worship: Charismatic worship styles emphasize the work of the Holy Spirit in the believer's life. These styles often involve more spontaneous expressions of worship, such as speaking in tongues, prophecy, and laying on hands. Charismatic worship aims to create a sense of connection to God through a powerful and transformative encounter with the Holy Spirit.

Fourth, there is evangelical worship. Evangelical worship styles focus on sharing the gospel and inviting people into a personal relationship with Jesus Christ. These styles often involve a high level of participation from the congregation, including singing, prayer, and Bible study. Evangelical worship aims to help people understand and respond to the message of salvation and encourage them to live out their faith daily.

Fifth, there is blended worship. Blended worship styles combine elements from different worship styles to create a unique and diverse experience. These styles often include traditional, contemporary, charismatic, and evangelical worship elements. The purpose of blended worship is to create a sense of unity and inclusivity among believers from different backgrounds and traditions.

Sixth, there is freestyle worship. It is a phenomenon of many independent Pentecostal, Apostolic, and charismatic churches. They conduct their services as the "Spirit leads." They have a set time to begin the service but no time to end. Anyone could bring "a word from the Lord."

Seventh, there is pandemonium worship. Some church services are exercises in total confusion. In worship services of this kind, every congregant seems to speak in tongues and prophecy at some point. There is no particular order to the worship; hysterics often borders on psychosis. Congregants often lose consciousness during the worship experience.

Styles of Christian worship serve different purposes, including connecting believers to the historical traditions of the church, creating a sense of relevance and meaning in contemporary contexts, emphasizing the work of the Holy Spirit, sharing the gospel, and inviting people into a personal relationship with Jesus Christ, and creating a sense of unity and inclusivity among believers from different backgrounds and traditions.

Sermon #29: Seven Mysteries of the Bible

Mysteries are truths or concepts that are not fully understood or revealed. Here are seven mysteries in the Bible. First, there is the mystery of iniquity. The mystery of iniquity is the fascinating nature of sin. Its tentacles are all-encompassing, and its roots are deep. How does sin grow? How cancerous is it to a person, community, or nation? What can make one sinful act become a way of life? No one can quantify the magnitude of sin; it is mysterious! But the ultimate consequence of sin is eternal separation from God; it is spiritual death, and the remedy for sin is repentance. God is forgiving and will pardon. The message of 2 Thessalonians 2:7 is clear: there is a power of lawlessness at work that opposes God's will and seeks to lead people away from the truth. The ultimate defeat of this power will come with the return of Jesus Christ, who will overcome all evil and establish His kingdom on earth.

Second, there is the mystery of godliness. The mystery of godliness refers to the revelation of God in Jesus Christ, who came to earth as a human being and revealed God's character and will to humanity. This mystery involves the incarnation, the atonement, and the resurrection of Christ, as well as the ongoing work of the Holy Spirit in the world. The incarnation of Jesus is a mystery, and that divinity could become humanity to procure redemption is a dynamic concept. Christianity shows the humility of God in assuming human nature. The gods of Greek mythology are aloof, condescending, and cruel, but the God of the Bible, though a God of justice, is a God of love and compassion. The mystery of godliness refers to the extent to which God will go to save sinners.

Third, there is the mystery of Christ. It refers to the plan of God to reconcile all things to himself through the person and work of Jesus Christ. This mystery was previously hidden but has now been made known through the Gospel. It involves the incarnation, crucifixion, resurrection, ascension of Christ, and the unity of all believers in him. The mystery of Christ is the idea that Christ is fully God and fully man. We must admit that the story of the promised, prophesied, and fulfilled Christ is not well-received by many, and some think it's a plagiarized story from antiquity. Thus, it becomes our duty to unravel the mystery of Christ and show that he is the Anointed One who was sent from God! They are on their "Road to Emmaus" (Lk. 24:13-35). And like the first travelers on that road, many do not recognize Christ.

Fourth, there is the mystery of the Gospel. How is the Gospel the power of God that leads to the salvation of people everywhere? Why did God choose to use the Gospel and not politics as the means of conversion? People should come to God freely. Forced conversions are troublesome for the church and adherents' mental health. The Gospel, when presented, carries the weight of eternity and forces people to consider the case for Christ and their eternal souls. It calls them to consider what God did for them through Christ and to accept his grace. No one should be forced to love God! Christian nationalism that seeks to impose Christian values on others is unbiblical and counterproductive. People have the right to reject Gospel at their perils.

Fifth, there is the mystery of the resurrection of the dead. Some religions believe in the resurrection, which is not unique to Christianity. But Christianity has evidence of the resurrection of Jesus, and history records it. Resurrection settles the idea of where there is life after death. It shows the power of God to change nature and science. It forces people to consider what they do in the present as it directly affects their afterlife experience. Resurrection can be a joyful or terrifying thought. Does it frighten you, or does it bring you joy and hope?

Sixth, there is the mystery of the kingdom of God (Mk. 4:11). Where is the kingdom of God? Is it here, there, or everywhere? When did it begin? Does it have an end? Because of this mystery, some people think the Bible is confusing or indirect. People do not want to search for things; they want them given to them. But the believer is a seeker, and whoever seeks finds. We must seek to understand the mystery of the kingdom of God. The Greek word for kingdom is Basilea which means rule or reign; it points to the "rule of God." Every kingdom has a king or ruler, realm or domain, citizens, laws, customs, powers, and destiny. But the Kingdom of God is here. It is a Kingdom of light, not darkness; it is a kingdom of power, hope, and peace. The "Basilea of God is a spiritual and ethical rule of God in the heart of the individual, both present and future. It is already but not full. It is here in those who do the work of Christ and those who resist evil, live righteously and oppose the evils of society. It is a kingdom of faith, love, moral purity, honesty, humility, and power! "For the Kingdom of God, is not meat nor drink, but righteousness, peace, and joy in the Holy Ghost." The kingdom of God was present in Christ, his disciples, and believers throughout the ages, and it has stood against the kingdoms of this world. Soon, the kingdom of God will be unveiled fully. Total righteousness, immortality, lack of diseases, peace, and complete victory over evil will characterize the final phase of the kingdom of God! God's kingdom does not consist of debauchery, whing, or dining; it is characterized by what God approves, the peace he gives, and the work of the Holy Spirit in one's life.

Seventh, there is the mystery of faith. Believers should defend the truths of Christianity. Hermeneutics and apologetics matter. Some wish to use Christianity to advance political agendas, and Christians must hold the realities of the faith conscientiously. To abandon the truths of Christianity for political expediency is to deny the faith.

Sermon #30: Seven Types of Obedience

Obedience means submission to authority. Submission is a voluntary sending oneself into service for another as support. Obedience means to give an ear to and obey.

There are seven Challenges to obedience: Laziness, pride, fear, cowardice, hastiness, doubt, and apathy; however, Scripture commands us to obey our employers, God, our parents, husbands, government, pastors, and each other.

Obedience to Employers/Obedience to God (1 Pet. 2:18). To foster respect, collaboration, and for the sake of the name of Christ, believers are asked to obey their employers. Employees are admonished to follow, which means listening and being submitted to their employers. "Eye service," or quiet quitting, performing well under supervision but working sluggishly after that, is not Christian. Alternatively, employers should obey God by providing good working conditions and a living wage. Slavery of any kind is not of God. All are made in the image of God. Workplace abuse must be prosecuted to the full extent of the law.

Obedience to God (Luke 22:42)

Man's obedience to God is important, and disobedience is the root of many problems. We must use Scripture as a guide to our practice of faith. Do you know what it means to obey God rather than man? Even demons obey Christ, and so should we!

Obedience to Parents. If longevity matters, consider obedience to your parents. Obedience helps to reduce stress, and we should obey and watch God's works. In Ephesians and Colossians, children are encouraged to obey their parents.

Obedience to Husbands. In Ephesians 5:22, Paul instructs wives to submit to their husbands "as to the Lord." This verse emphasizes the importance of submission within a godly marriage, assuming that the husband follows the Lord's guidance and will not lead his wife astray. However, the wife mustn't be naive or lack critical thinking skills. The passage acknowledges that the hearts of men can be wicked, and some husbands may display selfish and abusive behavior. While wives should not adopt an adversarial or confrontational approach, they are called to be wise and gentle in their interactions. Unfortunately, domestic abuse can occur even within households striving to follow God's principles.

Obedience to Rulers (Government). Should every citizen submit to their government even if they are tyrannical? "Let every soul be subject to the higher authorities. There is no authority but of God; God ordains the existing authorities. So that the one resisting the authority resists the ordinance of God, and the ones who resist will receive judgment to themselves" (Rom 13:1-2). Indeed, God would not want Christians to submit to a government that causes them to sin! Submission is not absolute, and it is conditional. German Christians submitted to Hitler until he began his acts of genocide against the Jews. Christians are called upon to courageously confront those in positions of authority with the truth, stand against wrongdoing, and boldly proclaim the message of truth.

Obedience to Pastors (Heb 13:7) A pastor is a gift to a church. Receive God's gift and the blessing he brings but be vigilant. Wolves are in sheep's clothing, and the church has become a haven for perverts and pedophiles. One should not worship on suspicion of a pastor, but he must understand the mystery of sin. Evil is present everywhere. Obedience is required, and vigilance is needed. Even a person described as being after God's own heart is susceptible to being influenced to commit heinous acts such as murder, resulting in horrific consequences. Ask King David. So, "Remember your leaders, who spoke the word of God to you. Consider the outcome of their way of life and imitate their faith" (Heb. 13:7).

Obedience to each other (Eph. 5:21). You should not submit to someone who did not earn your trust. "Submitting yourselves one to another in fear of God" is advocated in a non-abusive, safe, and positive environment. Why should you submit to the unlearned or spiritually immature? If you are to listen and follow someone's advice, such a person must have the capacity and intentions to help you to advance in your faith. But this advice is important for groups that will fight over the most minus things, thus hindering progress in a family or institution.

Sermon #31: Seven Satanic Strategies

Text: The thief comes only to steal, kill, and destroy; I have come that they may have life and have it to the full (John 10:10). How does Satan accomplish his tasks?

Strategy #1: Isolation.

Here Satan attacks one's emotional needs. He takes away one's connections. The individual is alone, away. Depression and regrets reign. When is a chicken most vulnerable? When it's by itself. There is strength in the group. "The poor are left friendless" Prov. 19:4 Isolation emphasizes total separation or detachment from others. You are detached, lonely, in solitude, sad, and hurt. In some countries, isolation separates the mentally ill, the diseased, and the worst of society. In the Bible, society isolated lepers as a punishment, subjecting them to social exclusion. This isolation served as a form of punishment or consequence for their condition.

Strategy # 2: Insulation

In this scenario, Satan launches attacks on one's ability to express emotions or seek support, resulting in isolation from all connections. Insulation occurs when individuals become excessively self-focused, distancing themselves from people and things. It acts as a barrier that restricts the flow of warmth, preventing the person from radiating positive energy or establishing connections with others. A hermit, for instance, intentionally chooses to live in seclusion and isolation from society. At the same time, solitude involves a lack of contact with people, often sought for concentration, reflection, or meditation. A recluse, on the other hand, hides away from public attention and lives in solitary seclusion. Situations such as job loss, the passing of a loved one, divorce, health issues, and fear of the future can contribute to insulation. Consequently, Scripture advises, "Now I plead with you, brethren, by the name of our Lord Jesus Christ, that you all speak the same thing, and that there be no divisions among you, but that you be perfectly joined together in the same mind and the same judgment" (1 Cor. 1:10).

Strategy #3: Interrogation.

It is a tactic employed by Satan to undermine our faith in God. Satan is often referred to as the accuser of the brethren, highlighting his role in attempting to sow doubt and confusion in our minds. Interrogation is a form of attack where Satan bombards us with questions that challenge our beliefs and sense of identity. These questions may include doubts about our purpose, thoughts of resignation or giving up, questioning the authenticity of our relationships with others, and even questioning the existence and love of God. These interrogative thoughts can create a sense of uncertainty and vulnerability, aiming to weaken our trust and confidence in God and His plans for our lives.

Strategy #4: Inaction.

It is a method employed by Satan to target your will and discourage you from actively participating in ministry. In this strategy, Satan instills thoughts such as not wanting to serve anymore and perceiving others as hypocrites. These negative thoughts aim to create apathy, disillusionment, and a loss of motivation, ultimately deterring you from engaging in meaningful service and impacting the lives of others through ministry.

Strategy #5: Infusion.

This Satanic tactic attacks our minds. An infusion of thoughts refers to a sudden and intense influx of ideas, impressions, or mental images that enter a person's mind. It can happen spontaneously or be triggered by external stimuli, experiences, or internal processes. This phenomenon often involves a rapid succession or overlapping of thoughts, where multiple concepts or perspectives present themselves simultaneously or in quick succession. Infusions of thoughts can be experienced as a surge of creativity, a flood of insights, or even intrusive or overwhelming streams of consciousness. They can occur in various contexts, such as during moments of inspiration, problem-solving, reflection, or even certain mental health conditions.

Strategy #6:

Indecision. Indecision refers to uncertainty or hesitation in making choices or decisions. The verse from James 1:8

and 4:8 highlights that a person with a double mind, meaning they are divided or conflicted in their thoughts and beliefs, tends to be unstable in all aspects of their life. This instability affects their dependability and reliability as they struggle to make firm commitments or decisions. In the context of faith, an indecisive person may experience doubts about their salvation and may have uncertainties regarding their level of involvement in their Christian journey. They may question the nature of their beliefs and harbor skepticism about life's meaning and purpose. Indecision can hinder personal growth and lead to unease and lack of clarity in navigating one's path.

Strategy #7:

Incarcerate. In this context, Satan mentally traps people, distorts reality, and makes them believe the opposite of what is true. For example, those rich in faith may feel unworthy and poor, while those engaged in wrong actions may think they are better than others. Satan can establish a pattern of mental slavery where people are physically free but mentally bound.

Sermon #32: Shalom

"Shalom," which is the Hebrew word for peace, lies in its broader meaning beyond the absence of conflict. Shalom encompasses a sense of wholeness, harmony, well-being, and flourishing in personal and collective relationships. Similarly, the Greek word for peace, "eireinei," carries the connotation of tranquility and unity. Peace, in both its Hebrew and Greek understandings, is not limited to an absence of war or strife but encompasses a state of balance, reconciliation, and thriving.

First, the peace of God (Phil. 4:7). 21st-century people are plagued with fear, anxiety, and depression, hence, the need for the peace of God. Such peace surpasses human comprehension, so people do not fully understand how to possess calmness and harmony in the presence of trouble or uncertainty. It is a gift from God – the gift of peace. People need God's peace when they are faced with the insurmountable.

Second, the peace with God. Before conversion, everyone is at enmity with God. People are born with an inherited Adamic disposition of rebellion, and one must accept his offer of peace to be at peace with God. The advent of Christ in the world is God's initiative to reestablish peace with humanity if we accept the atonement of Christ. Everyone needs to accept the "gospel of peace" to obtain the peace of God (Eph. 6:15). So, "Therefore, being justified by faith, we have peace with God through our Lord Jesus Christ" (Rom. 5:1).

Third, peace with all men. "If it is possible, as far as it depends on you, live at peace with everyone (Rom. 12:18). This is aspirational. Believers should live at peace with others without compromising their beliefs. There are the wicked, who, like the troubled sea, have no capacity for peace. Try as hard as you can. A narcissist will not be peaceful unless he's helped. But peacemaking must be a principle of our life. There is no need for revenge or getting even because God repays. Sometimes, it is the Christian who is creating conflict with his faith. Christians must learn to accept no and not seek to force their faith on others. It is their choice if people want to reject the Christian way of life.

Fourth, the peace with self. "When you find peace within yourself, you become the kind of person who can live at peace with others" (Peace Pilgrim). Internal conflicts can be torturous. The traumas and toxicity of the past can rob an individual of his contentment, but "if our hearts do not condemn us, we have confidence before God 22 and receive from him anything we ask because we keep his commands and do what pleases him" (1 John. 3:21-2). We should be your best cheerleaders, but self-doubt will ensue if our inner self points at condemnation.

Fifth, the peace with each other (Mk 9: 50). unsurprisingly, the Christian community has been asked to live at peace with each other and become a model of peace. The major factions of Christianity are still adversarial to each other. Since the 12th century, the Nuseibeh family, the oldest Muslim family in Jerusalem, has controlled the temple that is believed to contain the Tomb of Jesus by a Muslim family because Christians cannot be trusted with peace.

Sixth, the makers of Peace. "Blessed are the **peace**makers, for they shall be called sons of God" (Matt. 5:9). Those are the words of Jesus. Christians are not military warriors; they are spiritual warriors. We must be apt and ready to initiate peace if it does not compromise our faith. Peacemakers are blessed, and we are better for their friendship and fellowship.

Seventh, the Way of Peace. "And the way of **peace** they have not known" (Rom. 3:17). What is the way, manner, or process of peace? It is twofold: peace with God and man. It was exemplified in the life of Jesus, who "grew in wisdom and stature, and in favor with God and man" (Lk 2:52). The way of peace is the way of health in mind, body, and spirit.

In the context of prophetic teachings, the absence of peace in the world is often seen as an accurate indication of the end times. The lack of peace, both on an individual and global scale, is considered a significant sign pointing towards the fulfillment of prophecies regarding the culmination of human history. It highlights the brokenness and discord in the world as an integral part of the end-time narrative, prompting believers to reflect on the need for divine intervention and the ultimate establishment of lasting peace in the future. Christians are called to be peacemakers, and the Beatitudes provide governing principles for our lives. We must pray for the peace of Jerusalem and strive to spread Shalom in all aspects of our lives.

Sermon #33: Peace on Whom His Favor Rest!

The passage from Luke 2:14 proclaims peace is bestowed on those who have received God's favor. Throughout history, there has been a lack of peace on Earth, with conflicts and divisions among people persisting. Wars continue to loom in various world regions, and no century has been free from war. True peace cannot be guaranteed by material possessions or worldly success. The high rate of suicide among privileged individuals highlights their lack of inner peace. Research suggests that those without peace experience various negative effects, such as constant irritation, sleeplessness, anxiety, and internal and external strife. Despite appearances, even those who seem to prosper may not find true happiness, as evident by the pursuits of individuals like Bezos and Musk to escape to another planet. True peace is found through salvation and the favor of God.

God's favor rested on Noah. Noah experienced God's favor and had peace during the time of the flood, as he and his family were the only ones saved in the ark. His obedience to God led to favor and honor, as mentioned in Genesis 6:8. The story of Noah serves as a reminder of the coming of the Son of man, as stated in Matthew 24:37. Abraham also received God's favor, being chosen, blessed, and favored by God. Despite his old age, God allowed him to have a son, demonstrating favor. Abraham's obedience led to him becoming the "Father of many nations." Jacob, too, experienced the favor of God, which protected him from the wrath of his brother and the mistreatment of his uncle Laban. Similarly, Joseph received God's favor, although his eleven brothers did not. Joseph faced hardships, including being sold into slavery and spending time in prison, but eventually, God's favor elevated him to a position of authority in Egypt. Through his journey, Joseph had the opportunity to help and reconcile with his brothers. These examples show how God's favor operates and demonstrates that it is not experienced by everyone in the same way.

Moses is a prime example of God's grace. Despite the wicked command of Pharaoh to kill male Hebrew infants, Moses was spared and delivered into his mother's arms by God's grace. Throughout Moses' life, God's grace continued to protect and guide him. Moses received education as an Egyptian and was made aware of his Hebrew heritage through God's grace. After escaping Egypt, Moses spent forty years as a shepherd, away from Egyptian influence, where he could discern God's plan for his life. Ruth also experienced God's favor through her relationship with Naomi, her mother-in-law. Despite facing hardship and loss, Ruth's faithful journey led her to marry a wealthy man named Boaz and be included in the lineage of Jesus Christ. Both Moses and Ruth exemplify the workings of God's grace in their lives.

God's favor rested on King David. By God's favor, he defeated Goliath when his brothers couldn't. By God's favor, he was anointed King of Israel when his brothers thought the position would be theirs. As a king, David lived in God's favor, so much so that God referred to him as "a man after his own heart" (1 Samuel 13:14). Mary, the mother of Jesus, received God's Favor. God's favor was not limited to the Old Testament. In the New Testament, the angel Gabriel told Mary that she had "found favor with God" and would bear a son and name him Jesus (Luke 1:30). She needed it! Can you imagine how this young lady felt when she heard that she was to become the mother of Christ? We need the favor of God to rest on us for us to do the big things in life! Jesus said: "And Jesus grew in wisdom and stature, and in favor with God and man" (Lk. 2: 52). The father's summary statement of Jesus was: "This is my beloved son in whom I am well pleased" (Matt. 3:17).

God's favor rested on the apostle Paul. The apostle Paul had a "thorn in the flesh." It might have been a physical sickness, an emotional burden, or a mental or sexual problem, but God didn't answer his prayers. He did not take away the "thorn", but placed his favor on him: "My grace is sufficient for you, for My strength is made perfect in weakness."

The favor of God rests on those who are born again. They have received Eternal Life. Ephesians 2: 8-9 says, "For it is by grace you have been saved, through faith-and this is not from yourselves, it is the gift of God- not by works so that no one can boast." it is only by God's grace (or undeserved favor) that we can experience eternal life, and it is only by God's grace that we can live for the Lord during the difficulties of life.

God's favor rests on those who live a good life. Genesis 6:8-10 says, "But Noah found favor in the eyes of the LORD. Noah was a righteous man, blameless among the people of his time, and he walked with God. Noah had three sons: Shem, Ham, and Japheth." Anyone can find the favor of God: "For he says to Moses, "I will have mercy on whom I have mercy, and I will have compassion on whom I have compassion" (Rom 9:15, NIV). God is looking for people to whom he might show favor. "For the eyes of the Lord range throughout the earth to strengthen those whose hearts are fully committed to him. You have done a foolish thing, and from now on, you will be at war" (Chron. 16:9, NIV).

The entrance of God's favor brings peace. Blessing changes the trajectory or focus of your life. As a first-time homebuyer, I got an FHA loan at a reasonably good rate then, but someone was convinced he could get something better for me. I followed him and abandoned the FHA loan. Two weeks from closing, I learned that I was being offered a conventional loan which was a two-point percentage higher than the first. I was tricked. I was hurt. I knew that God's favor was resting on me. Hence, I walked into Chase Bank and met a banker who introduced me to her friend. In the end, I got a first-time buyer loan which was two percent less than the FHA loan that I got initially. And it only took two weeks. God's favor makes the difference. "But this is the one to whom I will look: he who is humble and contrite in spirit and trembles at my word" (Isa. 66:2).

God's favor rests on the "poor in spirit," who humbly recognize their need for God. Humility leads to exalting: pride leads to abasement! The favor of God rests on the humble. It rests on the contrite or repentant. These are those who not only confess their sins to God but can also ask forgiveness from their others if they offend them.

All of the characters of the Old and New Testaments who have had the favor of God on them and who lived with peace were people of humility like Noah, Abraham, and Moses; people with contrition like David who sinned with Bathsheba but who confessed, people of the early church like Peter who denied Christ, but wept bitterly when he came to his senses; but most importantly, they were all people who believed God's word and trusted him. Peace comes to those on whom God's favor rest!

References

Alewine, S. (n.d.). A Picture of God's Perfect Grace in the Life of Moses. Bible Study Tools. Retrieved from https://www.biblestudytools.com/bible-study/topical-studies/a-picture-of-gods-perfect-grace-in-the-life-of-moses.html

Sermon #34: Seven Ways Men Lead

The text of 1 Corinthians 11:3 guides the biblical basis of male leadership. We must celebrate godly men who lead, not in arrogance, but with wisdom. This scripture calls for men to lead with humility, integrity, compassion, wisdom, vision, courage, and servanthood.

First, men should lead with humility. Humility is the cornerstone of effective leadership, and it is a characteristic that allows men to lead respectfully, inclusively, and selflessly. Jesus Christ, our ultimate example, displayed profound humility throughout His earthly ministry, washing His disciples' feet and prioritizing service over self. As men, we must follow in His footsteps, seeking to understand and fulfill the needs of those we lead, putting their well-being before our own.

Second, men should lead with integrity. Integrity is another vital criterion for male leadership. It involves maintaining strong moral principles and consistently aligning our actions with our beliefs. Our character should be marked by honesty, transparency, and reliability. Leading with integrity inspires trust, builds meaningful relationships, and sets an example for others.

Third, men should lead with compassion. Compassion is a crucial attribute of godly leadership, and it entails showing genuine care, empathy, and understanding toward those under our guidance. Just as Christ exemplified compassion by ministering to the hurting and marginalized, we are called to lead with compassion, seeking to uplift and support those entrusted to our care.

Fourth, men should lead with wisdom. Wisdom is essential for effective leadership, and it involves seeking divine guidance, making sound decisions, and imparting knowledge to others. As men, we should strive to grow in wisdom through prayer, studying God's Word, and seeking counsel from those with wisdom and experience. By leading with wisdom, we can navigate challenges, resolve conflicts, and make decisions that honor God and benefit those we lead.

Fifth, men should lead with vision. Visionary leadership involves casting a compelling and God-centered vision for those we lead. It entails having clarity of purpose, setting goals, and inspiring others to join in fulfilling a shared mission. By leading with vision, we encourage unity, motivate others towards excellence, and empower them to contribute their unique gifts and talents.

Sixth, men should lead with courage. Courage is an indispensable quality in male leadership, and it requires stepping out in faith, taking risks, and standing firm in the face of adversity. Just as Joshua exemplified courage when leading the Israelites into the Promised Land, we must be courageous leaders who trust in God's strength and guidance. Leading with courage can overcome challenges, inspire others to persevere, and bring about positive change.

Seventh, men should lead with servanthood. Servant leadership is a transformative approach that Jesus taught, and it involves selflessly serving and uplifting those under our care. As men, we are called to imitate Christ's servant heart, placing the needs of others before our own and using our leadership positions to bring about positive transformation in the lives of those we lead.

The patriarchy has distorted the leadership of men. Men have done poorly in leadership at home, in the community, and in the world. Their hubris and arrogance should be tempered with compassion and empathy for others. Men should lead with humility, integrity, compassion, wisdom, vision, courage, and servanthood. By aligning our leadership with these principles, we can reflect the character of Christ, inspire others,

Reference

Covenant Keepers. (n.d.). How Does a Husband Lead His Wife and Family? Retrieved from https://www.covenantkeepers.org/online-articles/44-family-issues/330-how-does-a-husband-lead-his-wife-and-family

Sermon #35: Seven Secrets to Keep

James 5:16: "Confess your faults one to another, and pray one for another, that ye may be healed. The effectual fervent prayer of a righteous man availeth much."

First, personal matters belong to God, but what is revealed should be followed. Second, prayer should be done in private for God to reward. Third, fasting should also be done in secret for the reward from God. Fourth, one's source of strength should be kept secret. Fifth, if someone slanders their neighbor in private, they will be cut off. Sixth, giving to the needy should be kept a secret for God to reward. Lastly, gossiping about someone's secret betrays their confidence, but trustworthy people keep secrets.

Keeping personal matters secret is essential to follow God's law. Prayer and fasting are private acts of worship. Where we get our strength should be kept confidential, and we should not let anyone use it against us. We should not slander others privately and give to those in need without making it public. Lastly, we should not gossip about other people's secrets but rather keep them confidential if someone has confided in us. It is important to keep these seven things secret to maintain trust, integrity, and loyalty in our relationships with others and God.

Sermon 36: Seven Ways to Renew Strength

God's mercies are renewed daily, and His compassion never fails. His unfailing kindness and faithfulness sustain us. We can find strength and assurance in knowing that goodness and mercy will accompany us throughout our lives, allowing us to dwell in the presence of the Lord forever.

First, renewal comes through patience. When we wait, this is our part of the bargain. Isaiah 40:31 - But they that wait upon the Lord shall renew their strength; they shall mount up with wings as eagles; they shall run and not be weary, and they shall walk and not faint. (KJV)

Second, renewal comes through rest. God rested on the seventh day to demonstrate a principle to refresh and revitalize the body. Sleep helps the organs of the body need to rest. When the body is physically rested, it positively affects our attitude and temperament. Psalm 127:2 "It is vain for you to rise early, to sit up late, to eat the bread of sorrows: for so he giveth his beloved sleep." Getting enough sleep is essential for the body to repair and rejuvenate itself. Most adults require 7-8 hours of sleep per night, and it is important to establish a consistent sleep schedule.

Third, renewal comes with meditation. Practices like meditation and deep breathing can help reduce stress and promote relaxation, which can help reduce fatigue and increase mental clarity. Psalm 104:34 says, "My meditation of him shall be sweet: I will be glad in the LORD."

Fourth, renewal comes with exercise. What is the value of exercise? 1Ti 4:8 "For bodily exercise profiteth little: but godliness is profitable unto all things, having promise of the life that now is, and of that which is to come. The "little" in the above passage include increased energy and metabolism; improved muscle tone, self-esteem, and overall health; and stress reduction.

Fifth, renewal comes through goodness. Engaging in hobbies and social activities that bring joy and fulfillment can help reduce stress and provide a sense of purpose and meaning, which can increase energy levels.

Sixth, renewal comes through nutrition. You are what you eat; a balanced and healthy diet can give the body the proper nutrients to function correctly. Eating fruits, vegetables, lean proteins, and whole grains can help maintain energy levels throughout the day.

Seventh, renewal comes with connecting with nature. Spending time in nature has been shown to improve mood, reduce stress, and increase overall well-being. Walking in the park or hiking in the woods can help renew energy levels. – God's love is unconditional and unfathomable.

Sermon #37: Seven Ways Satan Kills

"The thief cometh not, but for to steal, and to kill, and to destroy, I have come that they might have life and that they might have it more abundantly" (John 10:10).

First, Satan kills through entrapment. Satan uses lies to trap people. He has the truth and always tries to distort it. Example: God said: "But of the tree of the knowledge of good and evil, thou shalt not eat of it: for in the day that thou eatest thereof thou shalt surely die" Gen. 2:17. But Satan entrapped Eve: "And the serpent said unto the woman, "Ye shall not surely die; For God doth know that in the day ye eat thereof, then your eyes shall be opened, and ye shall be as gods, knowing good and evil." This entrapment causes sin, which brings death. The solution to entrapment is this: Know the truth. "And you shall know the truth, and the truth shall make you free" John 8:3. Second, Satan kills through despair or hopelessness. "They repay me with evil for the good I do. I am sick with despair" Psalms 35:12. When all hope is gone, despair steps in. The solution to despair is hope in God: "Why art thou cast down, O my soul? And why art thou disquieted within me? Hope in God: for I shall yet praise him, who is the health of my countenance, and my God" Psa. 43:5. Isa. 61:3 states (God) "will provide for those who grieve in Zion— to bestow on them a crown of beauty instead of ashes, the oil of gladness instead of mourning, and a garment of praise instead of a spirit of despair."

Third, Satan kills through toxic stress. Everyone faces some form of stress, which can result from preparation for an exam, confrontation with someone, or just being stuck in traffic. But toxic or chronic stress is different. It can kill you. It includes anxiety and depression caused by a contentious home, work, or church environment. The Corinthian church, with some who were for Paul, some for Apollos, and some for Cephas, was a toxic environment. Toxic churches die. Fourth, Satan kills through fear. Do you live in fear of the future? Are you afraid of ghosts? Matt. 21: 26 states, "Men's hearts will fail them for fear and for looking upon those things which are coming on the earth; for the powers of heaven shall be shaken." Trust God. You are more than sparrows.

Fifth, Satan kills through others. Cain killed Able (Gen 5:2-12). Sixth, Satan kills through the world. 2 Corinthians 4: 4 states that Satan is the "god" of this world. He influences the ideals, opinions, views, and actions of many. Non-Christians are under the power of Satan, and he uses them to carry out his schemes.

Seventh, Satan kills through demons. Demons are evil spirits that form the entourage of Satan. Satan is not omnipresent; he uses demons to carry out his work.

Satan uses many strategies and methodologies to kill the unsuspecting and unprepared. But he does not have the last word in the life of a Christian. Be careful. Satan is a killer.

Sermon # 38: How to Keep Moving Forward

"**If you can**'t fly, then **run**. **If you can**'t **run**, then **walk**.
If you can't **walk**, crawl, but
whatever you do, you must **keep moving** forward"
Martin Luther King, Jr.

Inertia is a problem many people face, especially in their spiritual lives. However, we must keep moving forward to achieve our goals and fulfill the Great Commission. As Martin Luther King, Jr. said, "If you can't fly, then run. If you can't run, then walk. If you can't walk, crawl, but whatever you do, you must keep moving forward." This sermon will explore seven ways to keep moving forward and avoid becoming stagnant.

First, Walk. The first way to keep moving forward is to walk with God. Genesis 5:22 tells us that Enoch walked with God, and Psalm 1:1 also teaches us that walking in the way of the Lord brings blessings.

Second, Run. Sometimes walking is not enough, and we must run. Isaiah 40:31 states that those who wait on the Lord will renew their strength and run without growing weary.

Third, Ride. We can also keep moving forward by riding, as described in Judges 5:10. We should enjoy the journey as we travel towards our goals.

Fourth, Fly. Taking a plane is an excellent way to keep moving forward quickly. Psalm 90:10 reminds us that our time on earth is limited, so we should use it wisely.

Fifth, Swim. We may need to swim to keep moving forward when facing obstacles. In Acts 27:43, the centurion commanded those who could swim to cast themselves into the sea to reach land.

Sixth, Jump. Jumping can be an exhilarating way to keep moving forward, as shown in Mark 10:50 and Acts 3:8. These verses describe people jumping up and walking after being healed by Jesus.

Seventh, Sail. Finally, we can keep moving forward by sailing, as illustrated in Jonah 1:3. Although Jonah tried to flee from God, he ultimately realized he had to keep moving forward and followed God's plan.

Stagnation is not an option for Christians who want to fulfill their purpose in life. We must keep moving forward, even if it means walking, running, riding, flying, swimming, jumping, or sailing. As we move forward, we should keep our eyes fixed on God and trust He will guide us toward our goals.

Sermon #39: Ways to Overcome Temptation

"No temptation has seized you except what is common to man. And God is faithful; he will not let you be tempted beyond what you can bear. But when you are tempted, he will also provide a way out so that you can stand up under it." (1 Cor. 10:13). Temptation typically comes from external sources, such as the devil or worldly influences, and aims to entice us into sinful actions or attitudes. It appeals to our desires and weaknesses, luring us away from God's will and leading us into disobedience. The purpose of temptation is to lead us astray and separate us from God.

Conversely, a test of faith often originates from God Himself and is intended to strengthen and refine our faith. It may involve trials, hardships, or difficult circumstances that require us to trust God and rely on Him. The purpose of a test of faith is to develop our character, deepen our dependence on God, and prove our faithfulness to Him. It is an opportunity for spiritual growth and maturation.

Seven Ways to Overcome Temptations are as follows.

First, use the Word of God against Satan when attacked. Jesus did, and he was victorious. Second, renew your mind. Romans 12:1-2 calls us to saturate ourselves in the things of God. Think as Godly. Colossians 3:2 states, "Set your mind on the things above, not on the things on earth." And, "Finally, brethren, whatsoever things are true, whatsoever things are honest, whatsoever things are just, whatsoever things are pure, whatsoever things are lovely, whatsoever things are of good report; if there be any virtue, and if there be any praise, think on these things" (Phil 4: 8).

Third, practice avoidance. "Abstain from all appearance of evil" (I Thes. 5:22). Flee: "Now flee from youthful lusts, and pursue righteousness, faith, love, and peace, with those who call on the Lord from a pure heart" (2 Tim. 2:22). You might have to run away from someone or someplace like Joseph and Lot respectively. Fourth, walk in the Holy Spirit—pattern spiritual things (Gal. 5:16-25). Recognize the role of the Holy Spirit in our fight. "When the enemy shall come in like a flood, the Spirit of the Lord will lift up a standard against him and put him to flight" (Isa. 59:19).

Fifth, through submission to God. "Submit yourselves, then, to God. Resist the devil, and he will flee from you" James 4:7. Sixth, try prayer and fasting. Prayer is a deterrent to sin and helps us resist temptation as we affirm our positions in God and seek His help. Fasting is helpful– "Howbeit, this kind goeth not out but by prayer and fasting" Matt 17:21. Some temptations will not leave until you mix your prayer with fasting. Seventh, fellowship – "And they continued steadfastly in the apostles' doctrine and fellowship, and in the breaking of bread, and prayers" (Acts 2: 42). There is strength in unity. "*One shall chase a thousand*, and *two put ten thousand to flight*" (Deut 32:30).

Temptations are many and varied. To overcome them, we should use God's word, renew our minds, practice avoidance or abstention, pattern spiritual things, practice submission to God, live with prayer and fasting, and fellowship with and kingdom people.

While temptation seeks to lead us into sin, a test of faith challenges us to remain faithful and obedient to God even in the face of adversity. Temptation tempts us to turn away from God, while a test of faith encourages us to draw closer to Him and rely on His strength.

Sermon #40: How to Prepare for the Appointment with Death

We are all dying, literally! Death is an inevitable reality that affects everyone regardless of age, wealth, or background. It transcends boundaries and claims lives from every corner of the world, every race, culture, and belief system. No language is exempt from the sorrow of death, and no family can escape its impact. The antiquity of death serves as a reminder that it is a universal experience shared by all of humanity.

Seven Ways to Prepare for the Appointment with Death

In Hebrews 9:27-28, we are reminded that it is appointed for each of us to die once and then face judgment. However, as believers, we find hope in the sacrifice of Christ and the promise of His second coming. Today, we will examine seven ways to prepare for the appointment with death so that we may face it with confidence and assurance of eternal salvation.

First, we must embrace the reality of mortality. The first step in preparing for the appointment with death is to acknowledge the reality of our mortality. Death is not something we can escape or postpone indefinitely. By accepting this truth, we can live each day with a sense of urgency, making the most of our time to serve God and impact the lives of others.

Second, we must seek forgiveness and reconciliation. Death reminds us of the brevity of life and the importance of relationships. Take time to seek forgiveness from those we have wronged and extend forgiveness to those who have wronged us. Embrace reconciliation and mend broken relationships so that we may depart from this world with a heart free from bitterness and strife.

Third, we must cultivate a vibrant relationship with Christ. Our hope lies in Christ and His redemptive work on the cross. Cultivate a deep and personal relationship with Him through prayer, studying his Word, and fellowship with other believers. Strengthen your faith and anchor it in the unwavering promises of God's Word.

Fourth, we must live a life of purpose and meaning. In light of our impending appointment with death, let us live each day with purpose and meaning. Discover and pursue the calling that God has placed upon your life. Use your talents, time, and resources to positively impact this world, leaving a lasting legacy that honors God.

Fifth, we must store up treasures in heaven. Jesus taught us not to store up treasures on earth where moth and rust destroy, but to lay up treasures in heaven (Matthew 6:19-20). Invest in the things that have eternal value: love, kindness, generosity, and sharing the Gospel with others. Let us prioritize heavenly treasures over earthly possessions.

Sixth, we must prepare financially and practically. While we focus on spiritual preparation, making practical arrangements for our departure is also wise. Consider writing a will, or living trust, making funeral arrangements, and ensuring your loved ones are cared for. We can alleviate unnecessary burdens on our families during difficult times by addressing these practical matters.

Seventh, we must anticipate Christ's Second Coming. Finally, as we prepare for the appointment with death, let us eagerly anticipate the glorious return of our Lord Jesus Christ. He will come again to gather His people and grant them eternal salvation. Live with a sense of anticipation, knowing that our ultimate hope and destiny lie in His presence's eternal joy and peace.

Our appointment with death is a reality we cannot escape. Yet, as believers, we can face it with hope and assurance. By embracing our mortality, seeking forgiveness, cultivating our relationship with Christ, living a purposeful life, storing up heavenly treasures, preparing practically, and anticipating Christ's return, we can be ready to meet our Savior. May the Lord strengthen us as we walk this journey, and may we be found faithful until the very end.

Sermon #41: To Divorce or Not to Divorce

In Matthew 19:8-9, where Jesus responds to a question posed by the Pharisees about divorce. Divorce is a difficult and painful process for all involved, and unfortunately, it is becoming increasingly common in our society. It is important to understand the reasons behind divorce so that we can address them and work toward healing and restoration. In this sermon, we will discuss the seven main reasons for divorce and what we can do to prevent them.

First, there is infidelity. One of the primary reasons for divorce is infidelity. When one partner violates the trust and commitment of the marriage by engaging in an extramarital affair, it can be devastating to the relationship. Fidelity and honor are important in the covenant of marriage. Second, there is a communication breakdown. Another common cause of divorce is communication breakdown. When couples cannot effectively communicate their needs, desires, and concerns, it can lead to misunderstandings and resentment. People should to practice healthy communication in our relationships. Third, there are financial problems. Financial problems can also significantly strain a marriage. When couples cannot manage their finances and debts, it can lead to arguments and tension. As Christians, we are called to be good

191

stewards of our resources and to work together to manage our finances.

Fourth, there is domestic violence. Domestic violence is a serious issue that can lead to divorce. When one partner is abusive towards the other, it creates an unsafe and unhealthy environment for both spouses. People should respect one another and seek help and support if they are in an abusive relationship. Fifth, there is incompatibility: Sometimes, couples grow apart over time and find that they are no longer compatible. Incompatibility can be difficult, but it is important to acknowledge and address if it is causing significant strain in the relationship. Sixth, there is substance abuse. Substance abuse can also lead to divorce. When one partner struggles with addiction, it can significantly strain the relationship and create a cycle of dysfunction. People should seek help and support if they are struggling with addiction and support our partners in their recovery journey. Finally, there are religious differences. Religious differences can also lead to divorce. Couples with different beliefs and values can create significant tension and conflict in the relationship. Couples should respect each other's beliefs and seek common ground and understanding in their faith journey.

Divorce is painful and difficult, but it is often avoidable. To promote healing and restoration in marriages and families, addressing the following seven main reasons for divorce is crucial. Firstly, a lack of communication can lead to marital breakdown, emphasizing the importance of open and effective dialogue. Secondly, various forms of abuse, including sexual, physical, and emotional, must be confronted and addressed for healing. Thirdly, the inability to manage or resolve conflicts can erode the foundation of a relationship, highlighting the need for healthy conflict resolution skills. Fourthly, financial problems can strain marriages, necessitating wise financial management, and joint decision-making. Fifthly, unmet expectations regarding children, household chores, and other areas should be openly discussed and negotiated. Sixthly, external interference from in-laws, friends, or societal pressures can impact a marriage negatively, requiring boundaries and open communication with external influences. Lastly, incompatibility in sexuality, intellect, idiosyncrasies, culture, or religion should be acknowledged and addressed through understanding and compromise.

Sermon #42: God's Plan for You

Jeremiah 29:11 is part of the prophet's letter to the Jewish exiles in Babylon. The context of this verse is when the Israelites were in captivity in Babylon due to their disobedience to God. Jeremiah 29:11 is a specific promise from God to the exiles, assuring them that He has plans for their future and that those plans are good. It is a message of reassurance and comfort, reminding the exiles that even in their current circumstances, God has a plan and a purpose for their lives. This verse has been widely quoted and cherished by believers as a reminder of God's faithfulness and desire to bless and guide His people.

First, God's plan for you involves prosperity. This fact is confirmed in 3 John 1: 2 "Beloved, I wish above all things that thou mayest prosper and be in health, even as thy soul prospereth"

Second, God's plan for you involves posterity, our future generations, or our descendants. The apostle Paul writes:

"If you belong to Christ, then you are Abraham's seed, and heirs according to the promise" (Gal 3:29). Believers become part of Abraham's spiritual posterity and inherit the promises made to him. Not only does he want us to prosper, but he also wants us to have good health.

Third, God's plan for you involves provision, that is, favors even in difficult situations: "Behold, I will do a new thing; now it shall spring forth; shall you not know it? I will even make a way in the wilderness and rivers in the desert (Isa. 43:19).

Fourth, God's plan for you involves pleasure. The Bible also guides seeking pleasure in a way that aligns with God's will. It cautions against pursuing sinful pleasures that lead to harm, addiction, or distance from God. Instead, it encourages seeking lasting joy and fulfillment through a relationship with God and obedience to His commandments. Psalm 149:4 is written, "For the LORD takes pleasure in his people; he adorns the humble with salvation." This verse suggests that God finds joy and delight in His relationship with His people.

Fifth, God's plan for you involves paradise, a place of beauty, delight, and the presence of God. The term "paradise" is derived from the Greek word "paradeisos," which originally referred to a walled garden or park. Revelation 22:1-5 depicts a river of the water of life, the tree of life, and the absence of sorrow, pain, or evil. This portrayal suggests a future state of eternal joy, peace, and communion with God in a renewed paradise. "And God shall wipe away all tears from their eyes; and there shall be no more death, neither sorrow, nor crying, neither shall there be any more pain: for the former things are passed away" (Rev. 21:4).

Sixth, while were are on earth, God's plan involves prominence. Believers are called to be at the top and not the bottom. "And the LORD shall make thee the head, and not the tail, and thou shalt be above only, and thou shalt not be beneath; if that thou hearken unto the commandments of the LORD thy God, which I command thee this day, to observe and to do them." Deut. 28:13).

Seventh, God's plan involves purpose. You are no dead fish that's on its way to oblivion! God established purpose in every aspect of creation: *"When I consider your heavens, the work of your fingers, the moon, and the stars, which you have ordained, what is the man that you are mindful of him, and the son of man that you visit him? You have made him a little lower than the angels and crowned him with glory and honor. You have made him have dominion over the works of your hands. You have put all things under his feet"* (Psalm 8:3-6).

God's plan for your life involves prosperity, posterity, provision, pleasure, paradise, prominence, and purpose.

Sermon #43: To Christen or Not to Christen

The reasons for christening a child may vary depending on individual beliefs and cultural practices. Traditions of men are legalistic, but spiritual precedence is important.

First, christening is an act of thanksgiving: "Every good and true thing is given to us from heaven, coming from the Father of lights, with whom there is no change or any shade made by turning" (James 1:17). A child is a gift from God.

Second, it is an act of following the life of Jesus. Luke 2:52 states, "And Jesus increased in wisdom and stature, and in favor with God and men." This verse describes the growth and development of Jesus during His early years.

Third, it is an act of petitioning God. It is a moment of request, where parents ask for God's help to raise a child. In Mark 10:13-16, for example, people brought little children to Jesus for Him to touch and bless them, indicating Jesus' acceptance and care for children.

Fourth, it is an act of covering with divine protection. Some parents believe that christening their children gives them spiritual protection and blessings from their faith community. It is a way to invoke divine guidance and support for the child's well-being and future.

Fifth, it is an act to remove the generational curse and ask for a community's help to raise the child correctly. Christening ceremonies often involve the child's parents, godparents, and the wider religious community. It is an opportunity for the community to come together, offer support, and commit to helping raise the child following their religious values. It is a time to pray for a child's destiny (Lk 2).

Sixth, it is an act of baptism in Early Christian Practices. While the term "christening" itself may not be explicitly mentioned in the Bible, certain biblical passages and historical evidence support the concept of baptizing infants. Early Christian writings and historical records prove infant baptism was practiced in the early Church. For example, the writings of the early Church Fathers such as Origen, Tertullian, and Augustine indicate their belief in infant baptism.

Seventh, it is a time to bring parents closer to God in the rededication of their lives and the children. Bring the parents closer to God – Come unto me all he that are labor, and I will give rest.

Christening is an act of thanksgiving, an act that follows the example of Jesus, an act of petitioning God, an act of covering a child with divine protection, an act of removal of a generational curse, and soliciting the blessings of the community, an act of baptism, and an act of bringing parents closer to God.

Sermon #44: Consequences

Galatians 6:7 reminds us of personal responsibility and accountability for our actions. It encourages us to consider our choices' consequences and align ourselves with God's principles of righteousness and love.

First, do not sow to the wind. "To sow to the wind" is an expression that warns about the inevitable consequences of engaging in negative or morally questionable actions. It serves as a cautionary reminder that our choices have repercussions. If we sow seeds of unrighteousness or engage in empty and harmful behavior, we will eventually face the destructive consequences of those actions. Hosea 8:7 Israel sowed to the wind in their backsliding, corruptions, and idolatry. Israel reaped the whirlwind in 722 B.C. when Nebuchadnezzar took them into slavery in Babylon.

Second, sow in tears. "Sowing in tears" refers to investing effort or engaging in a task or situation amidst hardship or sorrow, expecting the future outcome to be joy and celebration. It encourages individuals to endure difficult times, knowing their perseverance will eventually lead to a positive effect. "They that sow in tears shall reap in joy" (Psa. 126:5).

Third, acknowledge God's providence. Birds do not sow. "Behold the fowls of the air: for they sow not, neither do they reap nor gather into barns; yet your heavenly Father feedeth them. Are ye not much better than they?" (Matt 6:26). .So, they show not reap. God provides for all his creatures.

Fourth, acknowledge what is promised to you already. The wealth of the wicked is stored up for the righteous. "And herein is that saying true, One soweth, and another reapeth" (John 4:37).

Fifth, acknowledge the strength in weaknesses. "So also is the resurrection of the dead. It is sown in corruption; it is raised in in corruption: It is sown in dishonor; it is raised in glory: it is sown in weakness; it is raised in power: It is sown a natural body; it is raised a spiritual body. There is a natural and spiritual body" (1 Cor. 15:42-44).

Sixth, love. It is more potent than retribution. "An eye for an eye, and a Tooth for a tooth" is shallow. This law of equivalence was right under the Mosaic law but barbaric under grace (Matt 5:38-39). Seventh, Forgive. "Therefore, as the elect of God, holy and beloved, put on tender mercies, kindness, humility, meekness, longsuffering; bearing with one another, and forgiving one another, if anyone has a complaint against another; even as Christ forgave you, so you also must do" Col. (3:12-13).

Do not sow to the wind; sow in tears and acknowledge God's Providence and promises; recognize the strength in weakness; love and forgive. By so doing, you will not reap the judgment of sowing evil.

Sermon #45: Life is Short

Exceptional longevity is recorded in the biblical narrative. Methuselah holds the record as the longest-lived person, reaching the age of 969 years. Jared lived for 962 years, while Noah, famous for building the ark, reached the age of 950. Adam, the first man, is said to have lived for 930 years, and his son Seth is believed to have lived for 912 years. Kenan's lifespan is mentioned as 910 years, and Enosh is recorded to have lived for 905 years.

The phrase "life is short" captures the idea that our time on Earth is limited and unpredictable. It reflects the transient nature of human existence, as described in James 4:14, where life is likened to a mist that appears briefly and then dissipates. This perspective reminds us to appreciate and make the most of our time.

First, life is short comparatively. When we compare human life to the vastness of the universe and the immense timeline of existence, our lifespans appear incredibly brief. The universe is estimated to be around 13.8 billion years old, and in comparison, a typical human life that spans several decades seems minuscule.

Second, life is short chronologically, and individual lives are relatively short regarding the overall duration of human existence. The recorded history of humanity spans only a few thousand years, and even the oldest civilizations are relatively recent. When considering the billions of years that have passed since the formation of the Earth, the timespan of human life becomes but a fleeting moment.

Third, life is short collectively. Human life is also short from a collective standpoint; each individual is just a small part of the vast human population. With more than 7 billion people currently inhabiting the planet, our time on Earth seems brief compared to the collective experience of humanity.

Fourth, life is short culturally. Cultures and societies have evolved over long periods, often spanning centuries or even millennia. Compared to the longevity of cultural traditions, customs, and knowledge accumulated over generations, an individual's lifetime can feel fleeting. Cultural progress and change occur over extended periods, making the brevity of human life apparent.

Fifth, life is short biological. From a biological standpoint, human life is relatively short compared to other organisms. Some species of trees can live for thousands of years, while certain tortoises can survive for over a century. In comparison, the average human lifespan of around 70-80 years appears limited. Life is short developmentally, and human life is short regarding our developmental stages. The journey from infancy to adulthood involves rapid physical and cognitive growth, which can seem fleeting when looking back. Childhood, adolescence, and early adulthood, during which significant developmental milestones occur, pass relatively quickly in the grand scheme of life.

Sixth, life is short personally. On a personal level, human life can feel short due to the limited time available to pursue personal goals, fulfill aspirations, and experience everything the world offers. With so many possibilities and experiences to explore, it is common for individuals to feel that life is passing by quickly.

Seventh, life is short environmentally, and human life is affected by the changing environment and the impact of climate change. As ecosystems transform and species face extinction, our time on Earth coincides with significant environmental shifts. These changes can alter the availability of resources, the stability of habitats, and the overall balance of the planet, highlighting the transience of human life.

Comparatively, our individual lifespans appear minuscule compared to the universe's vastness and the timeline of existence. Chronologically, human life is brief when considering the overall duration of human existence and the billions of years since Earth's formation. Collectively, as part of a vast human population, our time on Earth seems limited. Culturally, the brevity of life is evident when compared to the longevity of cultural traditions and knowledge. Biologically, our lifespans are relatively short compared to other organisms. Personally, the limited time available to pursue goals and experience the world can make life feel short. Environmentally, human life is affected by the changing world and the impact of climate change, emphasizing the transience of our existence.

Sermon #46: Tears

Tears and weeping are inherent to the human experience and serve as outlets for various emotions, including joy, gratitude, sorrow, and repentance. Whether found in religious texts or personal narratives, tears symbolize the depth of human sentiment and our capacity for empathy and compassion.

Crying and laughing are often regarded as distinct expressions of human emotion, and they are powerful manifestations of our experiences, capturing moments of profound sadness and immense joy. The significance of tears and weeping can be found in various religious texts and personal accounts.

In the Bible, Jesus is depicted as shedding tears on multiple occasions. The shortest verse in the Bible, "Jesus wept" (John 11:35), shows Jesus mourning the death of his friend Lazarus. Another verse from the Gospel of Luke states, "Blessed are you who weep now, for you shall laugh" (Luke 6:21), highlighting the promise of eventual joy for those who experience sorrow.

Throughout history, both men and women have openly expressed their tears. It is a misconception that strength is incompatible with vulnerability. For instance, Jesus wept for Lazarus and over Jerusalem, expressing deep compassion for the people. Jeremiah became known as the "weeping prophet," and his book of Lamentations reflects his sorrow. King David, too, wept over the loss of his son Absalom.

The personal experiences of individuals also illustrate the power of tears. Lurline Lamond, a minister and founding member of a church, was known as "Weeper" because of her deep empathy. She would weep for and because of the people, urging them to change their ways and seek repentance. Emma Coke, my grandmother, similarly exemplified a weeping disposition. She would pray and weep for them upon hearing of tragic events, even involving strangers, demonstrating her compassion and care.

There are different reasons why people cry. Firstly, tears of joy are shed to celebrate success, the fulfillment of long-awaited desires, the birth of a child, or answered prayers. Returning soldiers, for example, are met with tears of joy as their loved ones rejoice in their safe return. When Joseph was reunited with his family in the Bible, he wept tears of joy, grateful for the divine intervention that turned a dire situation into a blessing.

Secondly, tears can be expressions of repentance and gratitude. In the account found in the Gospel of Luke, a woman wept and used her tears to wash Jesus' feet, signifying her thankfulness for the forgiveness of her sins. Sometimes, tears are the most profound way to convey emotions when words fall short.

Third, there are tears of denial. When we experience failure or denial, tears can be a natural response. In

Psalm 6:6, the psalmist expresses their weariness: "I am weary with my groaning; all the night makes I my bed to swim; I water my couch with my tears." This vivid imagery portrays their sorrow and the abundance of tears in denial or distress. Similarly, in Matthew 26:75, Peter, one of Jesus' disciples, wept bitterly after denying his association with Jesus, realizing the weight of his actions and feeling remorseful.

Fourth, there are tears of compassion. Jesus, known for his empathy and compassion, shed tears at the grave of his friend Lazarus. The verse "Jesus wept" (John 11:35) succinctly captures the depth of his sorrow. It serves as a reminder that Christians should also shed tears for lost people, as mentioned in Psalm 126:6.

Fifth, there are tears of the abandoned. Crying in the present moment, rather than later, is emphasized in passages such as Matthew 8:12, which mentions "weeping and gnashing of teeth." This phrase alludes to the regret and anguish experienced by those left behind or abandoned.

Sixth, there are tears of regret. Regret can bring tears for a missed opportunity or a wrongful action. In the Psalms, King David expressed deep remorse for his sins and wept as a form of repentance. In Psalms 69:10-11, he writes, "I wept and chastened my soul with fasting... I also made sackcloth my garment," signifying his sorrow and desire for forgiveness. Similarly, the tears of Esau mentioned in Hebrews 12:16-17 demonstrate his regret for trading his birthright for a mere meal, as he later sought repentance but found no opportunity for it.

Seventh, there are tears of desperation. In the story of Queen Esther, she desperately cried out to save her people from a plot to kill all Jews. Esther 8:3 describes her falling at the king's feet and beseeching him with tears to intervene and prevent the harm planned by Haman the Agagite.

Eighth, there are tears of salvation. Tears can also be associated with salvation and finding solace. In Matthew 11:28, Jesus invites those who are burdened and weary to come to him for rest. The tears of the tired and heavy-laden can be wiped away, symbolizing the comfort and relief found in faith.

The ministry of tears involves the expression of joy, gratitude, denial, compassion, care, concern, and consolation. The psalmist David believed that his tears held significance to God, as expressed in Psalm 56:8: "Thou tellest my wanderings; put thou my tears into thy bottle; are they not in thy book?" This verse implies that God is attentive to our tears and takes note of our sorrows and struggles.

Sermon #47: When God Intervenes

The intervention of God in Joshua 5:13-15 marks a pivotal moment in Joshua's journey as the leader of the

Israelites. It affirms God's presence, guidance, and command in conquering the city of Jericho. Through this encounter, God reassures Joshua of His support and establishes the divine authority behind Joshua's leadership. God's intervention serves as a reminder that victory is not achieved by human strength alone but through humble reliance on the Lord and His divine assistance.

God is not a spectator. He is actively involved in world affairs and ordinary life affairs. He is not a mystical or aloof figure. The world is under His purview and influence. But God does not seem to intervene to heal everyone or always protect everyone. He works in sync with His plan of salvation. But God intervenes.

First, when God intervenes, he takes over and takes the side of the poor. Second, when God intervenes, he empowers (Acts 2). If you are in a room with a demon or evil spirit, that entity brings fear, heaviness of Spirit, burden, oppression, depression, and loneliness. On the contrary, when you are in a place where the Holy Spirit is present, there is light, freedom, joy, peace, and power. Prayer: "Lord, empower me at church, at home, in my job, wherever I am – empower me." Third, when God intervenes, he shines light into darkness. He brings clarity to a situation, and he removes the veil. Jesus is the light. When He comes into our lives, he shines and brings light.

Fourth, when God intervenes, he brings deliverance. After 400 years, God intervened to liberate enslaved Israelites. Fifth, when God intervenes, he overrules nature; for example, he allows Sarah, Abraham's older wife, to conceive, and she has passed the age of conception. Sixth, he blocks destruction when God intervenes, and the destroying agent cannot intervene.

Seventh, when God intervenes, he brings resurrection. Life is restored, and the status quo is permanently changed. With feet and hands bound, Lazarus came out of the grave. To the people, Jesus said, "Lose him and let him go." Peter raised Tabitha to life (Acts 9:40).

When God intervenes, he takes over, empowering, shining light into darkness, delivering, overruling, and blocking destruction. When God intervenes, everything changes. Our circumstances may seem overwhelming, and the world may offer no solutions, but our hope lies in a God who actively intervenes on our behalf. As we surrender to His will, exercise our faith, and eagerly anticipate His intervention, we position ourselves to witness His miraculous works and experience His transformative power. God is with us, ready to intervene and bring about His divine purposes in our lives. May we always seek Him, trust Him, and anticipate the moments when God intervenes.

Sermon #48: Angels

Angels are essentially "ministering spirits" (Hebrews 1:14) and do not have physical bodies like humans. What do angels do?

First, Angels are messengers of God. The word "angel" itself means "messenger," highlighting one of their primary functions. Angels frequently serve as divine messengers, delivering vital messages from God to humans. Throughout biblical history, they significantly delivered messages regarding God's plans, warnings, and instructions. Second, angels' worship and Praise: Angels are known for their worship and adoration of God. In heavenly realms, they constantly worship and praise God, glorifying His name and declaring His majesty. Their worship is seen in various passages, such as Isaiah 6:1-3 and Revelation 5:11-14. Third, angels are Guardians and Protectors. They are often portrayed as guardians and protectors, providing assistance and protection to individuals or groups. They watch over and defend God's people, ensuring their safety and well-being. Psalm 91:11-12 highlights their role as protectors, saying, "For he will command his angels concerning you to guard you in all your ways. They will bear you up on their hands lest you strike your foot against a stone."

Fourth, angels are Executors of Divine Judgment: At times, angels act as agents of God's judgment and justice. They carry out God's commands to execute judgment upon individuals, cities, or nations, as seen in various accounts throughout the Bible. For example, in Genesis 19, angels were sent to rescue Lot and his family while executing judgment on the cities of Sodom and Gomorrah. Fifth, angels are Assistants in Spiritual Warfare. They are involved in spiritual warfare against evil forces, fight against demonic powers and work to protect God's people from spiritual attacks

Sixth, angels are Agents of Provision and Miracles. They have been involved in providing for physical and spiritual needs throughout history. They can bring provision, guidance, and miraculous interventions according to God's purposes. An example is in Elijah's story, where an angel brings him food and water in his time of need (1 Kings 19:5-7). Seventh, angels Strengthen and encourage. They strengthened Jesus after His temptation (Matt 4:11), urged the apostles to keep preaching after releasing them from prison (Acts 5:19-20), and told Paul that everyone on his ship would survive the impending shipwreck (Acts 27:23-25).

Angels are created beings, serving as instruments of God's will. They serve as messengers, delivering important messages from God, engaging in worship and praise, glorifying God's name, acting as guardians and protectors, and watching over and defending God's people. Angels are involved in spiritual warfare, fighting against evil forces. They can provide for physical and spiritual needs and perform miracles according to God's purposes. Lastly, they strengthen and encourage individuals in their faith and journey.## #49: Sevenfold Significance of Mt. Hebron

"Therefore, give me this mountain" (Josh 14:12)

Hebron, located in the hill country of Canaan in the modern-day West Bank, holds various significant roles and characteristics. In Joshua 14:12, Caleb declares, "Therefore, give me this mountain" - Mt Hebron, expressing his desire for this particular region. Let's explore the different aspects associated with Hebron.

Firstly, Hebron is a place of affirmation or ratification, which signifies the formal approval and fulfillment of God's promises. God ratified His covenant with Abraham in Hebron, demonstrating His faithfulness and confirming His plans for His people.

Secondly, Hebron is a place of rebirth. Originally named Kiriath-Arba, it experienced transformation and renewal over time. It symbolizes the opportunity for personal growth, change, and new beginnings.

Thirdly, Hebron is a place of remembrance, holding positive and negative memories. Abraham resided there, enjoying blessings, fellowship, and abundant provisions. However, Hebron is also associated with losing and burying loved ones, serving as a reminder of life's fragility and the need to cherish meaningful relationships.

Fourthly, Hebron represents a place of promise, and Caleb, in his request, claimed the promise of inheriting the region. Similarly, believers today have promises from God to hold onto, such as the assurance of Christ's return and the fulfillment of His plans for His people.

Fifthly, Hebron is a place of challenge, and it is marked by difficulties and obstacles that need to be overcome. Caleb had to face and conquer the Anakim, representing the giants or strongholds we must confront and drive out.

Sixth, Hebron is a place of anointing, where kings were anointed and set apart to fulfill their roles as representatives of God's justice, truth, and service. The anointing symbolizes empowerment and divine appointment.

Seventh, Hebron serves as a place of refuge. It was designated as a city of refuge, providing safety and protection for those seeking asylum. It embodies finding solace and sanctuary in distress or unintentional harm.

Hebron encompasses multiple facets: affirmation and ratification, rebirth, remembrance, promise, challenge, anointing, and refuge. Each aspect holds significance and offers valuable lessons and insights for believers today.

Sermon #50: Positioned to Enter: New Rules of Engagement

Deuteronomy 8:2 establishes the concept of "rules of engagement," referring to the laws and principles set by God to govern the lives of His people in the promised land. From the time of Abraham, God established specific guidelines and entered into a dynamic relationship with His chosen ones. Moses was given standards to govern his behavior as the lawgiver while leading the Israelites toward the promised land.

A tragic event in the Bible is the Israelites' 40-year wilderness journey, a much longer duration than necessary. They wandered for four decades due to their failure to adhere to God's rules of engagement, and they forgot the directions and lost their way. To enter the promised land, the first rule of engagement is sanctification. Joshua 3:5 emphasizes the need for the people to sanctify themselves, setting themselves apart for God's service.

The second rule of engagement is to cross over Jordan, symbolizing overcoming obstacles in one's path. Jordan represents any challenges or hindrances one may face. Rather than succumbing to the difficulties, one must navigate through them, knowing that God is with them in the journey.

The third rule of engagement is to be strong and courageous. Instead of focusing on the challenges or giants that may intimidate, one should fix their gaze on

Jesus, finding strength in Him. Joshua received a direct command from God to be strong and courageous, as doubts had crept into his heart.

Rule number four emphasizes the importance of praying before taking action. Joshua 9:14 is a cautionary tale, illustrating what happens when God's people neglect to seek His guidance through prayer. The failure to inquire of the Lord led to deception and wrong decisions, highlighting the significance of seeking God's wisdom and direction before making choices. Leaders, in particular, are responsible for praying and seeking God's guidance to avoid failing those under their care.

Rule number five emphasizes the role of the Word of God as a guide. Joshua 1:7 emphasizes the importance of observing and practicing the laws given by Moses, emphasizing the need for believers to engage with the Scriptures regularly. Reading and meditating on the Bible cleanses the mind, provides perspective, and brings blessings. It serves as a compass for navigating life.

Rule number six involves knowing one's enemies and weapons. Recognizing that Satan, the world, and the flesh are adversaries, believers must equip themselves with the weapons of the Word, prayer, praise, fasting, and the power of Jesus' blood. Acknowledging Jesus Christ as the leader is crucial, relying on His guidance and strength in spiritual battles. Joshua's imperfection serves as a reminder that even good leaders can make mistakes. In one instance, Joshua's failure to consult the Lord led to a bad decision, underscoring the need for humility and dependence on God's wisdom in leadership.

Lastly, rule number seven emphasizes the importance of celebration. Just as the Israelites observed the Passover and celebrated in Gilgal, a balance between work and celebration is necessary. While hard work is vital, moments of celebration, both personal and collective, allow for rejuvenation and enjoyment.

It is essential to remember that Satan also operates with his own set of rules of engagement, including distraction, deception, disunity, disillusionment, diversion, disintegration, and death. Understanding these tactics can help believers remain vigilant in their spiritual journey.

There are seven rules of engagement: sanctify yourselves, cross over Jordan, be strong and courageous, pray before you act, let the Word of God be your guide, know your enemies, and celebrate. Applying these principles can help people to navigate through challenges, relying on God's strength, seeking His guidance, engaging with the Scriptures, equipping themselves spiritually, remaining humble and dependent on God's wisdom, and finding a balance between work and celebration. These rules help believers align with God's will and experience His blessings.

Chapter 3: Preface

The Moral Orator

The best way to preach is to live! A good example is better than a thousand words. A good preacher has a good character. He may fall because he's human, but he cannot live a life of perpetual sin and proclaim the unadulterated word of God. The private and public lives of the preacher matter. When a preacher's personal life is in stark contrast to his public life, he is a hypocrite. And people know a hypocrite when they see and hear one.

Some political dogma, xenophobia, and violence spur from pulpits are un-Christian, unholy, and unproductive. The world has begun to tune it out, and empty pews are a testament to this. After a while, people come to understand how shallow some preaching is. Those who proclaim the word of Christ must represent him in thought, word, and deed.

The Christian preachers and orators must 'feed the sheep." People need substance, not stimulation, stylistic expression, or sensationalism. Religious service must not only be passionate, but it must also be didactic and encouraging. Entertainment is a 21st Century phenomenon imposed on the church, and it is an unholy part of the commercialization and capitalization of Christendom. The 21st century is the age of nihilism, when people reject all forms of religious and moral principles and embrace the idea that life is meaningless. Christian orators must rigorously present the reasons for the relevance of the Christian life. Life is meaningful only when people know who they are, where they belong, to whom they belong, and where they are going.

When preaching, we must contend with much more than skepticism and cynicism. We must contend with solipsism, the idea that nothing can be confirmed except our existence. With new data comes new doubt. Biblical inerrancy is challenged. How do we present the authenticity of the canon of the Holy Scripture in the face of new revelations about the Bible? These are not days for just shouting, howling, perspiration preaching. We need those who will defend the faith and be true to inherit discrepancies or contractions in our Christian journey.

Sometimes, "people do what is right in their own eyes." In one case, Israel had no king and no leader. It was a time of civil war that brought the tribe of Benjamin to the brink of extinction. Israel's attempt to administer justice to the tribe of Benjamin brought unparalleled grief and bloodshed. Women and children became property (Jdg. 21:25). Whenever "people do what is right in their own eyes," their lack of a moral compass often leads them to commit atrocities. It took the rise of Samuel, the priest, judge, and prophet, to bring Israel out of their mental and spiritual fog and misdirection. The world is in a mental and spiritual fog! People are searching for direction. We need preachers and orators of the order of Samuel who are anointed, honest, and impartial.

Chapter 3: Sermons 51-75
Sermon #51: Lessons from the Walls of Jericho

The "Walls of Jericho" symbolize strongholds and barriers, that is, the physical walls of Jericho represent the obstacles, challenges, or strongholds that hinder individuals or communities from reaching their goals or entering into their promised land; Unbelief and doubt, that is, the fortified walls of Jericho, seemingly impenetrable, symbolize doubts, lack of faith, and unbelief that prevent people from experiencing God's power and promises in their lives; opposition and resistance, that is, the Walls of Jericho symbolize opposition or resistance faced by individuals or communities when pursuing their purpose or God's calling or the forces that stand in the way of progress and require faith, unity, and obedience to overcome; Redemption and deliverance so the collapse of the walls of Jericho signifies redemption and deliverance and liberation from bondage, freedom from captivity, and the fulfillment of God's promises, and is a reminder that God can bring down any barrier or stronghold in our lives and provide a way to victory, and spiritual transformation, that is, the story of the Walls of Jericho also holds symbolic significance in terms of personal or spiritual transformation. The walls falling represent the breaking down of old patterns, habits, and limitations, making way for new beginnings, growth, and spiritual progress.

Lessons from the Walls of Jericho

First, our greatest battle may require our least effort if God fights it: In Joshua 6:2, God assured Joshua that He would deliver Jericho into their hands. Sometimes, God calls us to rest and trust in His power. When we surrender our battles to Him, He becomes our strategist, leading us to victory. We must seek obedience rather than rebellion. Second, humility brings exaltation: Joshua had to learn humility as a warrior. Despite his military expertise, he had to follow God's unconventional instructions, including marching silently around Jericho for six days. This story teaches us that we must humble ourselves to be exalted as leaders. God opposes the proud but gives grace to the humble. Humility allows us to receive God's guidance and experience His exaltation.

Third, obstacles can be overcome through faith and obedience. The walls of Jericho seemed impenetrable, but they fell through faith and obedience to God's commands. This miracle serves as a reminder that our obstacles, no matter how formidable they may appear, can be overcome when we trust in God's guidance and follow His instructions. Fourth, persistence in following God's instructions leads to victory. The Israelites faithfully followed God's command to march around Jericho for seven days, even when it seemed repetitive or ineffective. Their persistence paid off, and the walls came tumbling down.

Fifth, trust in God's promises and His faithfulness: God had promised to deliver Jericho into the hands of the

Israelites, and He fulfilled His promise. This reminds us to trust in God's promises and have confidence in His faithfulness. When we trust Him, He will always come through for us. Sixth, victory is achieved through unity and teamwork: The Israelites acted as a unified force, following God's instructions together. They marched in unison, demonstrating the power of unity in achieving victory. This teaches us the importance of unity and collaboration within our communities and organizations. We can overcome even the most formidable challenges when we work together, guided by God's principles. Seventh, God's deliverance leads to praise and celebration: After the walls of Jericho fell, the Israelites celebrated and praised God for His faithfulness and victory. This reminds us to always acknowledge and give thanks for God's deliverance in our lives. Celebrating His faithfulness strengthens our faith and encourages others to trust in Him.

The lessons from the Walls of Jericho include the importance of crying out to God in worship and praise, recognizing the strength that comes from unity and collective effort, confusing the enemy through acts of joy and praise, knowing when to be silent and guard our words, and understanding the transformative power of faith. Applying these lessons can lead to spiritual victory and a deeper relationship with God

Sermon #52: Efficacies of the Blood of Jesus

Our text is Hebrews 9:14. The blood of Jesus is the means of atonement, salvation, cleansing, access to God, victory over Satan, reconciliation, and identification with Christ. It represents the core message of the Christian faith, emphasizing the sacrificial love and redemptive power of Jesus Christ.

First, the blood of Jesus procures eternal life for us. The blood of a person contains His life. Life is in Jesus' blood – it gives eternal life. John 6: 53-54, 56 "Jesus said to them, I tell you the truth unless you eat the flesh of the Son of Man and drink his blood, you have no life in you. Whoever eats my flesh and drinks my blood has eternal life, and I will raise him up on the last day. Whoever eats my flesh and drinks my blood remains in me, and I in him." Therefore, communion is so profound. When we take it, we affirm that we have eternal life.

Second, the blood of Jesus guarantees our victory over Satan. Revelation 12:11 says, "And they overcame him by the blood of the Lamb, and by the word of their testimony, and they loved not their lives unto the death." We need the blood in our warfare against Satan. He is afraid of it, and it reminds him of his past defeat at the cross and his future doom. The blood of Jesus brings us deliverance. Rahab was delivered because she had blood on her window. Joshua 2:18 says, "Behold when we come into the land, thou shalt bind this line of scarlet thread in the window which thou didst let us down by, and thou shalt bring thy father, and thy mother, and thy brethren, and all thy father's household, home unto thee." It is a covering and a source of protection.

Third, the blood of Jesus purchased our redemption. God used the blood of Jesus to repurchase us from the slavery of sin. "In whom we have redemption through his blood..." (Eph. 1:7). Fourth, we are justified or declared righteous through the blood of Jesus. Romans 5:9 says, "Since his blood has now justified us, how much more shall we be saved from God's wrath through him!" When God looks at you, he does not see your sins, but he sees the righteousness of Christ. We are declared righteous through the blood of Jesus.

Fifth, the blood of Jesus sanctifies us. Sanctification is the state of being set apart for God. Hebrews 10:29 says, "Of how much sorer punishment, suppose ye, shall he be thought worthy, who hath trodden underfoot the Son of God, and hath counted the blood of the covenant, wherewith he was sanctified, an unholy thing, and hath done despite unto the Spirit of grace?" We are saints or "sanctified ones." We should continue to live a life of holiness, and it is the sanctified life. Sixth, the blood of Jesus brings us deliverance. Rahab was delivered because she had blood on her window. Joshua 2:18 says, "Behold when we come into the land, thou shalt bind this line of scarlet thread in the window which thou didst let us down by, and thou shalt bring thy father, and thy mother, and thy brethren, and all thy father's household, home unto thee." It is a covering and a source of protection.

Seventh, the blood of Jesus brings us into a new covenant. "...This cup is the New Testament in my blood, which is shed for you" (Luke 22:20). We are in a new relationship with God because of the blood of Jesus. We are in the dispensation of grace, and the veil has been torn, and we are free to enter the throne of God anytime.

The blood of Jesus surpasses the temporary purification offered by the ashes of the red heifer. It can cleanse our hearts and remove all past, present, and future sins. It secures eternal life, grants victory over Satan, procures redemption, justifies us, sanctifies us, reconciles us with God, and brings deliverance and protection. Its significance lies in its profound impact on our lives and relationship with God.

Sermon #53: Sevenfold Empowerment

The empowerment of believers involves a series of actions and attitudes that contribute to their effectiveness in fulfilling their calling. The empowerment of the believer, as described in Acts 1:8, involves several key aspects:

First, Positioning is key to empowerment. Believers are positioned for empowerment by God, and they are predestined, called, justified, and glorified, indicating their qualification for empowerment. Additionally, believers are seen as a chosen people, a royal priesthood, and a holy nation, further affirming their positioning for empowerment.

Second, Training is key to becoming empowered. Examples from biblical figures such as Moses and Joshua, Elijah and Elisha, and the apostles highlight the importance of empowerment training. Mentoring and learning from experienced leaders contribute to developing effective and decisive leadership qualities, preparing individuals for their empowered roles.

Third, Waiting for God's timing! Timing is crucial in receiving empowerment. Just as Elisha and the 120 disciples were instructed to wait for their empowerment, believers are encouraged to exercise patience and trust in God's timing. Waiting allows for proper preparation and readiness to receive the power for empowerment.

Fourth, the Reception of empowerment. Believers receive the power for empowerment through the Holy Spirit. This power is not intended for self-promotion or self-glorification but rather to be effective witnesses of God. Through this empowerment, believers can fulfill their calling and carry out their mission to spread the message of faith.

Fifth, Going: Empowered believers are called to go and spread the message of faith. They are instructed to go to different places, starting from their own homes (Jerusalem), reaching out to their neighbors (Judea), and even extending their influence to those considered enemies (Samaria). This directive emphasizes the inclusive and expansive nature of the gospel.

Sixth, Doing. Empowered by the Holy Spirit, believers are encouraged to engage in acts of goodness and service. Following the example of Jesus, who went about doing good and healing the oppressed, believers are empowered to make a positive impact in the lives of others. Good works do not save, but they reflect the transformed lives of believers and demonstrate their commitment to God.

Seventh, Resting. Rest is an essential aspect of empowerment. Just as the Apostle Paul returned to his base in Antioch to rest and reflect after his missionary journeys, believers need reflection, relaxation, and recuperation moments. Rest allows for re-examination, accountability, and the replenishment of physical, mental, and emotional well-being. It is a reminder of God's provision and care for His beloved.

The empowerment of the believer involves God's positioning, training, waiting, and receiving the power of the Holy Spirit, going, doing, and resting. Each aspect contributes to the overall empowerment of believers, enabling them to fulfill their purpose and make a meaningful impact in the world. It is a process through which believers are equipped to carry out their responsibilities as effective witnesses and fulfill their divine purpose.

Sermon #54: When God Shakes A Nation

When God shakes a nation, he disgraces their gods or whatever they worship, contaminates what they cherish, destroys their capacity to procreate and have posterity, diminishes their sense of comfort and stability, and directs judgment specifically at the oppressors, and decimates their economy.

When God attacked Egypt, he brought judgment against Apis, Isis, and Khanum, the Egyptian gods of the Nile. Through frogs, he attacked Heqet, their God of fertility. The gnats were God's response to Set, the Egyptian God of the desert wind. And the flies reminded the people that Re, their God of the sun, has no power at all. A hail shower wiped out Egypt's livestock and rendered Hathor mute. No Egyptian god had a response to boils, locusts, or darkness that engulfed the nation. The pantheon of Egyptian God could not protect the best and brightest children, and the firstborn of every household was killed.

God has overthrown many nations! Is America on his list? It is 400 years since we have endured slavery, colonialism, segregation, Jim Crow, white supremacy, race biology, scientific racism, and systemic racism. Our ancestors suffered cruelty, injustice, robbery, rape, and violence. Like the Jews, who suffered 400 years of slavery in Egypt, the time is ripe for judgment to proceed from the courts of heaven on those who have oppressed black people.

Today, I want to bring our attention to a topic that holds great significance in the Scriptures: when God shakes a nation. We see throughout history that God intervenes in the affairs of nations, bringing about both judgment and restoration. Our text for today is Exodus 4:21-23. Let us explore together what happens when God shakes a nation.

First, when God shakes a nation, he disgraces its gods and idols. When God shakes a nation, He exposes the futility of false gods and idols. In the case of Egypt, we witness God's judgment against the Egyptian pantheon. Each plague was a direct assault on a particular deity, demonstrating their powerlessness before the one true God. Today, we must reflect on our own lives and ask if we have any idols or false gods that we place before the Lord. Let us remember that God alone is worthy of our worship and devotion.

Second, when God shakes a nation, he contaminates cherished things. When God shakes a nation, He confronts the people with the contamination of what they hold dear. The plagues of frogs, gnats, flies, and other afflictions disrupted the normalcy of life in Egypt. It made people aware of their reliance on false sources of security and comfort. As believers, we must examine our hearts and ensure we do not find security in worldly possessions or temporary pleasures. God desires that our trust be solely placed in him.

Third, when God shakes a nation, he diminishes comfort and stability: When God shakes a nation, He challenges the comfort and stability that people rely on. The plagues caused disruptions in the daily routines of the Egyptians, bringing discomfort and fear. This reminds us that our ultimate security should be in God alone, not material wealth, social status, or worldly success. God desires that we find our true comfort and stability in Him, even in the midst of uncertain times.

Fourth, when God shakes a nation, he addresses the oppressors and brings forth justice. In the case of Egypt, God's judgment targeted those who oppressed His people. Similarly, in our world today, God sees the oppression and injustice that occurs. As His followers, he calls us to stand up against oppression and advocate for justice. Let us not turn a blind eye to the suffering of others but be agents of change and instruments of God's righteousness in our society.

Fifth, he decimates the economy: When God shakes a nation, He can bring about economic consequences. The plagues in Egypt devastated their economy, impacting their livelihoods and prosperity. This story reminds us of the importance of stewardship and responsible use of resources. As Christians, we are called to be wise stewards of God's blessings, using them to bless others and advance His kingdom.

God's actions are not arbitrary or without purpose. When God shakes a nation, it is an opportunity for transformation, repentance, and restoration. We must align our priorities with God's will and stand against oppression and injustice.

Sermon #55: Stones of Significance

The command to pick up 12 stones, as mentioned in Joshua 4:5-7, holds significant symbolism. They represent commemoration and remembrance, historical documentation, identity and cultural preservation, healing and reconciliation, and didactic symbolism.

Seven Significances of the 12 Stones Taken from the Jordan

First, they are stones of remembrance. They will remember that the river, which seemed impassable, was open for passage, not by Moses' rod, but by divine intervention. "Roll back the curtains of memories now and then. Show me where you brought me from and where I could have been. Remember, I'm human, and human forgets, so remind me, remind me, dear Lord."

Second, they are stones that signify and attest to God's help from the Lord. Third, **the stones are a reminder of God's ability to defy nature of nature.** Josh. 3:16-17 "That the waters which came down from above stood and rose upon a heap very far from the city Adam that is beside Zaretan: and those that came down toward the sea of the plain, even the salt sea, failed, and were cut off: and the people passed over right against Jericho. And the priests that bare the ark of the covenant of the LORD stood firm on the dry ground amid Jordan, and all the Israelites passed over on the dry ground until all the people passed over Jordan." They attest to what God has done for His people before and what He can do for them anytime. So, we say, "Do it again, Lord. Do it again." First, it serves as a witness to Israel's neighbors. When they heard what God had done and how the people began to cross over, fear paralyzed them.

Fourth, **the stones represent the continuance of God's blessings on the 12 tribes of Israel.** These stones were about them. The promise made to Abraham and its fulfillment. How do you feel when God fulfills His promise to you? It brings joy and a sense of being special, separated from leadership in the world.

Fifth, the stones are witnesses only to the Israelites and their neighbors. They are witnesses to the world. The stones are witnesses of the might of God. Josh. 4: 24b "That all the people of the earth might know the hand of the LORD, that it is mighty ..." The stones remind us of WHO brought them through. They did not drown in the biggest challenge of their life.

Sixth, the stones are witnesses. In the church, it is often said, "Can I get a witness?" The stones or pillars of rocks are considered witnesses because they serve as enduring physical representations of past events and encounters with God. They testify to the faithfulness of God and the experiences of the people who set them up, reminding subsequent generations of their spiritual heritage. Believers must become living witnesses, like stones or pillars, testifying to their faith's reality and transformative power.

Seventh, the stones are sacred, and they are meant to help the people to fear God. Joshua 4: 24b says, "That ye might fear the LORD your God forever." Here, fear means reverence. Because the stones are sacred, the people should maintain respect and reverence for God. "And now, O Israel, what does the LORD your God ask of you but to fear the LORD your God, to walk in all his ways, to love him, to serve the LORD your God with all your heart and soul" (Deut. 10:12).

Memorials are good reminders; they are important because they preserve collective memory, honor the past, and provide opportunities for reflection, education, healing, and inspiration. The 12 stones from the Jordan River hold profound spiritual significance as they serve as stones of remembrance, attesting to the source of true help, defying the laws of nature, testifying to past and future deeds, representing the continuation of blessings, bearing witness to the world, and evoking a sacred reverence for God. They stand as tangible symbols of God's faithfulness, power, and the people's responsibility to honor and fear him.

Sermon #56: This Mountain

Joshua 14:12 "Now give me this hill country that the LORD promised me that day." "Give me this mountain" is a request of God to give us.

First, this mountain is promised. Caleb was asking God for the promise that was made to him before. Christians must ask God for the manifold promises entailed in the Bible. We must accept, receive, and apply them to our lives. "This Mountain" represents all of God's promises to us. 2 Corinthians 1:20 says, "For all the promises of God in him *are* yea, and in him Amen, unto the glory of God by us." Are you standing on the promises of God?

Second, this mountain is a plan or project. "This Mountain" can be a job, a duty, mission, commission, assignment, charge, or an undertaking. It could be the Great Commission as in Matthew 28:16-20, or it could be your cross as in Matthew16: 24-25 "Then said Jesus unto his disciples, if any man will come after me, let him deny himself, and take up his cross, and follow me. For whosoever will save his life shall lose it: and whosoever will lose his life for my sake shall find it." This mountain means give me my task, destiny, and purpose.

Third, this mountain is prosperous. Give me these mountain means give me prosperity as a child of the king of the mountain. If God's plans are meant to bring us prosperity and lead us to a secure end, then we must ask for this mountain of prosperity. Proverbs 13:22 reminds us, "The sinner's wealth is laid up for the just."

Fourth, this is a mountain of Possibility. This Mountain represents the possibilities that await the Christian. In Matthew 6:33, Jesus promises that if we seek first the Kingdom of God, everything we need will be added to us. These possibilities include empowerment through the Holy Spirit.

Fifth, this mountain is paradise. This mountain is a place of fulfillment. It is like heaven. Abraham looked for a city, and Jesus was gone to prepare one. Give me this mountain is a soul call for a glorious city whose builder is God. It is a call to live with the God of the mountain. Think of heaven. It is a place of rest, tranquility, and fulfillment. Everyone should say, "Lord, give me this mountain – the mountain of heaven.

Sixth, this mountain is a position. Your mountain could be a position or seat of power. Are you ready for it? Can you handle being the boss without being abusive? Christians are not called to be silent relics of society; we are called to be engaged in culture. We want to walk the streets of heaven, but first, we must do the work of Christ here on earth. Christian leaders can make a difference in the world. The time has come for Christians to be movers and shakers in the world.

Seventh, this mountain is a paradigm. "Give me this mountain" is an acceptance of a particular lifestyle. It is a lifestyle that upholds standards of holiness and love. Jesus is our paradigm for practice, and we must emulate his life. Styles and fashion change and rotate, but a Christian must maintain a certain way of life. Do you want such a mountain?

Sermon #57: Frightening Numbers (666)

What numbers frighten you? Some people fear their blood pressure numbers! Some people fear their blood sugar numbers! Some people fear their age! The number that frightens me the most is 666; it is the number of the Antichrist! The Bible says, "this is the last hour, and as you have heard that the antichrist is coming, even now many antichrists have come. This is how we know it is the last hour" (1 John 2:18). The world is primed, positioned, and predetermined for the arrival of the Antichrist – the one who will lead it out of chaos but will ultimately seek the place of God!

The Antichrists imitate Christ

Jesus is the Christ (Matt. 16:16). He is called the Antichrist (1 John 4:3). Jesus is the Man of Sorrows (Isa. 53:3), the Antichrist is the Man of Sin (2 Thess. 2:3). Jesus is the Son of God (John 1:34), the Antichrist is the Son of Perdition (2 Thess. 2:3). Jesus is the Seed of a woman (Gen. 3:15), the Antichrist is the seed of the Serpent (Gen. 3:15). Jesus is the Lamb (Isa. 53:7), the Antichrist is the Beast (Rev. 11:7). Jesus is the Holy One (Mark 1:24), the Antichrist is the Wicked One (2 Thess. 2:8). Jesus is the Truth (John 14:6), the Antichrist is the Lie (John 8:44). Jesus is the Prince of Peace (Isa. 9:6), the Antichrist is the wicked, profane Prince (Ezek. 21:25). Jesus is the glorious Branch (Isa. 4:2), the Antichrist is the abominable Branch (Isa. 14:19). Jesus is the Mighty

Angel (Rev. 10:1), the Antichrist is the Angel of the Bottomless Pit (Rev. 9:11).

A man is coming to fix, improve, and restore normalcy! And many will worship him. A great man is coming, but he is not Christ! The Antichrist comes up out of the bottomless pit (Rev. 11:7). Christ came to do the will of His Father (John 6:38), Antichrist will do his own will (Dan. 11:36). Christ was energized by the Holy Spirit (Luke 4:14), the Antichrist will be energized by Satan (Rev. 13:4). Christ submitted Himself to God (John 5:30), the Antichrist defies God (2 Thess. 2:4). Christ humbled Himself (Phil. 2:8), Antichrist will exalt himself (Dan. 11:37). Christ honored the God of His fathers (Luke 4:16), the Antichrist refuses to honor God (Dan 11:37). Christ cleansed the Temple (John 2:14,16), the Antichrist defiled the Temple (Matt. 24:15). Christ ministered to the needy (Isa. 53:7). The Antichrist robbed the poor (Psa. 10:8,9). Christ was rejected by men (Isa. 53:7). Antichrist will be accepted by men (Rev. 13:4). Christ leads the flock (John 10:3). Antichrist leaves the flock (Zech. 11:17). Christ was slain for the people (John 11:51), the Antichrist slays the people (Isa. 14:20). Christ glorified God on earth (John 17:4), Antichrist blasphemes the name of God in heaven.

The Antichrist will be an Intellectual Genius.

The Antichrist is an intellectual genius. He is well-read, a man of scholarship, and an erudite scholar. He will be well acquainted with industry, science, and technology. He will be a man of literature and art and an oratorical genius In Daniel. 7:20, we are read that he has "a mouth that spoke very great things." People like good speakers! They despise the inarticulate. He is confident, passionate, and self-assured, and he will know how to keep it short and sweet! He will have an uncanny capacity to connect with his audience, and they will love him! He will be possessed of extraordinary intelligence. He will be the Devil's imitation of that blessed One "in whom are hid all the treasures of wisdom and knowledge" (Col. 2:3). This Son of Perdition will surpass Solomon in wisdom. In Dan. 7:20, he is represented as "A horn that had eyes." It is a double symbol. The "horn" prefigures strength, and the "eyes" speak of intelligence.

The Antichrist will be a Political Genius

The Antichrist will be a political genius and a shrewd politician who can make deals and build alliances. He will be a commercial genius. "And through his policy also he shall cause craft to prosper in his hand" (Dan. 8:25)." He will be a military genius. "He will be endowed with the most extraordinary powers, so that "he shall destroy wonderfully, and shall prosper, and practice, and shall destroy the mighty and the holy people" (Dan. 8:24)."

The Antichrist will be a Governmental Genius

The Antichrist will be a governmental genius. "He will weld together opposing forces. He will unify conflicting agencies. Under the compelling power of his skill, the world Powers will be united. The dream of a League of

Nations will then be realized. The Orient and the Occident shall no longer be divided.

The Antichrist is a Religious Genius

The Antichrist will be a religious genius. He will proclaim himself God, demanding that Divine honors should be rendered to him, and sitting in the Temple shall show himself forth that he is God (2 Thess. 2:4). He will proclaim himself God, demanding that Divine honors should be rendered to him and sitting in the Temple shall show himself forth that he is God (2 Thess. 2:4). Such wonders will he perform, such prodigious marvels will he work, he would deceive the very elect did not God directly protect them.

The march to the final telos, the end of the world, has begun. The Antichrist is a master, an imitator, an academician, a politician, a tactician, an aesthetician, a motivator, and a religious fanatic. The AntiChrsit is a person with a particular system of governance!

Sermon #58: Sex: It is Controversial!

In a world that often distorts and misrepresents the beauty of human sexuality, it is crucial for us, as believers, to understand God's design and purpose for this precious gift. Let us explore the Scriptures to find guidance and discover the biblical historicity of sex. Our text is Genesis 2:18-25; it gives an account of creation where God established the foundations of the world and everything in it. In this narrative, we encounter the beautiful story of the creation of Adam and Eve, the first man and woman. It is within this context that we discover the biblical efficacy of sex.

First, sex was designed for procreation. Sex guarantees the continuation of the human species. Through sexual intercourse, the union of a man's sperm and a woman's egg can lead to conception and the birth of a child. Marriage is the biblical context for sex. In this way, a child is born with the presence and love of both parents.

Second, sex is designed for intimacy and bonding. Sex serves as a powerful means of deepening intimacy and bonding between partners. It can enhance emotional closeness, foster a sense of connection, and strengthen the bond of love and commitment within a relationship.

Third, sex is designed for pleasure and enjoyment. Another purpose of sex is the experience of physical pleasure and enjoyment. The human body is designed to experience sexual pleasure, and engaging in sexual activity can bring joy, fulfillment, and a sense of well-being.

Fourth, sex is designed for the expression of love and affection. Sex can express love, care, and affection between partners. It allows for the physical manifestation of deep emotional and romantic feelings, expressing and reinforcing the love shared within a committed relationship.

Fifth, sex is designed for communication and intimacy building. Sex can be a form of non-verbal communication, enabling partners to express desires, needs, and vulnerability uniquely. It can foster understanding, empathy, and a deeper emotional connection.

Sixth, sex is designed for stress relief and relaxation. Engaging in sexual activity can promote stress relief and relaxation. The release of endorphins during sex can lead to a sense of calm, relaxation, and improved well-being, helping individuals cope with daily stressors.

Seventh, sex is designed for spiritual union: For some, sex can hold spiritual significance, representing the union of souls or embody spiritual values such as unity, transcendence, and oneness with a higher power.

The purposes of sex mentioned here are not mutually exclusive and often overlap. Additionally, individual perspectives on the purposes of sex may vary based on personal beliefs, cultural norms, and religious teachings. Sex is a divine gift in biblical teachings, intended for fulfillment and enjoyment within the boundaries of marriage. However, society has distorted sex meaning through practices like pornography and objectification.

To restore its significance, people should consider having sex within the confines of marriage, align their lives with God's purposes, and cultivate healthy and loving relationships. By rejecting societal devaluation of sex, people can deepen emotional bonds, foster intimacy, and experience the blessings and joy of following God's design for sex.

Sermon #59: I Am Statements of Jesus

The "I Am" statements of Jesus in the Gospel of John hold deep theological significance, and they reveal Jesus' divinity, mission, and the nature of his relationship with humanity. Using these statements, Jesus identifies himself with the divine name "I AM" (which God revealed to Moses in Exodus 3:14) and asserts his unique role and authority.

First, I am the Bread of Life. Jesus declares himself as the living bread from heaven, offering eternal life to those who partake in him (John 6:51). He portrays himself as the spiritual sustenance that grants eternal life to those who believe in him.

Second, I am the Light of the World. Jesus proclaims himself as the world's light, offering guidance and deliverance from darkness to those who follow him (John 8:12). He presents himself as the source of divine illumination, leading people out of spiritual darkness and ignorance.

Third, I am the Door/Gate. Jesus identifies himself as the door through which people can find salvation and abundant life (John 10:9). He is the entryway to salvation, emphasizing the exclusive means through which people can find redemption and enter a relationship with God.

Fourth, I am the Good Shepherd. Jesus presents himself as the good shepherd who sacrifices his life for his sheep (John 10:11). He portrays himself as the caring and sacrificial shepherd who guides and protects his followers, even giving his life to them.

Fifth, I am the Son of God. Jesus affirms his identity as the Son of God, which some perceive as blasphemous (John 10:36). He claims a unique relationship with God, asserting his divine nature and authority.

Seventh, I am the Resurrection and Life. Jesus declares himself as the resurrection and the life, promising eternal life to those who believe in him (John 11:25). He asserts his power over death, promising eternal life to those who believe in him. Eight, I am the Way, Truth, and Life. Jesus states that he is the way, the truth, and the life, asserting that salvation and access to the Father are exclusively through him (John 14:6). He declares that he is the only path to the Father, the embodiment of truth, and the source of abundant life.

Ninth, I am the True Vine. Jesus refers to himself as the true vine, with his Father being the vinedresser, emphasizing the significance of abiding in him (John 15:1). He uses this metaphor to illustrate the importance of abiding in him for spiritual fruitfulness and connection to God.

The "I Am" statements of Jesus reveal his divine nature, establish his unique role in salvation, and invite people to enter into a transformative relationship with him. They challenge individuals to consider who Jesus truly is and respond to his claims with faith, surrender, and discipleship.

Sermon #60: Where are the Men?

"God gave them his blessing and said: Have many children! Fill the earth with people and bring it under your control. Rule over the fish in the ocean, the birds in the sky, and every animal on the earth" (Gen. 1:28).

The challenges some Christian women face in finding a husband can vary and may not have a single, universal explanation. It's important to recognize that individual circumstances and experiences differ greatly. However, here are a few factors that could contribute to this situation:

First, there have been many cultural shifts. Societal changes over time have led to shifts in gender roles, expectations, and priorities. Some men may delay marriage or prioritize other aspects of their lives, such as education, career, or personal goals. It can result in a smaller pool of eligible men actively seeking marriage.

Second, there are demographic imbalances. Certain regions or communities might have a demographic imbalance regarding gender ratios. It is due to migration patterns, cultural practices, or gender-specific issues in a particular area, leading to fewer available men.

Third, there are compatibility and expectations issues. Finding a suitable life partner involves compatibility in various aspects, including values, faith, personality, and life goals. Some women may struggle to find someone who meets their desired criteria or shares their beliefs and values.

Fourth, there are relationship dynamics at play. Building and maintaining healthy relationships requires effort, communication, and commitment from both individuals involved. Challenges may arise if there is a lack of commitment or a reluctance to invest in relationships, making it harder to find a suitable partner.

Fifth, there are individual circumstances that militate against women finding a mate. Each person's journey and timing for marriage are unique. Some individuals may face personal challenges, such as limited social circles, geographical constraints, past experiences, or specific preferences that can impact their ability to find a partner.

The Case of Black Women

Black women, many Christians, are very quality and are particularly disadvantaged. Many are asking, where are the qualified black brothers? The marriage rate for African Americans has been dropping since the 1960s, and today, we have the lowest marriage rate of any racial group in the United States (42%). Such statistics have caused Howard University relationship therapist Audrey Chapman to point out that African Americans are the most uncoupled people in the country. Why can't black women find a suitable black mate? Some of the reasons are as follows:

Some arguments put forth as to why some black Christian women may struggle to find a partner include:

248

First, there is a disproportionate Incarceration and Unemployment. The high incarceration rates and unemployment among black men can lead to a smaller pool of marriageable black men, creating challenges in finding compatible partners.

Second, there are cultural expectations. Traditional cultural expectations within the black community, such as the preference for same-race partners, can limit options for black Christian women seeking relationships.

Third, self-esteem and cultural Influence. Societal and cultural factors can influence black women's self-perception, leading to self-love and acceptance challenges. Negative portrayals in media and demeaning songs can contribute to these issues.

Fourth, there are independence and submission issues. The perception of black women as independent and lacking in submission can impact relationship dynamics, as some men may prefer partners who exhibit more traditional gender roles.

- Stereotypes and Attitudes: Stereotypes about black women, including those related to having a "bad attitude," can create biases and misconceptions that hinder relationship prospects.
- Financial Expectations: The perception that black women are too focused on financial stability or material gain may impact relationship dynamics.

- Perceptions of Nurturing: Some black men may gravitate towards white or Asian women due to perceptions of them being more nurturing or submissive, which can influence partner preferences.

- Compatibility and Interpersonal Challenges: Like in any demographic group, black women can face challenges related to compatibility, communication, and building relationships.

Fifth, there are changing social dynamics. The era of increased acceptance of diverse sexual orientations may result in some black men choosing same-sex partnerships.

Sixth, unfortunately, some men are at home; some are unemployed or uneducated; some are incarcerated in the new 21st-century slavery; some are in the gay community; and some have lost interest in women. Fortunately, some men are in workplaces, social gatherings, educational institutions, recreational venues, volunteer organizations, hobbies, interest groups, and online platforms and dating apps. The solution may lie in encouraging open communication, fostering healthy relationships, and seeking support from the community, and faith-based networks can be helpful for individuals navigating these challenges.

Men are ubiquitous, but finding a partner is a challenge.

Sermon # 61: The Seven Marvels of the Birth of Jesus

Our text is Luke 1:1-45. The seven marvels of the world today can include a combination of natural and human-made wonders that captivate and inspire people around the globe. They might consist of iconic landmarks like the Great Wall of China and the Taj Mahal, showcasing human achievements' architectural brilliance and cultural significance. Natural wonders such as the Amazon Rainforest and the Great Barrier Reef highlight our planet's extraordinary biodiversity and ecological importance. The technological marvels of the modern age, like the International Space Station and the Large Hadron Collider, push the boundaries of human knowledge and exploration. Finally, the awe-inspiring spectacle of the Northern Lights, with its dazzling colors dancing across the night sky, serves as a testament to the beauty and mystery of the natural world.

The first wonder of Jesus' birth is the incarnation of Jesus. The incarnation of Jesus is the divine act of God taking on human nature, where divinity is clothed in humanity, making Jesus fully God and fully man; through this, Jesus reveals the Father, fulfills the will of God, dies for reconciliation, serves as our high priest and mediator, destroys the works of the Devil, provides an example to follow, offers an adequate sacrifice for sin, and calls all people to repentance for ultimate salvation (John 1:14,

Heb 4:15, John 14:8-11, Heb 10:5-9, 1 Pet 3:18, 2 Cor 5:18-21, Heb 7:24-28).

The second wonder of Jesus' birth is the fulfillment of prophecy. The fulfillment of over 300 prophecies about Jesus, spanning from the earliest books of the Old Testament to the book of Revelation, serves as a remarkable testament to the divine plan and preparation for the coming of the Messiah. These prophecies cover various aspects of Jesus' life, ministry, death, and resurrection, providing compelling evidence of his identity as the promised Messiah and affirming the credibility and divine inspiration of the Scriptures. The comprehensive fulfillment of these prophecies throughout history underscores the significance of Jesus' role and mission in fulfilling God's plan for humanity.

The third wonder of Jesus' birth is the presence of "His star." The presence of "His star" holds significant symbolism within the narrative of the Christmas story, and it represents God's guidance, revelation, and divine intervention. The star served as a celestial sign that led the wise men to Jesus, signifying the fulfillment of prophecies and the arrival of the long-awaited Savior. It exemplifies God's guidance and direction to those who seek Him, emphasizing the divine nature of Jesus' birth and the heavenly proclamation of His arrival.

The fourth wonder of Jesus' birth is an angelic Announcement. Angels appeared to Mary, Joseph, and the shepherds, bringing messages of the birth of the Savior. These divine interventions signaled the extraordinary nature of Jesus' arrival and conveyed the significance of His mission.

The fifth wonder of Jesus's birth is the womb's communication. As soon as Mary greets Elizabeth, the baby in Elizabeth's womb (John the Baptist) leaps with joy, and Elizabeth is filled with the Holy Spirit (Lk. 1: 39-44).

The sixth wonder of Jesus' birth is Herod's Massacre. Matthew 2:16-18 recounts the brutal act of King Herod ordering the massacre of male infants in Bethlehem and its surrounding regions, a tragic event foretold by Jeremiah in Jer. 31:15. The exact number of victims is not specified. Still, it was a heinous act reminiscent of Pharaoh's attempt to eradicate the Israelite babies in Exodus 1:22. The purpose behind the killings included eliminating any potential threat from a male leader, diminishing the population and power, and causing widespread turmoil and grief among families. This dark event starkly contrasts the sixth marvel of God's love, described in John 3:16, which demonstrates God's unconditional love's practical, powerful, and passionate nature.

The seventh wonder of Jesus' birth is the love of God, and it is the very essence of the story itself. The advent of Jesus, the Son of God, in a humble manger profoundly demonstrates God's unconditional love for humanity. God chose to enter the world as a vulnerable baby, willingly taking on human form, revealing His love's depth and desire to reconcile and save humanity. The

Christmas story highlights God's sacrificial love, His willingness to dwell among us, and His ultimate plan to offer redemption and eternal life through Jesus. The love of God displayed in the Christmas story is a powerful reminder of His grace, mercy, and compassion, compelling us to respond with gratitude, worship, and love in return.

The significance of the seven wonders of the ancient world and the marvels of the modern world is undeniably remarkable. Each of these wonders showcases the ingenuity of human craftsmanship and the awe-inspiring beauty of nature. However, amidst these extraordinary achievements, none can compare in importance to the birth of one child - Jesus. The birth of Jesus transcends human achievements and natural wonders, for it represents the culmination of divine love, grace, and redemption. In the birth of Jesus, the world received the ultimate gift, the embodiment of God's unconditional love and the hope of salvation. The wonders of the ancient and modern worlds may inspire admiration and wonder. Still, it is in the birth of Jesus that the true wonder of humanity's spiritual journey and the divine connection with the Creator are found.

Sermon #62: Metaphors of Life

In James 4:14, the author describes life as a mist; it is a biblical metaphor that conveys a deeper meaning and insight into the complexities of life. Truthfully, life is a multifaceted concept, a precious and sacred gift encompassing physical, spiritual, and eternal dimensions.

Life is a gift. It is a precious and undeserved blessing God bestows, contrasting the consequences of sin and death with the gift of eternal life through Jesus Christ. Life is a vapor, and its brevity and transient nature are compared to a fog, a mist that quickly dissipates. It highlights the fleeting and fragile nature of human existence. Life is a race; it is a race that requires endurance, perseverance, and a steadfast focus on the goal. It encourages people to run their spiritual journey with patience and determination, pursuing the ultimate prize.

Life is a tale. This metaphor parallels life and a story or narrative, and it signifies that human life unfolds like a tale, with an exposition, climax, and resolution. It implies that life is limited but encompasses a complete story.

Life is a battle. This metaphor depicts life as a constant struggle against the spiritual forces of evil. It highlights the need for spiritual armor and readiness to withstand and overcome challenges and temptations. Life is a flower. This metaphor highlights the brevity of life by comparing it to the fleeting beauty of a flower. It underscores the transitory nature of human existence and emphasizes the importance of making the most of our limited time. Life is a mystery, acknowledges life's inherent complexity and unpredictability, recognizes that aspects of life are beyond human comprehension, and invites individuals to embrace the mysteries of life with faith and humility.

Life is a multifaceted journey filled with challenges, gifts, adventures, sorrows, and tragedies. It is a series of duties, games, mysteries, and songs. Life presents us with opportunities, journeys, promises, beauties, struggles, and goals. It is a puzzle we must solve and believe in its eternal nature. People are encouraged to embrace the diverse experiences it offers. Life is not a stagnant existence but a dynamic and ever-changing adventure. It requires us to face challenges head-on, accept the gifts it bestows upon us, and have the courage to dare greatly. Despite sorrows and tragedies, people can overcome them and find the strength to endure. Life is not meant to be passively observed but actively engaged, like playing a game enthusiastically and joyfully.

Within life's complexity, mysteries are waiting to be unraveled, and songs are waiting to be sung. Life carries promises that need our commitment and dedication to fulfill, and it is also a source of beauty that deserves our recognition and praise. Despite our struggles and obstacles, people should fight for what they believe in and strive to achieve their goals.

Sermon #63: But God

The phrase "but God" implies a shift or contrast in the narrative, highlighting God's intervention, power, or sovereignty in a particular situation. It signifies a turning point or resolution beyond human limitations or expectations. It acknowledges that despite challenges, obstacles, or human shortcomings, God can bring about change, provide solutions, and work in ways that surpass human understanding or capabilities. "But God" emphasizes the faithfulness, authority, and supernatural nature of God's actions in human circumstances.

"But God" signifies God's intervention and involvement in various situations, including preventing adultery, protecting individuals from harm, orchestrating appointments and positions of power, turning evil intentions into good outcomes, providing guidance and direction, supplying miraculous provisions, and delivering people from harm. The phrase highlights God's active role in changing circumstances and displaying His sovereignty. "But God" signifies divine intervention and showcases God's involvement in various situations.

First, "But God" intervenes. God appears in a dream to prevent Abimelech from committing adultery. Second, "But God" protects: Despite Laban's attempts to deceive Jacob, God safeguards Jacob from harm. Third, "But God" appoints. Joseph acknowledges that God orchestrated his rise to power in Egypt. Fourth, "But God" turns things around. Joseph reassures his brothers that although they intended evil, God used it for good to save many lives. Fifth, "But God" directs. God leads the Israelites through the wilderness, guiding them to the Red Sea. Sixth, "But God" provides. God miraculously provides water for Samson in a desperate situation. Seventh, "But God" delivers. Despite Saul's pursuit, God protects David and prevents him from falling into Saul's hands.

"But God" demonstrates how God exercises His authority and power in different ways: overruling human plans and decisions, providing strength in times of weakness, offering forgiveness for sins, speaking truth and judgment, knowing the depths of the heart, being present and supportive, and even raising the dead. The phrase emphasizes God's sovereignty and involvement in the affairs of humanity, and these instances illustrate how God's intervention brings positive outcomes, protection, guidance, and deliverance. The phrase "But God" emphasizes the pivotal role of God in changing the course of events and displaying His sovereignty.

Sermon #64: The Christian Narcissist

The modern church needs liberation from the tentacles of Christian narcissists. In 3 John 9-10, Diotrephes is mentioned as a leader in a local church who loved to have preeminence and refused to acknowledge the authority of the apostle John, known for spreading malicious gossip and using his position to manipulate and control others for his gain. His behavior exemplifies the traits of a religious narcissist, including the desire for power, manipulation, and disregard for authority. Christian narcissists can exhibit various characteristics indicative of their manipulative and self-serving nature. First, Grandiosity. Think of hats, suits, and shoes. Christian narcissists love to announce their arrival. They often have an inflated sense of self-importance and believe they possess special knowledge or insights that others lack. They can discern everyone's problems except their own. They may claim to communicate directly with God or consider themselves superior to others in matters of faith.

Second, they use manipulation and deception to get what they want. These individuals are skilled at manipulating others to serve their agenda. They may use charismatic charm, emotional manipulation, charity, or even spiritual coercion to gain control and influence over their followers.

Third, they lack empathy. They are people who do not know love and cannot exhibit it. Christian narcissists tend to be self-centered and lack genuine empathy for others. They exploit people's vulnerabilities and manipulate their emotions for personal gain without considering their followers' emotional or spiritual well-being. Of them, Jesus said, "You travel over land and sea to win a single convert, and when you have succeeded, you make them twice as much a child of hell as you are" (Matt. 23:15).

Fourth, they have an excessive need for admiration. Christian narcissists " love to be first" and crave constant attention, admiration, and praise from their followers. They may demand unquestioning loyalty and use flattery or rewards to maintain a devoted following. And they will do the abomination to get this attention. If ignored, they move to another place to get this narcissistic supply.

Fifth, they lack accountability: Like Diotrephes, Christian narcissists are often not accountable to leadership; they are part of a strange oligarchy in the church. And when they strike, they avoid taking responsibility for their actions or admitting wrongdoing. They may deflect criticism, shift blame onto others, or use spiritual justifications to rationalize their behavior.

Sixth, they violate boundaries. In their quest for information on others, they disregard personal boundaries and invade their followers' or colleagues' privacy or personal lives. They may seek to control every aspect of their followers' lives, including their beliefs, relationships, and decision-making.

Seventh, they are good at exploitation and financial abuse. Christian narcissists know how to make people give money; they frequently exploit their followers financially, encouraging excessive giving or demanding financial contributions for personal gain. They may live lavish lifestyles while their followers struggle financially.

Not every Christian leader is a narcissist, but the church culture makes congregants vulnerable to them because a church is where people are supposed to trust their leaders. Leaders or teachers exhibit these traits, and discernment is crucial when evaluating the authenticity and integrity of spiritual figures. In navigating the challenges presented by Christian narcissists, we must remember that our ultimate allegiance is to Christ; hence, to deal with these narcissists rely on God's Word, the guidance of the Holy Spirit, and the support of a loving Christian community. Respond to them with wisdom, grace, and discernment, and seek to extend God's love. Remember, some have passed the place of repentance, and you can do nothing for them.

Sermon #65: Seven Crowns

Stephanos and diadema are crowns. Jesus received both. Which do you have? While Christians are considered royalty in Christ, the crowns are not automatically bestowed upon them; they must be earned. The Stephanos crown symbolizes the rewards and victories obtained through faithful endurance and service to God. It emphasizes that our crowns are not inherited but achieved through our dedication and commitment to Christ.

First, there is an imperishable or incorruptible crown. The apostle Paul compares earthly achievements and a heavenly, eternal reward (1 Cor. 9:25). He explains that athletes undergo rigorous training and discipline to obtain a perishable crown, a temporary symbol of victory. However, believers in Christ hope to receive an imperishable or incorruptible crown, which represents an eternal reward that cannot be tarnished or diminished. The imperishable crown is not subject to decay or fading and is unaffected by external factors such as cheating or dishonesty. It emphasizes the eternal nature of the reward awaiting those who faithfully follow Christ and endure in their spiritual journey.

Second, the crown of righteousness. 2 Timothy 4:8 represents the ultimate reward and recognition for a life of holiness, faithfulness, and anticipation of Christ's return. It underscores believers' hope and assurance in their future glorification and eternal fellowship with God. Third, the crown of life (Rev. 2:10). The crown of life is closely associated with overcoming trials and remaining steadfast in one's commitment to God. It signifies victory over spiritual battles and the assurance of eternal life with God. The crown symbolizes honor, reward, and the ultimate triumph of faith.

Fourth, there is a crown of rejoicing. (1 Thes. 2:19) The crown of rejoicing signifies the joy and satisfaction that Paul and his fellow apostles would experience in the presence of the Lord when they see the Thessalonian and Philippians believers standing strong in their faith and being faithful to Christ. It represents the shared joy between those who have been instrumental in leading others to salvation and seeing them continue their faith journey. Fifth, there is a crown of glory. The "crown of glory" signifies the eternal and unfading nature of the reward that awaits those who faithfully fulfill their roles as spiritual shepherds, pastors, or leaders within the Christian community. It symbolizes the special commendation and recognition that God will bestow upon those who have faithfully shepherded and cared for His people, exhibiting a genuine love for God and His flock. Sixth, there is a crown of lovingkindness and tender mercies. (Psa. 103:4). The imagery suggests honor, dignity, and authority.

Seventh, a crown of thorns (Matt. 27:29). The crown of thorns foreshadowed the suffering and sacrifice that Jesus would endure on the cross.

Sermon #66: Let Us

A command is imperative. "Let us" is a statement of encouragement to act. Let us not defy God, as seen in the story of the Tower of Babel where people sought to build a tower to reach heaven. The result was confusion and the scattering of people due to their defiance of God. (Gen. 11:4).

Let us not act in desperation, exemplified by the actions of Lot's daughters, who resorted to incestuous acts to preserve their family's lineage. It resulted in an abomination (Gen. 19:3).

Let us rise and worship God, as demonstrated by Jacob's decision to go up to Bethel and build an altar to God. It led to a change of heart and a renewed commitment to worship (Gen. 35:3).

Let us fall into the hand of God, as expressed by David when he faced a difficult situation. He trusted God's mercy and restoration rather than falling into man's hands (I Chron 21:13).

Let us rise up and build, as Nehemiah inspired the people to rebuild the walls of Jerusalem. They united and strengthened their hands for this important work (Neh. 2:18).

Let us worship and praise God, as encouraged in various Psalms. People should bow down, sing joyfully, exalt His name, and come into His presence with thanksgiving and songs of praise (Psa. 95:6).

Let us go into the house of the Lord and come before Him with thanksgiving, as expressed in Psalms. The invitation is to eagerly enter God's presence and offer our worship and gratitude (Psa. 122:1). These "let us" statements motivate and encourage us to live in alignment with God's will, pursue righteousness, and actively participate in acts of worship, service, and unity. They encourage us to do the following:

- Avoid defying God and face the consequences of disobedience.

- Refrain from desperate actions that compromise our values.

- Rise and worship God, committing ourselves to His presence and service.

- Trust in God's mercy and seek His intervention in times of trouble.

- Unite and work together for constructive purposes.

- Engage in heartfelt worship, expressing praise and exaltation to God.

- Eagerly enter the house of the Lord, approaching Him with gratitude and reverence.

Sermon #67: Let Us: Hebrews

In the book of Hebrews, we encounter a recurring phrase throughout this epistle: *Let Us.* These two simple words hold immense significance and beckon us to action. Today, we will delve into the various *Let Us* statements in Hebrews and uncover their transformative power in our lives. Let us open our hearts and minds to these divine invitations.

First, *Let Us* come boldly to the Lord. Hebrews 4:16; Hebrews 10:22. The writer of Hebrews urges us to approach the throne of grace with boldness and confidence. We are invited to come before our merciful God, knowing he will provide us with the mercy and grace we need in times of trial. Let us draw near to God, not with fear or hesitation, but with sincere hearts and unwavering faith. Second, *Let Us* go on. In our spiritual journey, we are called to move forward and progress beyond the foundational principles of our faith. Let us not remain stagnant but press on toward maturity and spiritual perfection. By continually growing in understanding and applying God's Word, we align ourselves with His divine purpose for our lives.

Third, *Let Us* hold fast (Hebrews 10:23). In a world filled with distractions and challenges to our faith, we are encouraged to hold fast to our confession of faith. Let us remain steadfast and unwavering in our belief, for our God is faithful to His promises. Through His strength, we can endure trials and remain anchored in Him.

Fourth, *Let Us* consider one another (Hebrews 10:24). People should be mindful of one another. Let us actively encourage one another to love and do good work. We can build each other up and exemplify Christ's love in our relationships through our encouragement and support. Fifth, *Let Us* lay aside (Hebrews 12:1). We must lay aside the burdens hindering our progress to run the race before us. Let us cast off every weight and the sins that entangle us, fixing our eyes on Jesus, our ultimate example. Let's run this race with patience and endurance, focusing on the eternal prize. Sixth, *Let Us* have grace (Hebrews 12:28). God has bestowed upon us an unshakable kingdom; in response, let us live with grace. Let us humbly serve God acceptably, with reverence and godly fear. May His grace empower us to fulfill His purpose, reflecting His character to the world around us.

Seventh, *Let Us* offer the sacrifice of praise (Hebrews 13:15). Finally, let us continually offer the sacrifice of praise to God. Let us express gratitude and adoration for His goodness and faithfulness through our lips. Our praise must testify to our unwavering trust in him, even in challenging times.

 The *Let Us* statements in Hebrews unveil a roadmap for our spiritual journey. They call us to action, urging us to approach God boldly, grow in faith, support one another, and run the race with perseverance. Let us heed these divine invitations, allowing them to shape our lives and draw us closer to our loving Savior. The transforming power of the "Let Us" commands in Hebrews are guided by the Holy Spirit and empowered by God's grace.

Sermon #68: Embracing God's Restoration

The Year of the Lord's Favor was associated with the proclamation of the jubilee year in ancient Israel. During this jubilee, which occurred every fifty years, debts were canceled, enslaved people were set free, and the land was restored to its original owners. It was a time of resetting, renewal, and release from bondage. If people embrace rest, release, reception, revival, restoration, restitution, and recompense they can experience their Year of Jubilee. Let us delve into each of these R's and discover the transformative power they hold. First, Rest. God invites us to find rest in Him in a world filled with anxiety and restlessness. Hebrews 4:1 reminds us of the importance of entering His rest. Fear can consume us, affecting our physical and mental well-being. Let us cast our worries upon Him, for our God is a God of peace.

Second, Release. God calls us to release and forgive. Just as in Deuteronomy 15:1, the release of debts every seven years, we are urged to forgive and set others free. Release the burdens, grudges, and hurts that weigh us down. Doing so allows God's love to flow through us and bring healing to our relationships.

Third, Reception. Jesus invites us to come to Him and find rest for our souls. Matthew 11:28 assures us that weary and burdened can find solace in His arms. As we open the door of our hearts to Him, He enters and dines with us, bringing us comfort, companionship, and peace.

Fourth, Revival. Like the man who was revived upon touching the bones of Elisha in 2 Kings 13:21, God desires to bring revival to our lives. He can breathe life into our dry and weary spirits, igniting a renewed passion for Him. Let us seek His presence, allowing His Holy Spirit to revive us and set us on fire for His purposes. Fifth, Restoration. God is the ultimate restorer. Through Jesus Christ, He reconciles us to Himself, as stated in 2 Corinthians 5:18. He takes the broken pieces of our lives and mends them, transforming our pain into purpose. He restores what was lost and brings wholeness to every area of our being. Trust in His faithfulness and believe in His restoration power. Sixth, Restitution. Restitution calls us to make amends for our wrongdoings. Exodus 22:5 teaches that we must repay what we have taken or damaged. Let us seek reconciliation with those we have wronged and make things right. Doing so reflects God's love and righteousness in our actions.

Seventh, Recompense. Lastly, we come to recompense, a payment, or judgment. As in 2 Samuel 22:25, the Lord rewards us according to our righteousness. God sees and honors our faithfulness and integrity. Trust in His divine justice, knowing that he will recompense us according to His perfect plan.

Sermon #69: The People God Seeks

The text of Ezekiel 22:31 depicts God as searching for a person who could act as a mediator or intercessor on behalf of the people. The purpose was to find someone who would stand up for righteousness and justice, intercede and make a positive impact, thereby preventing the destruction of the land. God laments that He found no one who fulfilled this role among the people. It highlights the lack of righteous individuals willing to step forward and act according to God's desires. Despite God's omnipotence, He chose to work through human agency and sought someone to align their will with His and be a force for good.

By extension, God is in search of people in our society today. First, as the text implies, God is searching for people of prayer who will intercede. God sought someone who would mediate between Himself and the people, appealing to God on behalf of the community and seeking mercy or forgiveness. The Bible says, ""The effectual fervent prayer of a righteous man availeth much." (James 5:16). These intercessors must pray for political, religious, and social leaders, many of whom were proclive to do evil.

Second, God seeks people with passion; they must have fervor, enthusiasm, zeal, and intense emotion that compels them to seek change. John Lewis and CT Vivian were prominent figures in the Civil Rights Movement who demonstrated intense desire and a hunger to bring about positive change and fight for justice. Their actions and sacrifices exemplified their deep commitment to their cause.

Third, God seeks people with perseverance. Sometimes passion runs out; when that happens, we must lean on persistence. God desires men of determination who "Trust in the Lord with all your heart and lean not on your understanding, in all your ways submit to him, and he will make your paths straight." (Pro. 3:5-6).

Fourth, God seeks people of peace. In the text, there was no peace between the religious and the secular, the privileged and the poor, and God and Israel. Fifth, God seeks people with moral purity. Public and private morality is important. John Lewis has been called "the conscience of the U.S. Congress." It meant that in all things moral or ethical, he was the standard by which all actions should be judged. He was an institution of morality.

God has always used imperfect people committed to rising to an occasion to do his will: Throughout the Bible, we encounter a diverse array of individuals who confront various challenges and possess their imperfections. Abraham engaged in deception, Sarah expressed disbelief at God's promises, Moses struggled with speech, and David's armor did not suit him. Paul spurned John Mark, Timothy battled ulcers, and Hosea's wife engaged in prostitution. Amos gleaned wisdom from nature, and David committed adultery. Solomon possessed excessive wealth, while Jesus experienced poverty. Abraham faced advanced age, and David was regarded as youthful. Peter harbored a fear of death, Lazarus experienced death, and John displayed self-righteousness. Naomi became a widow, Paul and Moses were involved in acts of murder, and Jonah fled from God. Miriam engaged in gossip, Gideon and Thomas harbored doubts, and Jeremiah grappled with depression and thoughts of suicide. Elijah endured exhaustion, John the Baptist spoke boldly, Martha grappled with anxiety, Noah struggled with alcoholism, and Moses, Peter, Paul, and numerous others exhibited quick tempers. They serve as a reminder that despite their weaknesses, God can employ them for His purposes and utilize them to achieve remarkable feats.

Sixth, God seeks people with principle. A principle is a basis for action! There is something that helps a person know what is right and wrong – the Bible! It must influence thoughts and actions! But there are those in religious leadership without a moral compass!

Seventh, God seeks men and women who are "Present, Available, and Ready to GO! Like Isaiah the prophet, do you hear the voice of God? "Then I heard the voice of the Lord saying, "Whom shall I send? And who will go for us?" And I said, "Here am I. Send me!" (Isa. 6:8).

God actively seeks individuals who will step forward and make a difference. They exemplify passion, perseverance, prayerfulness, peace-loving nature, and moral purity. They are human, with flaws and imperfections; however, they hold firmly to their principles. God desires individuals who are present, available, and ready to act when called upon.

Sermon #70: A Church Without Jesus!

The text of Revelation 3:14-22 states that metaphorically and literally, Jesus is standing outside the door of His church signifies His desire for a personal and intimate relationship with individuals and the church as a whole. It conveys that Jesus seeks to be welcomed and invited into people's and their community's lives.

The setting of the text is important. Laodicea was once a wealthy, dynamic city in the Lycus River Valley of the province of Phrygia, and it was a lively commercial center of industry, medicine, and trade. The church of Laodicea was rich, but Jesus was not in it! Getting into a church can be funny: some repent, get baptized, and receive the right hand of fellowship. Some pay for their membership and have specific seats; others get in because of their connections, while some are accepted because they have talent. Some church people are not believers, but they are a part of the oligarchies of a particular assembly.

A man made several attempts to become a member of a particular church, but the church people rejected his application. One night, having prayed about his frustration, he went to bed. While he was asleep, Jesus came to him and encouraged him. Jesus told him not to become frustrated because he was not alone. In the dream, Jesus told the man that he, as the head of the universal church, had been trying to get into it himself.

What catastrophe or spiritual disaster must have occurred for Jesus to be outside of his own church?

First, Jesus is outside of a church that has abandoned the truth, and it is a church that worships the mythical, not the historical Jesus. Second, it is a church with many activities, even wealth, but it has lost its witness. The church must bear witness to Christ and represent him in words, deeds, and God's representation on earth! It must be faithful to represent all that Jesus is. Jesus stood at the door of this church "as the true and faithful witness." So, the church that locks out Jesus is not a church that is a true and faithful witness! In other words, it is a church without commendation! Jesus has nothing good to say about it – that sounds like the evangelical church in America. Let us look at all the seven churches mentioned in the early parts of Revelation.

Third, it is a church that is in spiritual blindness. Laodicea, the lukewarm church, like Sardis, the dead church, had no commendation to its credit! It is a church that stands condemned: "I know your deeds, that you are neither cold nor hot. I wish you were either one or the other! So, because you are lukewarm—neither hot nor cold—I am about to spit you out of my mouth. You say, 'I am rich. I have acquired wealth and do not need a thing.' But you do not realize you are wretched, pitiful, poor, blind, and naked" (Revelation 3:15-17). Fourth, it is a worldly church where wealth has become its God! The angel said, "You say, 'I am rich, and I have acquired wealth and do not need a thing.' Yet, their wealth had become their God! Is Jesus standing outside of your church?

275

Sermon#71: Criteria for Voting!

Make the most of every opportunity because the days are evil" (Eph 5:16). "Your kingdom come, you will be done, on earth as it is in heaven (Matt. 6:10).

Today, the Great United States is a classic example of an imploding empire! Every institution of democracy, decency, and duty is disintegrating! From the church to the courts, every institution has been corrupted! The vampires of economics are sucking the blood of the people. In 10 months, American billionaires have earned over 845 billion dollars because of a pandemic that has made thousand homeless, hungry, and hopeless.

How should Christians vote? The casting of lots is not an adequate criterion! First, you must be a citizen of the United States and have public and private morality. A candidate must support broad ethical values, and he must be a candidate who loves justice and mercy and walks humbly before God! Use the following scriptures to guide your vote. Do not vote for a divisive person. It is an abomination to the Lord: "There are six things the LORD hates, seven that are detestable to him: haughty eyes, a lying tongue, hands that shed innocent blood, a heart that devises wicked schemes, feet that are quick to rush into evil, a false witness who pours out lies and a person who stirs up conflict in the community" (Prov. 6:16-19).

Second, vote for the candidate who looks beyond wedge issues.

Third, voting for the candidate with humility and pride is set on a tangent of catastrophe. Fourth, vote for a candidate with a holistic foreign policy, not a policy of isolation! Fifth, vote for a candidate who promotes family values in its truest sense. One who protects our home – earth – the environment!

Sixth, vote for the candidate who protects the least amongst us, one who protects the vulnerable in society. One who loves humanity, not just his race, and upholds the common good! A candidate who values the sanctity of all human lives: Do not vote for a candidate who is pro-life in words but not in deeds. A candidate who calls himself pro-life and is against abortion, but is pro-wars, ignores the pain of his people, ignores racial injustice and inequalities, and supports the death penalty (most of the incarcerated are of one race and are without proper legal representation).

Seventh, vote for a candidate who respects the diversity of humanity. Respecting diversity within a country is essential for a politician to foster inclusivity, unity, and a thriving society.

A Political Candidate

First, he should embrace equality and promote and uphold the principle of equality for all individuals, regardless of their race, ethnicity, religion, gender, sexual orientation, or any other characteristic. They should advocate for laws and policies that ensure equal rights, opportunities, and protections for everyone. Second, he should foster inclusive governance and actively involve diverse voices and perspectives in decision-making. Politicians should create platforms for marginalized communities to be heard and actively seek input from various groups when formulating policies. Third, he should combat discrimination by taking a strong stance against it in all its forms. They should work to eliminate systemic biases and prejudices that hinder the full participation and advancement of individuals from diverse backgrounds. Fourth, promote multiculturalism and intercultural dialogue by celebrating and encouraging cultural diversity within the country. They should support initiatives that promote multiculturalism, such as festivals, cultural exchanges, and educational programs that foster intercultural understanding. Promoting dialogue and interaction among different cultures can enhance social cohesion and appreciation for diversity. Fifth, support inclusive policies and services by advocating for policies that address diverse communities' specific needs and challenges by giving access to quality education, healthcare, housing, employment opportunities, and social services.

Sixth, lead by example by demonstrating respect for diversity through their behavior and language. They should refrain from engaging in discriminatory rhetoric or actions and actively promote tolerance, respect, and understanding among citizens.

Vote

In the crucible lies the American citizen's voting might,
Where equity, dignity, and posterity take flight,
At stake is our ability to build a just society's height,
Resting on the tenets of justice.

For every abused, used, and refused American soul,
In the name of our ancestors who paid the toll,
Who bled and died, securing our voting role,
Let our voices unite and rise, making history whole.

As Jesus taught us to pray, "Thy will be done,"
Embrace the power within, let your vote be the sun,
From morning's rise to evening's fall, let it be spun,
Illuminate the darkness, and ensure justice is won.

Awake from your slumber, ignite your resolve,
Rise from the sofa, let your voice evolve,
Take action, make a difference, let your vote absolve,
The weight of indifference lets democracy revolve.

In this opportune moment, seize the hour,
There's a time to make a change, wield power,
To learn from past mistakes and rise even bolder,
To kindle hope's flame, make our future grow taller.

Vote, it is a candle, dispelling despair,
With each mark on the ballot, show that you care,
Vote! Vote! Vote! Let freedom's song blare.

Sermon#72: Choosing the God Way

Scripture: John 8:12 - "When Jesus spoke again to the people, he said, 'I am the light of the world. Whoever follows me will never walk in darkness but will have the light of life.'" The text encourages us to choose God in various aspects of our lives; let us anchor our reflections in the powerful words of Jesus: "I am the light of the world. Whoever follows me will never walk in darkness but will have the light of life." This scripture reminds us that choosing God means embracing His light, love, liberty, excellence, and truth. Let us dive deeper into this passage and discover how it shapes our choices and transforms our lives.

First, choose light over darkness. The words of Jesus declare that he is the world's light. We are led out of darkness and into His marvelous light by choosing to follow him. Accept God's light, walk in his truth, reject the deceit of darkness, and radiate his love and grace to those around us.

Second, choose love over hatred. Jesus' proclamation of being the light of the world is rooted in love. His life, death, and resurrection demonstrate the ultimate act of love. People should choose love over hatred in all their interactions. By accepting his love and extending it to others, we break down walls of animosity and division, paving the way for reconciliation and restoration.

Third, choose liberty over bondage. Jesus came to set the captives free and bring liberty to the oppressed. When we choose God, we choose to break free from the bondage of sin, fear, and worldly attachments. His liberating power empowers us to live a life of purpose and authenticity, unencumbered by the chains that once held us.

Fourth, choose excellence over mediocrity. In proclaiming himself as the world's light, Jesus invites us to pursue excellence in all we do. In choosing God, we embrace the call to offer our best, live with integrity and diligence, and honor him with our talents and abilities. As we strive for excellence, we become living testimonies of God's transformative work. Fifth, choose truth over lies. Jesus, as the light of the world, embodies truth. By choosing him, we align our lives with His truth and reject the lies surrounding us. His truth sets us free from the deception and confusion that the world presents. Walk in wisdom, discernment, and authenticity.

As we reflect on the text about Jesus as the light of the world, we are invited to make intentional choices to follow Him. Choosing God means choosing light over darkness, love over hatred, liberty over bondage, excellence over mediocrity, and truth over lies. Continue to seek his guidance and empowerment to make these choices, knowing that it is in him that we find abundant life, purpose, and transformation.

Sermon#73: A Lack of Knowledge in the Age of AI

Title: A Lack of Knowledge in the Age of AI

Text: Hosea 4:6 (NIV) - "My people are destroyed from lack of knowledge. Because you have rejected knowledge, I also reject you as my priests; because you have ignored your God's law, I will also ignore your children." In the age of Artificial Intelligence (AI) and rapidly advancing technology, we live in a time of great progress and innovation. However, amidst this technological marvel, a pressing concern deserves our attention - the lack of knowledge. Today, we will explore the implications of this knowledge gap and how it impacts our relationship with God and our responsibilities as His children.

First, AI or artificial intelligence comes with promise and peril. It promises a better future along with the dangers of technology. AI has the potential to enhance our lives, improve efficiency, and tackle complex problems. Yet, it also risks leading us astray if we rely solely on its capabilities while neglecting our pursuit of true knowledge and wisdom. Second, the danger of rejecting knowledge. The prophet Hosea reminds us that a lack of knowledge destroys the people of God, and it does not refer to worldly knowledge alone but primarily the knowledge of God's truth, laws, and ways. When we reject this knowledge and ignore His commands, we distance ourselves from God and the blessings He desires to pour out upon us.

Third, the impact on our spiritual lives. In this age of information overload, it is easy to be swayed by conflicting beliefs, ideologies, and opinions. Without a solid foundation of knowledge rooted in God's Word, we risk being led astray by false teachings and misleading voices. Our spiritual lives suffer when we lack discernment and fail to cultivate a deep understanding of God's truth. Fourth, our Responsibility. People should seek knowledge and truth and diligently study Scripture, prayer, and reflection, and we should seek to understand God's ways, character, and will for our lives. By pursuing knowledge, we equip ourselves to discern between right and wrong, navigate life's complexities, and faithfully follow God's path. Fifth, embracing Wisdom in the Age of AI. While AI can provide us with vast information, it cannot replace true wisdom. Wisdom is the application of knowledge in alignment with God's purposes and values. We must seek the wisdom that comes from God, which surpasses the limitations of human understanding. Wisdom helps us to navigate the challenges posed by AI and make decisions that honor God and benefit humanity.

The age of AI should extend our knowledge to the most crucial knowledge of all—the knowledge of God and His truth. People should commit to seeking wisdom, discern truth from falsehood, and faithfully follow the path that leads us closer to God.

Sermon#74: Rising from the Ashes!

We are at a critical and crucial juncture in the history of the United States. We are a dangerous fork in the road. There are two roads ahead – one is a continuation of the godless road we now trod, and the other – is a new road of justice, loving-kindness, and humility.

The African, Jewish, and Chinese civilizations are among the few groups of people to have emerged from antiquity! The Mayans have disappeared! The jungles of Central America swallow up their great monuments, cities, and roads, and their peoples are scattered to small, inconsequential villages. They do not exist as a great civilization anymore! The Indus Civilization that ran from India and Pakistan to Afghanistan does not exist today! These are three separate countries. In his book Collapse, Jared Diamond sums up what many scientists now believe to be the cause of the collapse of the Easter Islander Civilization, namely, their methods were not sustainable. Their methods were not sustainable.

Where is the Babylonian civilization today? It has fallen. And, what say we of the life of the Great Nebuchadnezzar? He is relegated to the garbage heap of history! Our Text, Isaiah 61:3 (NIV), says, "...to bestow on them a crown of beauty instead of ashes, the oil of joy instead of mourning, and a garment of praise instead of a spirit of despair."

Today we gather to explore a profound question: How can a nation arise from the ashes of history? As we examine nations' struggles and challenges throughout time, we will find hope and guidance in the Scriptures. Our text from Isaiah 61:3 reveals God's promise to bestow beauty, joy, and praise in the place of ashes, mourning, and despair.

First, the path to national restoration begins with acknowledging the Ashes. Before a nation can arise, it must acknowledge its history's ashes. Just as individuals must confront their past mistakes and failures, nations must face the consequences of their actions. It requires humility, repentance, and a willingness to learn from past mistakes.

Second, the path to national restoration is embracing restoration through God's Grace. We must find God's grace and redemptive power. He promises to replace mourning with joy, despair with praise, and ashes with a crown of beauty. Restoration begins by turning to God, seeking His forgiveness, and surrendering to His transformative work in the hearts and lives of individuals and the nation.

Third, the path to national restoration begins with pursuing justice and reconciliation: A nation can only truly arise when it addresses the injustices of its history. It involves seeking justice for the marginalized, reconciling with those wronged, and working toward unity and equality for all citizens. True healing and restoration can only occur when a nation commits to justice and reconciliation.

Fourth, cultivating a vision of hope and renewal. A nation must develop a vision of hope and renewal to rise from the ashes. This vision requires leaders and citizens who believe in the potential for positive change, work towards a common purpose, and invest in the nation's well-being and progress. A renewed sense of purpose and collective effort can inspire a nation to overcome adversity and build a brighter future.

Fifth, nurture a culture of love and compassion. Central to national restoration is cultivating love and compassion. It includes caring for the vulnerable, embracing diversity, promoting empathy, and fostering a spirit of generosity and kindness. A nation can rebuild its physical infrastructure and moral and social fabric by embodying these virtues.

The journey of a nation arising from the ashes of history is not easy, but it is a path marked by hope, redemption, and transformation. As we turn to God and embrace His grace, justice, and love, we can witness the restoration of our nations. Let us commit ourselves to the pursuit of truth, justice, reconciliation, and a vision of hope as individuals and as a community. May we be instruments of change, sowing seeds of love and compassion as we witness the glorious rise of nations from the ashes into a future filled with God's beauty, joy, and praise.

Sermon#75: The First Christmas

The Alignment of the Prophets

The verse Galatians 4:4 states that God sent forth His Son in the fullness of time. The birth of Jesus happened at the perfect moment, aligned with numerous prophecies from the Old Testament. The first Christmas marked the fulfillment of around 300 prophecies, such as Isaiah's prophecy about the virgin birth of Immanuel. Jesus' birth connected all the prophetic words of the significant biblical figures, from Genesis to Malachi. Each book foreshadowed a different aspect of Jesus' role, emphasizing Him as the Seed of the Woman, Passover Lamb, High Priest, Prophet, Shepherd, Prince of Peace, and many more. The birth of Jesus revealed a prophetic alignment, signifying that it was the ideal time for Him to enter the world.

Linguistic Alignment

Classical Greek was the dominant language of industry and commerce, but the New Testament was written in koine Greek, the language of everyday people. This linguistic alignment played a significant role in the rapid spread of the gospel because most people in the Mediterranean world widely understood koine Greek. Using a language accessible to the ordinary population facilitated the communication of the gospel message and contributed to its rapid dissemination.

Governmental Alignment

When Jesus was born, the world was governmentally alignment. No major wars were being fought at the time! The Pax Romana, or time of Roma peace, existed. The world in which Jesus was born had a unified Government: Rome. And the Romans had built a unified Empire. Having conquered Israel, the Roman Government built many roads through which the disciples would travel to bring the Gospel throughout the Roman Empire and turn the world upside down for God!

An Alignment of Peace and Tranquility

At the time of Jesus' birth, there was an alignment of peace and tranquility in the world. However, the present state of the world is marked by chaos and distress, including the mercurial nature of the current American President. In contrast, Jesus was born when peace prevailed, as the Romans established a period of peace and prosperity. However, this era of peace also coincided with moral decay and the loss of moral values. Societies tend to turn to God during hardships but may forget Him in times of prosperity.

An Alignment of Hope

Jesus was born in a world that had an alignment of hope. When Jesus was born, there was a profound anticipation and longing for the Messiah to come and liberate the people from the powers of Rome. The people longed for a liberator! They longed for a deliverer.

An Alignment of the Divine Order

The world in which Jesus was born was aligned by divine order. It was the fullest of time, the most appropriate or suitable moment, when all necessary conditions or preparations have been fulfilled, and something significant or significant event occurred. It refers to the perfect timing or culmination of events leading up to a particular moment or occurrence.

The birth of Jesus occurred in the perfect alignment of various factors. It was the fulfillment of numerous prophecies, showcasing the divine timing and preparation that led to His arrival. The linguistic alignment of the New Testament being written in koine Greek facilitated the spread of the gospel to the common people. Additionally, the governmental alignment during the Pax Romana provided a unified empire and infrastructure for the disciples to carry the message of the Gospel. Jesus' birth also represented an alignment of peace and tranquility, although it coincided with moral decay. The world at that time was filled with hope and anticipation for the Messiah's arrival. Ultimately, the birth of Jesus reveals the divine order and control that God exercises over human history.

Chapter 4: Preface

The Gospel – The Most Transformative Force on Earth

The Gospel is the most transformative force on earth. Nothing can replace bold, balanced, biblical, and prophetic preaching! The Gospel, and not politics, science, nor prodigious lies, is the power of God to bring salvation! And God needs people to declare it! Like first-century Christians, those who proclaim the unadulterated word of God must be prepared to die for it! The word of God is surgical and salvific. Many of whom we have revered as authentic preachers have been misleading colonizers, evangelical grifters, and those from the synagogue of Satan. Where are the preachers who demand righteousness and truth in public and private life? God is removing generations of corrupt preachers from the pulpit and infusing a new dynamic breed of vibrant, committed firebrand preachers willing to speak truth to power and die for it!

Everything is for sale except the power of God that leads to salvation! We need power for the hour! The sons of Sceva were amazed to see the power of God at work in the apostle Paul. He was able to exorcist demons and perform great miracles. Thus, they sought to buy that power (Acts 19). Such power will re-emerge in the church in the resolution of history! The latter rain cometh! And all fake healers and preachers will seek it too! The release of unparalleled power presents a precarious situation for seekers who hunger and thirst after righteousness; they must be careful. Wolves in sheep's clothing are always close! But the final harvest of souls is imminent. The last soldiers on the battlefield must be armed with the skill of exegesis, but more so, the power of authenticity. There is nothing worse than a fake preacher! He is not called, anointed, or appointed, yet he has the credentials, titles, and grabs of religiosity! That's a dangerous person! That's like Antiochus Epiphany IV on the altar of the temple!

People need freedom from the consequences of sin, release from the results of slavery and segregation, freedom from bad theology that taught the supremacy of one race above the other, freedom from church trauma, and freedom to seek God although he's omniscient and omnipresent! Because very soon,

The Lord will lay bare his holy arm

in the sight of all the nations,

and all the ends of the earth will see

the salvation of our God (Isa. 52:10).

Global economic, political, and social tumults are indicators of the cry for a new dimension to our life experience. People crave a new dawn of uprightness and equity. The prophetic voices of the Old and New Testaments were God's oracles to bring societies in check and to re-direct them when they were out of alignment with God. God is searching for men and women who will be obedient to him and live uncorrupt lives so they can be vessels of honor in a dishonest, disgraceful, and dying society. When the preacher is corrupt, he becomes an ineffective pretentious pariah. Corrupt preachers become peddlers of conspiracy theories rather than bearers of the light. They become a joke and anathema to the world. The 21st Century is the era for the latter rain that will bring unparalleled empowerment to the preachers of the Gospel and an unprecedented harvest of souls for the kingdom of God. So, our task is threefold: "Arise, shine, for your light has come, and the glory of the Lord rises upon you" (Isa. 60:1). First, Christian preachers must rise from their slumber of indifference and inertia. Second, they must begin to shine as models of Christ in a world of abject darkness after such obedience. Third, glory cometh. Like the sun that rises from the east, the glory of the Lord, God's grace, mercy, and favor, will become a reality in their lives and those who call on the name of the Lord.

Chapter 4 Sermons #76-100

Sermon #76: Move Forward in Marriage

Ladies and gentlemen, esteemed guests, and most importantly, the beautiful bride and groom,

Welcome to this joyous occasion, the solemnization of Holy Matrimony between [Bride's Name] and [Groom's Name]. Today, we gather here on a day filled with love and gratitude, and it is a day to celebrate and give thanks; it is a day the Lord has specially crafted for us to rejoice and celebrate.

[Bride's Name] and [Groom's Name], after a long wait, this moment has finally arrived, and it is truly a special one. So, take a deep breath and let all your worries fade away. Remember the wise words of Bob Marley, who once said, "Don't worry about a thing because every little thing is gonna be alright." As we stand here today, God is present with us, and the support of your dear friends and loving families surround you.

Sermon

This sermon focuses on the theme of moving forward in marriage, drawing inspiration from the scripture Jeremiah 29:11. We admonish the bride and groom to do the following:

1. Move forward together. As a married couple, operating as a team and not living as individuals

is important. Embrace the unity and shared responsibilities that come with marriage. By moving forward together, you strengthen your bond and tap into the strength of togetherness.

2. Move forward with a plan. Have a clear plan for your marriage and set short-term and long-term goals. Find a balance between spending and saving, and prioritize what is important for your future. Remember, communication and agreement on financial matters are crucial.

3. Move forward with love. Take care of each other's needs, including satisfying each other sexually. Encourage openness and understanding in your intimate relationship. Recognize each other's preferences and create a loving and fulfilling physical connection.

4. Move forward with leisure. Enjoy life and have fun together. Embrace fun and laughter, and create an atmosphere of joy in your marriage. Find activities and experiences that bring you happiness and create lasting memories.

5. Move forward with secrecy. Be cautious about sharing every detail of your life with others. Not everyone will be supportive or happy for your relationship. Maintain a healthy boundary between your marriage and external influences, including family and friends. Keep your personal

affairs private and avoid unnecessary interference.

6. Move forward with confidence. Believe in the strength of your marriage and have faith in each other. Your mindset and attitude play a significant role in the success of your relationship. Cultivate an optimistic outlook as you face challenges and navigate life together.

7. Move forward with God. Keep God at the center of your marriage. Seek His guidance, rely on His strength, and invite His presence into your relationship. When God is involved, goodness and mercy will follow you, bringing blessings and fulfillment.

Moving forward in marriage with unity, love, purpose, confidence, and faith in God will help cultivate a strong and thriving relationship.

Marriage Vows

Dear friends and loved ones, we are gathered here today in the presence of God and among this wonderful company to witness the joining of this man and this woman in holy matrimony. Marriage is a beautiful and sacred commitment that holds deep meaning in our modern world, and it represents the profound connection between Christ and His Church, a symbol that has endured through the ages.

Just as Christ adorned and blessed the institution of marriage with His presence and performed His first miracle in Cana of Galilee, we recognize the significance and sanctity of this union. It is a union that deserves our utmost respect, for it is an honorable bond commended by the apostle Paul, and it holds a special place among all people.

Therefore, let us remember that entering into marriage is not a decision to be taken lightly or without thoughtful consideration. It should be approached with reverence, wisdom, and a profound awe before God. Today, as these two individuals embark on this journey together, let us celebrate the love and commitment that has brought them here.

If there is anyone present who can show just cause why these two may not lawfully be joined together, let them speak now or forever hold their peace.

Opening Charge, I solemnly require and charge both of you, knowing that one day we will all answer before the judgment seat of Christ when all secrets are revealed. If you know of any impediment preventing a lawful union in matrimony, I urge you to confess it now. Is there anything you need to disclose?

1. You are giving Away the Bride. Who presents this woman to be married to this man? Thank you. You may be seated.

2. Exchange of Vows – Groom. I will now read the first part of your vow. If you agree, please respond with "I do." Will you, ..., take .... as your lawful wedded wife to live together according to God's ordinance in the sacred bond of matrimony? Will you love, comfort, honor, and remain faithful to her as long as you both shall live? Reply: I do.

3. Exchange of Vows – Bride. The same question goes to you, and if you agree, please respond with "I do." Will you, ..., take .... to be your lawful wedded husband, to live together according to God's ordinance in the sacred bond of matrimony? Will you love, comfort, honor, and remain faithful to him in sickness and health, forsaking all others, as long as you both shall live? Reply: I do.

4. Personal Vows – Groom. I, ..., take you, ..., to be my wedded wife. From this day forward, I promise to have and hold you, for better or worse, for richer or poorer, in sickness and health. According to God's holy ordinance, I vow to love and cherish you until death do us part. This is my pledge to you.

5. Personal Vows – Bride. I, ..., take you, ..., to be my wedded husband. From this day forward, I promise to have and hold you, for better or worse, for richer or poorer, in sickness and health. According to God's holy

ordinance, I vow to love and cherish you until death do us part. This is my pledge to you.

Presentation of Gifts and Blessing of Rings
Minister: As a symbol of your love and commitment, we have now come to the presentation and blessing of the rings. These rings represent the unending circle of love, a constant reminder of your vows to one another. Let us bless these rings and pray for the love and union they signify.

[Minister holds up the rings]

Minister: We gather here today in the presence of [the divine power or the higher power of your choice] to bless these rings, symbols of the love and commitment shared between [Groom's Name] and [Bride's Name].

[Minister or couple's chosen representative may offer a prayer or blessing over the rings]

Minister: Let us declare peace, love, and harmony over these rings, invoking the blessings of [the divine power or the higher power of your choice] upon them. May they serve as a constant reminder of the vows and promises made between [Groom's Name] and [Bride's Name].

[Groom takes the ring]

Groom: With this ring, I thee wed: in the name of the Father, Son, and Holy Spirit. Amen.

[Bride takes the ring]

Bride: With this ring, I thee wed: in the name of the Father, Son, and Holy Spirit. Amen.

[Minister or couple's chosen representative may offer a final prayer or blessing over the rings]

Minister: May these rings always shine as a symbol of the love, commitment, and unity between [Groom's Name] and [Bride's Name]. May they bring joy, strength, and enduring happiness throughout their journey together. We bless these rings in the name of [the divine power or the higher power of your choice]. Amen.

Closing Statement

Minister: In the presence of God and this gathering, [Groom's Name] and [Bride's Name] have joined their lives together in holy wedlock. They have expressed their commitment and love by exchanging rings and joining hands. As an authorized marriage officer in the state of ...., I now declare them to be husband and wife. I pronounce that [Groom's Name] and [Bride's Name] are now united in the bonds of matrimony in the name of the Father, and of the Son, and of the Holy Spirit. Amen.

[Minister may pause to allow for applause or congratulations]

Minister: And now, for the moment you've been waiting for, you may now seal your vows with a kiss to your beautiful bride, your wife.

[Groom and Bride share a kiss]

Minister: As a symbol of the unity they have formed today, [Groom's Name] and [Bride's Name] will now perform the Ceremony of Unity Sand (Optional).

Minister: Before we conclude, let us bow our heads in a prayer of dedication for [Groom's Name] and [Bride's Name]'s journey together as husband and wife.

[Minister or chosen individual offers a prayer of dedication]

Minister: And now, it is my honor to present to you, Mr. and Mrs. [Last Name], as they begin their new life together.

Minister: Please rise and join me in celebration as we recess from this joyful occasion.

[Minister, couple, and guests proceed with the recessional]

Sermon #77: This Jesus

There is a renewed search for the historical Messiah – the Yeshua of Nazareth! I've seen many posts on social media where people are trying to deconstruct their faith. I've heard the testimonies of ex-evangelicals, ex-pastors, pastors' children, and ex-pastors' spouses trying to separate the Jesus they were presented from the historical Jesus. And, with the advancement in technology and the increase in knowledge, many have been asking the question: Who is Jesus?

Is the historical Jesus the same as the one worshipped in white supremacy?

The historical Jesus refers to the historical person who lived in the first century CE and is the subject of historical analysis and research. Scholars use various methods, such as historical documents, archaeological findings, and textual analysis, to study Jesus and understand his life, teachings, and the socio-cultural context of his time. The historical Jesus is the focus of academic study and seeks to uncover the most accurate understanding of who Jesus was based on available evidence. On the other hand, the concept of Jesus worshiped in white supremacy is a distorted and perverted interpretation of Jesus adopted by some individuals or groups within white supremacist ideologies. This distorted view of Jesus misuses religious symbols and beliefs to support racist and supremacist ideologies. White supremacist interpretation of Jesus goes against the core teachings of Christianity, which advocate for love, compassion, equality, and the dignity of all human beings. The historical Jesus, as revealed through scholarly research, did not promote or endorse racism, discrimination, or the superiority of one race over another.

This Jesus is not limited to a particular nationality!

Jesus transcends nationalities, ethnicities, political affiliations, and racial divisions. He cannot be confined to any specific cultural or political identity. Jesus is beyond the boundaries of human constructs and is not limited by our human divisions. Any particular race or political ideology does not define him. Jesus' message of love, compassion, and salvation is universal and extends to all people, regardless of their background. It is important to recognize that Jesus cannot be reduced to any narrow or exclusive representation. Instead, Jesus calls us to embrace a broader understanding of humanity and to seek unity and love for all.

This Jesus is a Savior!

Jesus is a savior, not a savage, representing love and salvation for all people. Jesus transcends the concept of nationalism and is the Lord of the entire Earth. It is important to avoid molding Jesus into our image and instead recognize that he is the image of the invisible God and the firstborn of all creation. Jesus deserves our worship and acknowledgment as the Lord of all.

This Jesus is the Christ!

This Jesus is the Christ, the Messiah (Acts 17:3). According to Matthew 16:13-20, "This Jesus" refers to Jesus Christ, the central figure of Christianity. In this scripture passage, Jesus asks his disciples who people say he is, and Peter responds by proclaiming that Jesus is the Christ, the Son of the living God. Jesus acknowledges Peter's confession and declares that upon this rock, he will build his church, and the gates of Hades will not prevail against it. This passage highlights the divinity of Jesus and his role as the Messiah, the Son of God.

This Jesus is exalted, and he conquered death and hell. This Jesus is not fake; he's real! He's described in the text transcends divisions such as nationality, ethnicity, politics, and race. He is a savior who embodies love and salvation for all people. He is acknowledged as the Christ, the Messiah. This Jesus is holy and victorious over death and hell. He is not a false figure but a real and powerful presence.

Sermon #78: Important Questions

The Bible contains significant questions addressing fundamental aspects of human existence and our relationship with God. These questions include inquiries about accountability, justice, knowledge, purpose, identity, salvation, compassion, and divine power. They challenge individuals to reflect on their beliefs, values, and actions. These thought-provoking questions encourage introspection and guide individuals toward deeper understanding and spiritual growth.

Psalm 11:3 poses an important question: "If the foundations are destroyed, what can the righteous do?" King David wrote this verse during a time of turmoil when his son Absalom sought to overthrow him and take the throne. Absalom, known for his beauty and cunning, used deceitful tactics to gain popularity and support. David advised to flee to Gilead to protect Jerusalem, divided his army, and ultimately emerged victorious in the battle against Absalom's forces. While David did not desire his son's death, Absalom was killed by one of David's captains. This story highlights the challenges and trials the righteous face when foundations are shaken and the importance of seeking refuge and guidance from God in times of adversity.

Negatively, if the foundation of a nation is in the process of destruction, the populace must respond with wisdom and discernment. The people should rise above these negative reactions instead of resorting to complaints, protests, ignorance, denial, or apathy. Complaining without action achieves little, protests can escalate tensions without addressing the root causes, ignorance perpetuates ignorance, denial hinders progress, and apathy allows the decline to continue unchecked. Instead, people should strive for constructive engagement, seeking understanding, unity, and collaboration. They should educate themselves about the issues, engage in peaceful dialogue, participate in democratic processes, and work towards positive change. By rejecting detrimental attitudes and embracing proactive and responsible citizenship, the people can contribute to restoring and advancing their beloved country.

Positively, the test points to three ways to act. First, renew your Faith in God. Psalm 11:1 says, "In the LORD put I, my trust." When the foundations of a person – your character, courage, and confidence are destroyed – renew your faith in God. When the foundations of a family, finances, fellowship, and future are being destroyed (here, David's own Son was trying to kill him for the throne). Renew your faith in God when the foundations of a church, that is, its vision and vitality, the church need to renew its faith in God, when the foundations. Why should we renew our faith in God? Because God is not asleep. Verse 4-5 says, "The Lord is in his holy temple, the Lord is on his heavenly throne. He observes everyone on Earth. His eyes examine them.

Second, renew your courage. Take Courage. We must determine whether to fight or flee. Verse 1 says, "In the Lord, I take refuge. How then can you say t me: "Flee like a bird to your mountain?" King David didn't flee because he was afraid; he left Jerusalem to regroup and prepare for war.

If the foundations are being destroyed, stop the destruction, and begin to rebuild. Restore the foundations. In David's case, the foundations of family, community, and government were on the path of destruction. Rebuilding the foundations requires several steps. First, prayer is essential, seeking guidance and strength from a higher power. Second, providing an alternative and setting a good example can inspire and motivate others to follow a positive path. Third, pointing people to the scriptures and their wisdom can offer guidance and principles for rebuilding. Fourth, invoking the power of Jesus' sacrifice is efficacious. Fifth, developing a comprehensive action plan that outlines specific steps and goals is crucial for organized and focused efforts. Sixth, being prompt in acting and not delaying necessary measures is vital to prevent further deterioration. Lastly, practicing moments of silence to reflect, listen, and gain clarity can help make wise decisions. It is essential to be among those who make things happen rather than passively observing or being oblivious to what transpires.

Sermon #79: The New Life

Do you like the quality of your life? I am not talking about your neighbor's life, your opponent's life, or the life of your competitor. Are you living your best life yet? Some people have their dream marriage, career, car, house, friends, and families but are still unhappy. I have often heard people say they are ready for a new page or chapter in their lives, but the truth is that they need a new life. A new page or chapter in a sinful, sorrowful, or sagging life is meaningless if life is not fulfilling! The truth is: They need a complete transformation! They need a new life.

A New Life

In Romans 6:4, the apostle Paul compares Christ's resurrection to the new life we find in Him. Let us explore the characteristics of this new life and how it impacts our faith journey.

1. The Experience of Light. The resurrection of Jesus was an experience of light generated by and for the glory of God. When Saul encountered the transforming power of Christ on the road to Damascus, a light shone, a voice was heard, and directions were given. Similarly, we cannot emerge from the darkness of lethargy or spiritual death except through the power of the resurrection. The new life in Christ is a radiant

experience that illuminates our path and fills us with the glory of God.

2. Liberating Experience. Just as resurrection brings liberation, the new life in Christ sets us free. Jesus said, "He who hears My word, and believes Him who sent Me, has eternal life and does not come into judgment but has passed out of death into life" (John 5:24). In Christ, we are liberated from the chains of sin and no longer face condemnation. This new life offers freedom from guilt, shame, and the fear of judgment.

3. Active Experience. The new life in Christ is not a one-time but an ongoing, active experience. As believers, we are continually being transformed by God's grace. The apostle Paul affirms that God changes us daily, leading us from glory to glory. When we accept Christ, something marvelous happens to us, but this experience continues throughout our lives. Each day presents an opportunity for growth, renewal, and deeper intimacy with our Lord.

4. Transformational Event. Similar to the resurrection of Jesus, the new life is transformational. It marks a profound shift from death in sin to life in Christ. Through His death and resurrection, Jesus conquered sin and granted us the power to overcome its grip on our lives. This transformation enables us to live

according to God's purposes and align our will with His.

5. Victory Over Sin. Just as the resurrection of Jesus was a victory over death, the new life in Christ grants us victory over sin. The grave could not hold His body down, and now, sin no longer has dominion over us. The power of Christ's resurrection enables us to resist temptation, turn away from sinful habits, and live a life pleasing to God. We can overcome every temptation through the indwelling Holy Spirit and walk in righteousness.

6. A Life of Hope and Service. The new life in Christ is filled with hope. Romans 5:5 assures us that the hope we have in God's promises will never disappoint us. This hope is poured abundantly into our hearts through the Holy Spirit. Furthermore, this new life compels us to serve others. James 1:27 teaches us that true religion involves caring for orphans, widows, and the vulnerable. Our focus should not be on divisive issues but on protecting the weak and showing love to those in need.

7. An Eternal Life. The new life in Christ is not limited to this earthly existence, and it is a life that stretches into eternity. The wages of sin is death, but the gift of God is eternal life through Jesus Christ our Lord (Rom 7:23). Through faith in Jesus, we receive the gift of eternal life. Our

earthly life is just the beginning, and our citizenship is in heaven (Philippians 3:20). We eagerly await the return of our Savior, Jesus Christ, who will usher us into the fullness of eternal life with Him.

8. A Life of Healing. The new life in Christ brings healing—spiritually, psychologically, and physically. Spiritually, we find healing from the scars of sin through the forgiveness and redemption found in Jesus. Psychologically, Christ offers healing from the burdens and stressors of life. He invites us to cast our anxieties upon Him because He cares for us (1 Peter 5:7). Moreover, Jesus is the Great Physician who can bring physical healing. By His stripes, we are healed (Isaiah 53:5). While complete physical healing may not always occur in this life, we have the assurance of ultimate healing in the resurrection.

9. Holiness. The new life in Christ calls us to pursue holiness, and Hebrews 12:14 instructs us to follow peace with all people and holiness, without which no one will see the Lord. Personal holiness is the gradual work of grace in the believer's life, and it involves watchfulness, prayer, perseverance, and the ongoing transformation of our character to be more like Jesus. As we grow in holiness, we reflect the image of our Lord and draw closer to Him.

10. Harmony with God. Once, we were enemies of God, but through the new life in Christ, we are reconciled to Him and become His friends. The barrier of sin has been broken, and we can now enjoy a harmonious relationship with our Creator. This relationship is founded on love, grace, and the indwelling of the Holy Spirit. The new life in Christ allows us to fellowship with God, communing with Him through prayer, worship, and obedience to His Word.

The new life in Christ is a profound and transformative reality that encompasses our existence. It brings light, liberation, transformation, and victory over sin. This new life offers hope, eternal life, healing, holiness, and harmony with God. While challenges and disappointments may still arise, the Christian life is directed by God for His honor and glory. Let us embrace this new life with gratitude and joy, continually growing in our relationship with Christ. By walking in the power of His resurrection, our lives can reflect His love, grace, and compassion, shining as beacons of light in a world that needs hope. May the newness of life in Christ be evident in all we say and do.

Sermon #80: Make a Choice

The word of God calls on us to make a choice. Both making choices and refraining from making choices carry significant implications. Every decision we make or choose not to make has consequences that shape our lives and influence our paths. Not making a choice can be seen as a choice, as it indicates a deliberate decision to allow circumstances or others to dictate the outcome.

The implications of making choices are multifaceted; they can lead to personal growth, learning opportunities, and realizing our goals and aspirations. They enable us to exercise our autonomy and shape our lives according to our values and priorities. Making choices empowers us to take ownership of our actions and accept responsibility for the outcomes, fostering a sense of agency and self-determination.

On the other hand, not making choices can also have profound consequences. It can result in missed opportunities, stagnation, and a sense of passivity or indecisiveness. When we avoid making choices, we relinquish control over our lives and allow external factors or circumstances to determine our path. Not making choices can lead to feelings of regret, frustration, and a lack of fulfillment.

The implications of our choices extend beyond ourselves, and our decisions can affect those around us, influencing relationships, communities, and future generations. By actively making choices, we can positively impact the world and contribute to the greater good.

In the text, Joshua 24:15, we read: "But if serving the LORD seems undesirable to you, then choose for yourselves this day whom you will serve. But as for me and my household, we will serve the LORD." In this passage, Joshua presents the people of Israel with a profound choice. They are urged to decide whom to serve - whether to commit themselves to the Lord or turn to other gods. Similarly, we are confronted with choices that require us to make a deliberate decision about the direction of our lives. But why should we choose this context?

First, there is power in intentional decision-Making. It clarifies our values. Making choices forces us to examine our values and priorities. When we are faced with a decision, we must evaluate what truly matters to us. By intentionally choosing to serve the Lord, we align our lives with His principles and values, finding meaning and purpose in our journey of faith.

Second, it forces us to take responsibility. Making a choice empowers us to take responsibility for our actions and their consequences. It demonstrates our willingness to be accountable for the direction of our lives. When we deliberate to follow the Lord, we accept the responsibility to live according to His will, relying on His guidance and grace.

Third, it helps us to avoid complacency. Not choosing can lead to complacency and a lack of progress in our spiritual lives. Indecision or apathy can hinder our growth, keeping us in stagnation. By actively choosing to serve the Lord, we embrace a path of continuous growth, seeking deeper intimacy with Him and becoming more Christ-like in our character.

Fourth, there are blessings for choosing to serve the Lord:

1. Abundant Life. Serving the Lord opens the door to a life of abundance and fulfillment. The Lord desires to bless His children and lead them into a purposeful and joyful existence. When we choose to serve Him, we position ourselves to experience His blessings and walk in the fullness of His promises.

2. Guidance and Direction. Following the Lord allows us to tap into His wisdom and guidance. He promises to lead us on the right path and guide our lives. As we surrender our choices to Him, He illuminates our way and grants us discernment to navigate the complexities of life.

3. Strength and Support. Serving the Lord means embracing His strength and support in every circumstance. He promises to be with us, to uphold us, and to give us the strength to overcome challenges. By choosing to trust in Him, we can

experience His presence and experience supernatural empowerment.

We are faced with countless decisions, each carrying the potential to shape our destinies. In this sermon, we will delve into a passage emphasizing the importance of making a choice and reflecting on why it is crucial. Making a choice is crucial in the context of our spiritual journey, and it clarifies our values, instills a sense of responsibility, and guards against complacency. We invite abundant life, divine guidance, and unwavering support by serving the Lord. Today, let us reflect on the choices before us and, like Joshua, declare with conviction, "But as for me and my household, we will serve the LORD." May our choices be intentional, guided by faith, and rooted in our commitment to obedience to our loving and faithful God.

Sermon #81: Breakthrough

A spiritual breakthrough is a powerful intervention by God that propels His people forward. It is a transformative moment where a Christian gains a deeper understanding of biblical truth through direct divine intervention. It serves as a boost, a quantum leap, a remarkable advancement, and an enrichment of one's spiritual journey. A spiritual breakthrough is often sought when individuals face setbacks and stagnation, indicating the need for divine intervention to overcome obstacles hindering their progress. It is evidence of God's intervention to release individuals or circumstances into their God-appointed path.

There are different types of breakthroughs. Some are gradual, akin to childbirth, where there is a period of carrying the burden, intense labor pains, and finally, the moment of joy when the new life is born. Others experience breakthroughs through practices such as the Daniel fast, which can lead to spiritual growth and transformation over time. Additionally, sudden breakthroughs resemble the eruption of a volcano or the breaking of a dam or reservoir, bringing forth a significant and immediate shift in one's spiritual journey.

Are you prepared for a new spiritual ascension? A breakthrough takes you to a new level of spiritual experience, where you transition from defeat to victory, from sin to righteousness, from religious rituals to authentic relationship with God, from fear to love, from dead works to living faith, from sadness to joy, and from poverty to abundance. You become fruitful rather than fruitless in a breakthrough, showing God's transformative work in your life.

May we earnestly seek spiritual breakthroughs, recognize the areas where we need God's intervention, and eagerly embrace the new levels of spiritual growth and blessings He has prepared for us. Let us open our hearts to the transformative power of God, trusting Him to lead us on a journey of breakthrough and fulfillment in our walk with Him.

Strategies

A spiritual breakthrough is a transformative experience where God intervenes mightily on behalf of His people, propelling them forward in their spiritual journey. To understand and embrace the strategies for a breakthrough, we look to the life of David, anointed as king over Israel and Judah. Through his example, we can learn valuable lessons on positioning ourselves for divine intervention and experiencing breakthroughs.

First, anointing. The anointing represents God's empowerment and consecration for a particular purpose. As believers, we are anointed by the Holy Spirit and authorized as empowered agents of God. Understanding our anointing enables us to tap into the power that God has given us. Just as David sought God's guidance before engaging the Philistines, we must rely on the leading of the Holy Spirit to activate our anointing and experience breakthrough. 2 Corinthians 1:21-22: "Now it is God who makes both us and you stand firm in Christ. He anointed us, set his seal of ownership on us, and put his Spirit in our hearts as a deposit, guaranteeing what is to come."

Second, appointing. Authority for Breakthrough David's appointment as king came at God's appointed time. His appointment gave him the authority and right to lead the people. Similarly, when we recognize that God has appointed us for a specific purpose, we can step into the authority He has given us. Like police officers with power and authority, our appointment from God empowers us to overcome obstacles and lead confidently. Embracing our divine appointment positions us for a breakthrough. Matthew 28:18-20: "Then Jesus came to them and said, 'All authority in heaven and on earth has been given to me. Therefore, go ...'"

Third, assisting. Help for Breakthrough David accepted help from others in his journey to a breakthrough. Likewise, we must open our eyes and recognize that God often sends aid in the form of people, resources, and opportunities. One can chase a thousand, but two can put ten thousand to flight. We are not meant to walk this journey alone. By accepting assistance and aligning ourselves with the right connections, we position ourselves for breakthroughs. Ecclesiastes 4:9-10: "Two are better than one, because they have a good return for their labor: If either of them falls down, one can help the other up. But pity anyone who falls and has no one to help them up."

Fourth, attacking. We need courage for breakthroughs. David engaged the enemy in battle, but before doing so, he sought guidance from the Lord. It is important to seek God's direction before using our anointing and engaging in spiritual warfare. By seeking His guidance, we gain courage and clarity in our actions. We can confidently move forward despite opposition, knowing God is fighting on our behalf. As we attack the strongholds and obstacles in our lives, we experience breakthroughs and see the defeat of our enemies. Joshua 1:9 says, "Have I not commanded you? Be strong and courageous. Do not be afraid; do not be discouraged, for the Lord your God will be with you wherever you go."

Fifth, shaking. Sometimes, a breakthrough is incomplete on the first attempt. We must look and listen for God's shaking divine movement. Just as David heard the sound of marching on the tops of the poplar trees before moving forward, we need to be attentive to the leading of the Holy Spirit. God's timing and methods may differ from our expectations, but as we wait and trust His guidance, we will witness the breakthrough He has prepared for us. Isaiah 43:19: "See, I am doing a new thing! Now it springs up; do you not perceive it? I am making a way in the wilderness and streams in the wasteland." Habakkuk 2:3: "For the revelation awaits an appointed time; it speaks of the end and will not prove false. Though it lingers, wait for it; it will certainly come and will not delay."

God desires to release breakthroughs in our lives. We position ourselves for spiritual advancement and victory by embracing these God-given strategies. Let us recognize and activate our anointing, embrace our divine appointment, accept God's help, courageously engage the enemy, and expectantly wait for the shaking of divine movement. As we do so, we will experience breakthroughs, stepping into new spiritual growth and impact levels.

Sermon #82: When God Steps In

Text: Isaiah 41:10 (NIV) - "So do not fear, for I am with you; do not be dismayed, for I am your God. I will strengthen you and help you; I will uphold you with my righteous right hand."When God steps into our lives, everything changes. Our struggles, lack, rejection, confusion, and battles are transformed into abundance, favor, guidance, clarity, discernment, deliverance, and a life no longer marked by constant struggle. Let us dive into the Word of God and discover the promises that give us hope in the midst of life's challenges.

First, lack becomes abundance: When God steps in, lack is transformed into abundance. Our Heavenly Father is the God of provision and can more than meet our every need. In Philippians 4:19, the apostle Paul assures us that God will supply all our needs according to His glorious riches in Christ Jesus. As we trust in Him and seek His kingdom, we will experience His abundant provision pouring into our lives.

Second, rejection becomes favor and acceptance: God's acceptance and favor replace the sting of rejection. In Psalm 27:10, we read that even if our earthly parents forsake us, the Lord will never leave or forsake us. When we trust him, we become children of God, recipients of His unfailing love and favor. No matter what others may say or do, we can find solace and security in God's unwavering acceptance.

Third, there is guidance instead of confusion. When God steps in, confusion is replaced with divine guidance. Proverbs 3:5-6 reminds us to trust in the Lord with all our hearts and lean not on our understanding. As we acknowledge Him in all our ways, He promises to direct our paths. Our Heavenly Father, who knows the end from the beginning, will lead us with His wisdom and guidance, illuminating our way amid uncertainty.

Fourth, there is clarity of thought. God brings clarity of thought to our minds. In 1 Corinthians 2:16, the apostle Paul declares that we have the mind of Christ. When we seek God's presence, spend time in His Word, and surrender our thoughts to Him, He transforms our minds and aligns our thinking with His truth. His clarity replaces confusion, allowing us to make decisions that honor Him and bless others.

Fifth, there is discernment. When God steps in, He imparts discernment to us. In James 1:5, we are encouraged to ask God for wisdom, and He will generously give it to us. As we submit ourselves to His leading, He grants us the ability to discern between right and wrong, truth and deception. Through the power of the Holy Spirit, we can navigate the complexities of life with godly discernment, avoiding pitfalls and walking in His ways.

Sixth, there is deliverance. God brings deliverance from the struggles we face. Psalm 34:17 assures us that the Lord hears them and delivers them from all their troubles when the righteous cry. Whatever challenges we encounter— physical, emotional, or spiritual—our God is a mighty deliverer. He fights on our behalf and sets us free from every bondage that seeks to hold us captive.

Seventh, life is no longer a struggle. Finally, life is no longer a constant struggle when God steps in. Jesus invites us in Matthew 11:28-30 to come to Him and find rest for our souls.

When God steps in, lack becomes abundance, rejection becomes favor, confusion gives way to divine guidance, and clarity of thought and discernment are bestowed upon us. God brings deliverance and grants us rest from life's struggles. We can trust that His promises are true and will never fail us. Remember to invite God into those situations whenever you face lack, rejection, confusion, or battles. Seek His presence, His wisdom, and His guidance. Trust in His faithfulness and believe He can turn your trials into triumphs. Allow Him to transform your circumstances and bring forth His blessings unexpectedly.

Sermon #83: Demons or Mental Issues?

Sermon: Demons or Mental Issues?

Not every mental health issue is a demon issue! In a world where mental health issues are on the rise, we, as believers, must understand the importance of caring for our mental well-being. The Bible addresses the spiritual aspects of our lives and provides wisdom and guidance for maintaining a healthy mind. We can discover how to cultivate a sound and resilient mind through biblical mental health. Let us turn our attention to an appropriate text that speaks to the relevance of this topic. Our text is apropos. Philippians 4:6-8 says, "Do not be anxious about anything, but in every situation, by prayer and petition, with thanksgiving, present your requests to God. And the peace of God, which transcends all understanding, will guard your hearts and minds in Christ Jesus. Finally, brothers and sisters, whatever is true, whatever is noble, whatever is right, whatever is pure, whatever is lovely, whatever is admirable—if anything is excellent or praiseworthy—think about such things."

We must acknowledge the reality of mental health issues in the church. Exorcism is often the only remedy that exists. The most superficial mental issues are called demon possessions or oppressions. The Bible acknowledges the existence of struggles, anxieties, and worries that can affect our minds. We must not neglect or dismiss the importance of our mental well-being but rather embrace it as an integral part of our overall health.

First, seek God's peace through prayer and fasting. In the face of anxious thoughts and overwhelming situations, the Bible encourages us to bring our concerns to God through prayer and petition. By entrusting our worries to Him and seeking His guidance, we invite His peace to guard our hearts and minds. Prayer and fasting connect us to the source of true peace and allow us to experience God's calming presence.

Second, cultivate a positive thought life. The Scriptures urge us to focus our minds on true, noble, right, pure, lovely, admirable, excellent, and praiseworthy things. Our thought life has a significant impact on our mental well-being. By intentionally directing our thoughts towards positive and uplifting things, we create an environment that nurtures a healthy mind.

Third, embrace gratitude and thanksgiving: Thanksgiving is a powerful antidote to negative thinking and anxious thoughts. The act of giving thanks shifts our focus from our problems to the goodness of God. When we choose gratitude, we invite God's perspective into our lives and allow Him to transform our thoughts, leading to a more positive and healthy mental state.

Fourth, engage in self-care and seek support: Taking care of our mental health also involves practical actions. It may include self-care activities promoting relaxation, rest, and rejuvenation. It may also involve seeking support from trusted friends, family, or professional counselors. The Bible encourages us to bear one another's burdens, reminding us that we are not alone in our struggles.

The Bible provides valuable guidance for taking care of our mental health. We can cultivate a sound and resilient mind through prayer, positive thinking, gratitude, and seeking support. As we embrace the wisdom in God's Word, we position ourselves to experience the peace that surpasses all understanding. Let us prioritize our mental health, recognizing that it is vital to our overall well-being.

Sermon #84: Detox the Mind

Title: Detox the Mind Text: Proverbs 4:23 - "Above all else, guard your mind, for everything you do flows from it."

We cannot overlook our mental health. In a world filled with stress, negativity, and constant information overload, we must learn how to detox our minds and nurture a healthy thought life. Our text for today, Proverbs 4:23, reminds us of the importance of guarding our minds because everything we do flows from it. Let us dive deeper into this topic and discover how we can detox our minds according to the wisdom found in God's Word. We must recognize the need for mind detox. Our minds are like sponges, absorbing information and experiences from the world around us. Unfortunately, we can also absorb harmful influences that negatively impact our mental health. From negative thoughts and toxic relationships to excessive media consumption and unhealthy habits, our minds can become cluttered and burdened. We must recognize the need for a mind detox and commit ourselves to pursue a healthier thought life.

First, have a holistic approach to life; every aspect is intertwined. Mental health detoxification should be approached holistically, considering all aspects of our well-being—physical, emotional, spiritual, and social. Diet and exercise are integral components of this holistic approach, working synergistically with spiritual practices, emotional healing, and social support systems to achieve overall mental health and detoxification.

Second, filter your thoughts and influences. Just as we filter what we eat and drink to maintain physical health, we must filter our thoughts and influences to safeguard our mental well-being. Philippians 4:8 instructs us to focus on whatever is true, noble, right, pure, lovely, admirable, excellent, and praiseworthy. We can create a positive and uplifting environment that promotes mental health and spiritual growth by intentionally choosing what we allow into our minds. Let us be mindful of the media we consume, the company we keep, and the content we engage with, ensuring they align with God's principles.

Third, renew the mind with God's Word. God's Word is the most powerful detoxifying agent for our minds. Romans 12:2 encourages us not to conform to the patterns of this world but to be transformed by renewing our minds. As we immerse ourselves in Scripture, we discover God's truth, wisdom, and promises that counteract the negative and destructive thoughts that may plague us. The Bible is a source of comfort, guidance, and hope; when we meditate on it day and night (Psalm 1:2), our minds are cleansed and refreshed.

Fourth, seek God's presence through meditation. Prayer and meditation are vital tools in detoxing our mind. They allow us to connect with God, cast our anxieties upon Him, and find peace and stillness in His presence. Taking intentional moments of silence to commune with God, reflect on His goodness, and release our burdens helps us declutter our minds and invite the peace of God to dwell within us. Through prayer and meditation, we align our thoughts with His truth and experience the transformative power of His love.

Fifth, seeking support and professional help. While our faith and spiritual practices are essential, it is important to acknowledge that seeking support and professional help is not a sign of weakness but a step toward healing and growth. Just as we may consult a doctor for physical ailments, it is wise to seek the assistance of mental health professionals when needed. They can provide valuable insights, tools, and therapies to navigate challenges and promote mental well-being. As we detox our minds, let us be open to seeking professional help when necessary and trust that God can work through these avenues of support.

Sixth, watch your diet. Your gut is your second brain, and our food directly affects our brain chemistry and functioning. A healthy and balanced diet provides the nutrients, vitamins, and minerals for optimal brain function. It is important to nourish our bodies with whole foods, including fruits, vegetables, lean proteins, whole grains, and healthy fats. These foods provide the building blocks for neurotransmitters, such as serotonin and dopamine, vital for mood regulation and overall mental health. Avoiding excessive sugar, processed foods, and caffeine can also contribute to a more stable and balanced mental state.

Seventh, exercise. Physical exercise has numerous benefits for mental health. Engaging in regular exercise releases endorphins, known as "feel-good" hormones, which can boost mood and reduce symptoms of anxiety and depression. Exercise also helps reduce stress, improves sleep quality, increases self-confidence, and enhances cognitive function. Whether walking, jogging, dancing, swimming, or any other form of physical activity, finding an exercise routine that suits your preferences and capabilities can greatly contribute to mental health detoxification.

Finally, chronic stress can harm mental health, leading to anxiety, depression, and other mood disorders. Regular exercise can help alleviate stress by increasing the production of endorphins and reducing levels of stress hormones, such as cortisol. Additionally, practicing relaxation techniques such as deep breathing, meditation, or engaging in hobbies and activities that bring joy and relaxation can help detoxify the mind from stress and promote overall mental well-being. Mental detoxification is spiritual, physical, psychological, and social.

Sermon #85: Reverse the Curse

Various types of curses are mentioned in the Bible, each with its significance and implications. One type of curse is the divine curse, a consequence of disobedience or rebellion against God's commands. This curse can affect individuals, families, or even entire nations. Another type is the generational curse, which refers to the negative consequences that pass down through successive generations due to the sins or actions of ancestors. Additionally, there are curses spoken by individuals against others, known as imprecatory curses, where individuals call for harm or judgment upon someone. Curses can also result from witchcraft or occult practices involving the invocation of evil spirits or supernatural forces. However, it is important to note that the power of curses is ultimately broken through the redemptive work of Jesus Christ, who offers liberation and forgiveness. Through faith in Christ, believers can experience freedom from curses and the blessings of God's grace and love.

In Deuteronomy 28, there are seven blessings and seven curses mentioned. The blessings include exaltation, reproduction, health, prosperity, success, victory, and being the head, not the tail, and above and not beneath. These blessings signify God's favor and abundance in various areas of life. On the other hand, the curses mentioned in the same chapter include humiliation, barrenness, sickness of every kind, poverty, failure, defeat, and being the tail and not the head, and below and not above. These curses represent the negative consequences of disobedience and turning away from God. Through prayer and faith, we seek to align ourselves with God's blessings, trusting in His grace and provision to avert the curses and experience His abundant goodness.

How to Reverse a Curse

It is said that black people may face challenges such as the trauma of enslavement, absent fathers, health disparities such as diabetes and high blood pressure, feelings of emasculation, distorted gender roles, and struggles with self-esteem. But these can affect individuals from various backgrounds; they are not peculiar to black people. Addressing them with empathy, understanding, and a commitment to justice and equality is essential. It is not accurate or fair to attribute these challenges solely to one racial or ethnic group.

The challenges or curses that people face can be removed. First, curses can be broken through acts of repentance, forgiveness, prayer, and invoking divine intervention.

Second, curses can be broken by addressing the negative effects or patterns in one's life can involve personal growth, self-reflection, seeking counseling or therapy, cultivating positive relationships, and making positive changes in behavior and mindset. Focusing on healing, self-care, and pursuing a healthy and balanced life physically, emotionally, mentally, and spiritually is important.

Third, epigenetics. It can play a role in breaking curses by fostering positive adaptations and changes over time. Through epigenetics, certain traits and behaviors can be inherited and passed down through generations. In the context of breaking curses, it is important to recognize the positive qualities and strengths ingrained within a community, such as innovations, artistic competencies, intuition, empathy, and a strong conscience to empower individuals further to care for and support other oppressed people worldwide. Additionally, understanding and reclaiming the historical narrative and having the courage to persevere in adversity are vital in breaking curses.

Break every curse! Destroy every yoke! Curses, no matter their origin or impact, are not permanent and can be resolved through various means, leading to healing, restoration, and a renewed sense of empowerment.

Sermon #86: Medicines

Proverbs 17:22 says, "A joyful heart is good medicine, but a crushed spirit dries up the bones." This text sends us on a journey through the pages of the Bible to explore the remarkable medicines it offers us. Medicine has been a vital aspect of human life for centuries, and the Bible contains wisdom that extends beyond spiritual guidance, encompassing principles for our physical and emotional well-being. Our focus today is to uncover the remedies and prescriptions hidden within the Scriptures. Let us begin.

First, the healing power of a joyful heart. Our text from Proverbs 17:22 reveals a profound truth: a joyful heart is good medicine. It reminds us that our emotional state significantly affects our overall health. Joy, happiness, and laughter have healing properties that can uplift our spirits, strengthen our immune systems, and improve our well-being. As followers of Christ, we have the privilege of experiencing the joy that comes from our relationship with God. Let us cultivate a joyful heart and share the gift of laughter and positivity with others.

Second, the balm of forgiveness. One of the most potent medicines offered in the Bible is forgiveness. Holding onto grudges and harboring bitterness can harm our physical and mental health. The Scriptures implore us to forgive others as God has forgiven us. We release anger and resentment by extending forgiveness, and experiencing healing and freedom. Let us embrace the balm of forgiveness and allow it to restore our relationships and well-being.

Third, the comforting pillar of hope. Hope is another powerful medicine found abundantly in the Bible. In times of adversity, uncertainty, and despair, hope becomes a guiding light that sustains us. It lifts our spirits, strengthens our resolve, and enables us to persevere through life's challenges. The promises of God provide us with a firm foundation of hope. Let us cling to His promises and find solace and strength in the enduring hope that only He can provide.

Fourth, the transformative power of love. Love is the supreme medicine prescribed by the Bible. It has the remarkable ability to heal wounds, restore broken relationships, and bring unity. The Scriptures teach us that love covers a multitude of sins and that it is the greatest commandment. Love has transformative power, not only in our relationships with others but also within ourselves. Let us embrace the love of God and allow it to flow through us, bringing healing and restoration to our lives and those around us.

The medicines of the Bible go far beyond physical remedies; they touch the depths of our souls and address our emotional, mental, and spiritual well-being. As we delve into the Scriptures, we discover that God has provided us with abundant remedies that bring healing, joy, forgiveness, hope, and love. We need the physical healing that comes from these medicines' transformative power in our lives. May we find solace, restoration, and abundant life through the medicines of the Bible.

Sermon #87: The Test Before the Blessing

Let us analyze a powerful narrative from the book of 1 Samuel, where we encounter a test that preceded a great blessing. Our text in 1 Samuel 30:1-6 unveils a significant moment in the life of David, reminding us that sometimes before we experience the fullness of God's blessings, we must first face a test. Let us explore this story and draw valuable lessons for our own lives.

First, it was a time of desolation. As we enter 1 Samuel 30, we find David and his mighty warriors returning to their home in Ziklag. However, to their dismay, they discover that the Amalekites had raided their city, burned it with fire, and taken their families captive. Instantly, their joy turned into anguish, their security shattered, and their hearts burdened with grief. We can relate to times when unexpected trials leave us devastated and hopeless.

Second, the weight of suffering. In the face of this immense loss, we witness the profound impact suffering can have on our spirits. The text tells us that David and his men wept until they had no more strength to weep and were overwhelmed with sorrow and anguish. In our own lives, we may face moments when the weight of suffering feels unbearable, leaving us drained, questioning, and seeking answers.

Third, look at David's response. Amidst his anguish, David finds strength in the Lord his God. Instead of succumbing to despair or allowing bitterness to take root, David chose to seek God's guidance. He inquired of the Lord, asking whether he should pursue the Amalekites and if he would recover all that was lost. At this moment, David models the power of turning to God in times of adversity.

Fourth, encountering the test. God answers David's inquiry with assurance and a divine directive to pursue the enemy. However, little did David know that this pursuit would lead him to a significant test. Some of his own men, who were already weary and distressed, began to turn against him, blaming him for their misfortune. It was a moment of immense pressure where David had to face the test of leadership and maintain his faith in God.

Finally, hold onto faith. In the face of adversity and the weight of the test, David finds strength in the Lord his God. He encourages himself in the Lord, seeking divine guidance and rising above the discouragement around him. David's faith anchors him during this challenging time, reminding us that it is in our darkest moments that our faith can shine the brightest.

The story of David's test before the blessing is a powerful reminder that the most formidable tests often precede the greatest blessings. In times of desolation and suffering, we have a choice—to succumb to despair or to turn to God and seek His guidance. Like David, may we find strength in the Lord, hold onto our faith, and navigate through the tests with unwavering trust in His promises. As we do, we position ourselves for the blessings that lie ahead.

The test before the blessing is an opportunity for growth, refinement, and a deeper intimacy with our Heavenly Father. We should embrace the tests in our lives, knowing that God is faithful to bring about His blessings in due time.

Sermon #88: Man's Rejection: God's Direction

A powerful truth resonates throughout the pages of Scripture: "Man's rejection can be God's direction." This profound statement reminds us that even when we face rejection or opposition from others, God can work in mysterious ways to bring about His perfect plan. Our text for today, Psalm 118:22, will serve as our guide as we dive into the stories of individuals in the Bible who experienced rejection that ultimately led to God's divine direction.

First, Joseph's Journey. We begin with the story of Joseph, whose brothers rejected him and sold him into slavery. Though it seemed devastating, God orchestrated His divine plan through Joseph's rejection. In the end, Joseph became a powerful leader in Egypt, saving his family and bringing about God's purposes. What man intended for evil, God used for good. Joseph's rejection became God's direction.

Second, Moses' Call. Next, we encounter Moses, who was rejected by his own people, the Israelites, when he first attempted to deliver them from slavery in Egypt. Despite their rejection, God used Moses' time in the wilderness to shape and prepare him for the great task ahead. Ultimately, Moses became the instrument through which God led His people out of bondage and towards the promised land. God's direction unfolded through Moses' rejection.

Third, Jesus, the Cornerstone. In Psalm 118:22, we find the words, "The stone the builders rejected has become the cornerstone." These prophetic words find their fulfillment in Jesus Christ. Jesus, the Son of God, was rejected and despised by men. The religious leaders, the very builders, rejected Him. However, God used this rejection to bring about human history's greatest act of salvation. Through Jesus' rejection, God provided the way for humanity's redemption and eternal life. Man's rejection of Jesus became God's ultimate direction for the salvation of humanity.

Fourth, our personal experiences. As we reflect on the stories of Joseph, Moses, and Jesus, we can draw parallels to our own lives. Sometimes we face rejection from others—rejection in relationships, careers, or even within the church. In those moments, it is easy to become discouraged and doubt God's plan for our lives. However, we must remember that God can use even our rejections as stepping stones toward His perfect purpose.

The truth that man's rejection can be God's direction is before us. Just as God worked through the rejections experienced by Joseph, Moses, and Jesus, He can work through our own rejections. In times of rejection, let us seek God's guidance and trust in His sovereign plan. God's perspective differs from ours, and He can use rejection to position us for His greater purposes. As we surrender to His leading and trust in His faithfulness, we will witness how He turns rejection into a direction, bringing forth His blessings and fulfilling His divine plan. Take comfort and encouragement in this truth, and continue to follow God's path, even in the face of rejection.

Sermon #89: Complaining has no Value

Recently, a group of New Yorkers took a non-complaining challenge. They were asked not to complain about anyone or anything for one week. The results were astonishing, and they all failed. Why do you think they failed? The free online dictionary defines a complaint as "To express feelings of pain, dissatisfaction, or resentment." If complaining involves pain, why is it so straightforward, spontaneous, involuntary, or natural? Do people like to express pain rather than pleasure? Are humans more sadistic than happy?

If complaining involves the expression of dissatisfaction, why do people take pleasure in expressing discontent and unhappiness? Are people more barbaric than nice? If complaining means the expression of resentment, why do people tend to show displeasure and indignation? Are humans essentially evil? Complaining is a learned behavior. We were not born complaining about why we are here; I think the answer is in our education. As a form of manipulation, we have learned to complain instead of giving thanks.

Christians are the first to say, "I am too blessed to be stressed," or "God is so good, I can't complain." But Christians are some of the worst complainers I have ever met. They complain about everything. They complain when they are unemployed and when they find jobs.

They complain when it's cold, and they complain about the heat of summer. Therefore, I know some of them will not make it into heaven because they would complain about how beautiful it is if they did. They would charge God for being wasteful. In my many years of ministry, I have heard church people assert, "There is no order in this church." The truth is that by complaining, they are the ones who are creating the disorder they hope to see. There is no order because their many complaints have engendered disorder.

There is a consequence for complaining. The Israelites paid that price. Except for Caleb, Joshua, and the Levites, all Jews aged twenty and above died in the wilderness and did not enter the Promised Land (Num. 14: 1-30). They complained their way out of God's blessings. If Israel paid the price for complaining, what price will we pay as a church if we continue to be complainers? What happened to church leaders who complained against their pastors? Miriam complained about Moses and was publicly humiliated. She was hit with leprosy (Num. 12:1-15). Remember, complainers are selfish. They are more interested in their feelings than the church's unity. By their complaining, they sow the seeds of discord. They can hurt a church profoundly. The tongue also is a fire, a world of evil among the parts of the body. It corrupts the whole body, sets the whole course of one's life on fire, and is set on fire by hell (James 3:6).

God hates complaining to the point where he promised to remedy the situation through a new language. Yes. For this reason, he will give us a new language – with new words. God will give us a vocabulary without the word complaint. Zephaniah 3:9 states, "For then will I turn to the people a pure language, that they may all call upon the name of the LORD, to serve him with one consent." Language is the central core of a culture. By changing our language, God will change our culture of negativity and pessimism that keeps us in doubt and shame. For the present, God wants us to be unified to obtain his blessings, so we are encouraged to "Do all things without murmurings and disputing: That ye may be blameless and harmless, the sons of God, without rebuke, amid a crooked and perverse nation, among whom ye shine as lights in the world, Holding forth the word of life, that I may rejoice in the day of Christ, that I have not run in vain, neither labored in vain" Phil 2:14-16.

Complaining is primarily an improper use of the tongue. When people complain often, a culture develops. Seeds of discontent and discord are sown, and an opposition group form is formed. A complainer says, "You are not doing something right, and I can do it better."

Is there a legitimate place for complaining? Yes. Yes. Yes. In Acts 6, there was a legitimate reason to complain: the Greek-speaking Jews complained against the Hebrew-speaking Jews when their widows were neglected in the daily food distribution. The result of this complaint was corrective action. The twelve apostles appointed what we have come to describe as deacons to correct the disparity. Pastors and church leaders must not close their ears to legitimate complaints from their congregation. If there is a problem, the question must be, "What can the church do to fix or improve it?" Then, move on. Galatians 5:22 says, "But the fruit of the Spirit is love, joy, peace, forbearance, kindness, goodness, faithfulness, gentleness, and self-control. Against such things, there is no law." Nonetheless, we should not build a culture of complaining. It displeases God and men too!!

Sermon #90: Vision Assassins

A Poem

You should not share your goals with everyone!
You cannot share your vision with the wrong person!
Vision assassins are ready!
Vision assassins are steady and international!
Like the prince of the power of the air, they want to intercept and disrupt your blessings!

Vision assassins are jealous! They are evil! Vision assassins want to kill you!
They hate the call of God on your life!
They hate that you are above and not beneath
They hate to see the halo of God's blessings on your face!
They are frenemies who hate to see you soar!

Arise, Oh Lord, and take your place in my life!
You are the commander of the army of the living God!
Break and destroy the power of Jezebel!
Break and destroy the hold of the warlock!
Break and destroy the influence of the witch!
For though it tarries, let the vision come to pass!

Sermon #91: Education vs. Intelligence

In 1 Kings 3:5-14, we learn about the momentous occasion when King Solomon approached God with a humble heart and a specific request. He asked God for wisdom and understanding to govern the people of Israel with justice and discernment. Solomon recognized his inadequacies and the weighty responsibility of leading a nation, so he sought divine guidance and insight to fulfill his role as king. Education vs. Intelligence is our topic for today. We need to understand the meanings of both terms, recognize their differences, and explore their significance in our lives. By doing so, we can gain valuable insights into how these elements shape our understanding, growth, and impact on the world.

First, defining education. In its simplest form, education refers to acquiring knowledge, skills, values, and attitudes through formal instruction or training. It involves structured learning within educational institutions such as schools, colleges, and universities. Education equips individuals with foundational knowledge, imparts discipline, and provides the tools to navigate various life aspects. It encompasses academic subjects, practical skills, and social development.

Second, understanding intelligence. On the other hand, intelligence is the ability to comprehend, reason, learn, and apply knowledge effectively. It involves cognitive capabilities, problem-solving skills, adaptability, creativity, and emotional intelligence. Intelligence goes beyond formal education and is not solely determined by degrees or academic achievements. It encompasses various mental faculties and aptitudes that enable individuals to process information, make decisions, and engage with the world. Intelligence is wisdom on display.

Third, the differences. While education and intelligence are interconnected, they are distinct. Education provides the framework and structure for learning, whereas intelligence represents an individual's innate capacity to grasp, assimilate, and utilize information. Education can be obtained through formal channels, while intelligence is an inherent aspect of an individual's mental abilities. One can be highly educated but lack intelligence; conversely, one can possess high intelligence without formal education.

Fourth, the importance of education. Education plays a crucial role in our personal and societal development. It equips us with the knowledge and skills necessary for various professions, fosters critical thinking, and broadens our understanding of the world. Education enables us to communicate effectively, engage in meaningful dialogue, and contribute positively to our communities. It empowers individuals to pursue their passions, discover their potential, and make informed decisions. Education provides opportunities for personal growth, social mobility, and the advancement of society.

Fifth, the significance of intelligence. Though distinct from formal education, intelligence is equally important. Intelligence allows individuals to adapt to new situations, solve complex problems, and apply knowledge creatively. It enables us to make sound judgments, perceives nuances in different contexts, and navigate life's challenges with wisdom. Intelligence influences our ability to learn, acquire new skills, and adapt to changing environments. It fosters innovation, leadership, and resilience in the face of adversity.

Sixth, balancing education and intelligence. While education and intelligence are distinct, both are not mutually exclusive. The ideal approach is to cultivate both aspects in our lives. Education enhances our knowledge base, equips us with essential skills, and provides opportunities for personal growth. However, education alone is insufficient without the application of intelligence. Intelligence helps us think critically, question assumptions, and apply knowledge practically, and it enables us to adapt, innovate, and contribute meaningfully to society.

Our focus on Education vs. Intelligence forces us to recognize both aspects' value and significance in our lives. Education equips us with knowledge and skills, while intelligence empowers us to apply that knowledge effectively. Let us strive for a balanced approach, pursuing education with a hunger for knowledge and wisdom while nurturing our intelligence to think critically, solve problems, and positively impact our spheres of influence.

Sermon #92: Dilemmas of Fatherhood

A dilemma is a predicament, a tricky situation, and a problem. Let us examine a father's social, religious, ethical, spiritual, emotional, and mental dilemmas in the 21st Century. Today, we have come to celebrate, honor, elevate, and affirm Fatherhood. Happy Father's Day to fathers everywhere!

We honor fathers who have provided for their children's physical, emotional, and cognitive development. The National Retail Federation says Father's Day is the smallest American gift-giving holiday. Some studies rank Halloween 3rd as the most celebrated holiday, whereas Father's Day is ranked number 11. Even ghosts have greater honor than Dads in America. Some contend that "Father's Day " is a joke because it recognizes people who do not deserve it. Ah, that hurts!

Close relationships between children and their fathers or father figures have numerous positive effects. These children are less likely to engage in high-risk behaviors, have sex at a young age, or develop psychological problems. They tend to achieve higher IQ test scores, have high-paying jobs, and develop healthy, stable relationships as adults. Fatherhood is emphasized as more than just a biological and financial role; fathers shape character, instill confidence, and serve as spiritual leaders, guides, and coaches. The presence of a father is seen as essential for stability and is not only a societal requirement but also a spiritual and eternal need. The adverse effects of fatherlessness are well-documented, including diminished cognitive development, poor school performance, low self-esteem, increased likelihood of sexual promiscuity, emotional problems, drug abuse, and violence. Despite often receiving less recognition, fathers play a crucial role in the lives of their children, exemplified by Joseph, the husband of Mary, in the biblical narrative.

Dilemmas

Today's text says, "When Mary had been engaged to Joseph, but before they lived together, she was found to be with a child from the Holy Spirit" (Matt 1:18). The concept of dilemmas is explored concerning fatherhood, using the context of Joseph's dilemma in the biblical narrative. Several dilemmas faced by fathers are highlighted. Firstly, fathers face social dilemmas where societal expectations and perceptions can label them negatively if they deviate from prescribed roles. Secondly, religious and ethical dilemmas arise concerning their spiritual roles and responsibilities within the family. Joseph's ethical dilemma and compassionate response exemplify the challenges fathers may encounter. Thirdly, fathers confront spiritual dilemmas as they navigate their roles as spiritual guides and leaders for their families, with limited guidance or training available. The significance of Joseph's foster fatherhood role in raising Jesus is emphasized as an illustration of God's use of men in adoption. Fourthly, fathers experience emotional dilemmas, often overwhelmed and insufficient, while societal expectations discourage emotional expression. The detrimental impact on men's health, including heart disease, is mentioned. Lastly, fathers may face mental dilemmas, doubting their abilities and struggling with uncertainty.

The importance of recognizing and respecting the value of fathers, highlighting the significance of their roles and the challenges they encounter, must not be minimized. Do fathers deserve more respect than what has been given? Fathers matter! Yes, fathers' matter. Fathers are the prophets, priests, and kings of their homes. And, like mothers, they are not perfect.

Sermon #93: Drinks

We have come to an examination of the various drinks mentioned in the Bible, and we will seek to uncover the lessons they teach us about nourishment, symbolism, and our spiritual lives. From water to wine, the Bible provides insights into the importance of what we drink and the profound messages these beverages convey. Let us delve into this ancient wisdom and discover the nutritious value and spiritual significance of the drinks mentioned in the Bible.

First, the life-sustaining power of water. Water is a vital element of life; we witness its significance throughout the Bible. In John 4:14, Jesus declares, "But whoever drinks of the water that I will give him will never be thirsty again. The water that I will give him will become in him a spring of water welling up to eternal life." Water is essential for our physical survival and holds spiritual implications. Just as water quenches our physical thirst, Jesus offers living water, which satisfies our deepest spiritual longings. Water in the Bible symbolizes cleansing, purity, and the Holy Spirit's transformative work in our lives.

Second, the symbolism and moderation of wine. Nothing is wrong with a drink of wine. What was good for Jesus and the people of his time is good enough for me. Wine, often mentioned in the Bible, holds symbolic and nutritional significance. In moderation, wine can bring joy and celebration. In Psalm 104:15, we read, "And wine to gladden the heart of man." Wine symbolizes the abundance and blessings of God, as exemplified in Jesus' miracle of turning water into wine at the wedding in Cana. Wine also symbolizes the new covenant in the Lord's Supper, representing the blood of Christ shed for our redemption. However, the Bible also warns against the abuse of alcohol and the perils of drunkenness, reminding us to exercise moderation and self-control.

Third, the nourishing value of milk. Milk, a staple drink mentioned in the Bible, is a source of sustenance and nourishment. In 1 Peter 2:2, we are encouraged to "like newborn infants, long for the pure spiritual milk, that by it you may grow up into salvation." Milk symbolizes spiritual growth and the foundational truths of the gospel. From a nutritional standpoint, milk provides essential nutrients like calcium, protein, and vitamins, supporting the growth and strength of our bodies. Just as milk nourishes our physical bodies, let us seek spiritual nourishment from the Word of God, which brings our souls growth, strength, and maturity.

Fourth, the healing properties of Herbal Tea. While not specifically mentioned in the Bible, herbs and teas are referenced indirectly in passages that speak of plants' healing and restorative power. The Bible acknowledges the value of plants such as mint, hyssop, and balm, which were used for medicinal purposes. These herbs remind us of God's provision for our health and well-being. Herbal teas, like chamomile and peppermint, offer relaxation, aid digestion, and provide comfort.

The drinks mentioned in the Bible carry significant lessons for our lives. Water represents Christ's life-sustaining power and the Holy Spirit's cleansing work. Wine symbolizes both celebration and the blood of Jesus, calling us to moderation and self-control. Milk nourishes and signifies spiritual growth, while herbal teas remind us of God's provision for our health and rest. As we partake in drinks of the Bible, we must remember the spiritual truths they convey, the importance of moderation, and the blessings of God's abundance.

Sermon #94: Biblical Foods

Today I want to take you on a journey through the pages of the Bible to investigate the foods mentioned within its sacred verses and discover the valuable lessons they hold for our health and well-being. The Bible, the inspired Word of God, guides our spiritual lives and offers profound wisdom regarding the care and nourishment of our physical bodies. The Bible contains timeless wisdom and an understanding of foods that can enhance our health.

First, the blessing of fruits and vegetables. In the book of Genesis, we find the creation story, where God brought forth a bountiful variety of fruits and vegetables, declaring them suitable. These gifts from God are delicious and rich in essential nutrients, vitamins, and minerals. Fruits and vegetables, such as figs, grapes, pomegranates, olives, and lentils, are natural sources of healing and nourishment. Their vibrant colors and refreshing flavors remind us of the abundance of God's provision and the importance of incorporating them into our daily diet.

Second, the nourishment of grains. Throughout the Bible, grains play a significant role in sustaining life and symbolize nourishment and provision. In the Old Testament, we read about the importance of grains like wheat, barley, and spelt. Biblical grains were used for bread and making wholesome porridge, unleavened bread, and cakes. Grains are a valuable source of complex carbohydrates, fiber, and essential nutrients. They provide sustained energy, aid digestion, and promote a healthy heart. Let us remember that just as grains are vital for our physical well-being, the Word of God is the spiritual sustenance that nourishes our souls.

Third, the power of fish and seafood. Jesus performed miracles involving fish in the New Testament, emphasizing their significance. Fish and seafood, such as salmon, tuna, and shrimp, are excellent sources of lean protein, omega-3 fatty acids, and essential minerals like iodine. These nutrients contribute to healthy brain function, cardiovascular health, and overall well-being. As followers of Christ, we are called to be fishers of men, spreading the gospel to all corners of the earth. Let us also be mindful of the valuable lessons the fish in the Bible teach us about incorporating these nutritious foods into our diets.

Fourth, the gift of honey and olive oil. The Bible often mentions honey and olive oil as symbols of God's goodness and blessings. Honey, with its natural sweetness and medicinal properties, provides an instant energy source and can soothe a sore throat. Olive oil, referred to as the "oil of gladness" in the Scriptures, is packed with healthy monounsaturated fats and antioxidants. It promotes cardiovascular health, reduces inflammation, and supports radiant skin. Let us be grateful for the sweetness of God's love and the anointing of His Holy Spirit, which bring healing and joy into our lives.

People should honor God not only in their spiritual lives but also in the care and stewardship of their bodies. The foods mentioned in the Bible offer us a wealth of wisdom and guidance for maintaining optimal health. Through fruits and vegetables, grains, fish and seafood, honey, and olive oil, we witness the provision and blessings of our loving Creator. Let us embrace these valuable foods to nourish our bodies, honor God, and fulfill our purpose in serving others. May we seek His guidance and grace to make wise choices in our diet, for our bodies are temples of the Holy Spirit.

Proper health encompasses physical and spiritual well-being. By recognizing the significance of the foods mentioned in the Bible and incorporating them into our diets, we take steps towards a healthier lifestyle and align ourselves with God's divine wisdom and care.

We should follow the biblical teachings on food. Gluttony is a health hazard; it is sinful. Biblical teachings on food extend beyond mere physical nourishment, reminding us of the importance of gratitude, moderation, and self-control. Just as we exercise self-discipline in our food choices, let us exercise self-control in our speech, actions, and thoughts, honoring God in every aspect of our existence. As we journey through this life, we must be cognizant of God's abundance and provisions in the past, his desire for our well-being, and our responsibility to care for the bodies He entrusted us. Let us approach our meals with mindfulness, giving thanks for the sustenance they provide and using them as opportunities for fellowship and nourishment of both body and soul. In 1 Corinthians 10:31, the apostle Paul exhorts us, saying, "So, whether you eat or drink, or whatever you do, do all to the glory of God." Let us, therefore, honor God in our choices of food, recognize their value for our health and well-being, and let our lives be a testament to His goodness and grace. Food nourishment for our bodies is a tangible reminder of God's love, provision, and care.

Sermon #95: The Power of Two

The number two holds great significance, as seen in the relationship between the sun and the moon, the Old and New Testaments, and the natural and supernatural realms. Two create pairs, correspond, harmonize, synchronize, concur, blend, and fit together. Through divine mathematics, two can ultimately become one, highlighting the power and beauty in the unity and connection of the number two. Today, we gather here to explore marriage's profound and transformative power; when two become one. Our text, Ecclesiastes 4:9-12, encapsulates the Bible's wisdom and truth on marriage.

First, the power of two in combination. The first point we discover is that "the power of two" lies in its combination. When two individuals join together in marriage, they bring their unique resources, talents, and strengths, allowing them to move forward faster and achieve greater success. Even the world recognizes this power of partnership, as the IRS offers tax breaks to married couples. The Bible confirms this truth, stating that "two are better than one because they have a good return for their labor" (Ecclesiastes 4:9). Together, spouses can accomplish more than they could on their own.

Second, the power of two in companionship: Another aspect of "the power of two" is found in the companionship it brings. God, in His infinite wisdom and humor, created a longing for companionship within Adam and provided him with a woman as his suitable companion and friend. In marriage, couples experience the joy of friendship and togetherness, nurturing a deep bond and sense of belonging. True companionship is a precious gift that enriches our lives and strengthens the marital relationship.

Third, the power of two in comfort. The Scriptures remind us of the comfort that arises from the union of two individuals. Ecclesiastes 4:11 states, "Also, if two lie down together, they will keep warm. But how can one keep warm alone?" In marriage, couples share a physical and emotional closeness that brings warmth, solace, and security. Sleeping together signifies more than just physical proximity; it symbolizes the intimate connection and care that spouses provide for one another.

Fourth, the power of two in congruence. Congruence, or harmony, is essential in any relationship, especially in marriage. The Bible teaches that two are needed for agreement, compatibility, and unity. When two individuals come together with a shared purpose and commitment to each other, they create a harmonious partnership that can weather the storms of life. Seeking congruence in values, goals, and priorities is crucial for a strong and lasting marriage.

Fifth, the power of two in collaboration. Marriage provides a platform for collaboration, where spouses can pool their strengths and work together to overcome challenges. Ecclesiastes 4:12 declares, "Though one may be overpowered, two can defend themselves." In marriage, couples can face adversity with a united front, supporting and uplifting one another. Collaboration allows for sharing burdens, the multiplication of joys, and the achievement of greater victories.

Sixth, the power of two in connection. The power of the two is also evident in the deep connection and interdependence spouses share. Ecclesiastes 4:10 emphasizes this truth: "If either falls down, one can help the other up. But pity anyone who falls and has no one to help them up." In marriage, couples become each other's pillars of strength, offering support, encouragement, and assistance in times of need. The bond between two individuals in marriage creates a safety net, ensuring that neither spouse walks through life alone.

Seventh, the power of two in celebration. The power of the two is reflected in the ability to celebrate together. While it can be challenging for one person to experience joy and celebration fully, two can amplify the pleasure and get the party going. Constant big and small celebrations should mark a marriage, as couples cherish their shared moments, accomplishments, and milestones. Together, spouses can create a culture of celebration

The power of two in marriage is a divine design encompassing various aspects, as we have explored today. A combination of resources, talents, and strengths propels couples forward. It brings companionship, friendship, and a deep sense of togetherness. It offers comfort, warmth, and security in the embrace of a partner. It fosters congruence, harmony, and compatibility, creating a solid foundation for a thriving relationship. It encourages collaboration, enabling couples to face challenges and conquer them together. It establishes a profound connection, ensuring that spouses are never alone in their journey. And it ignites a constant spirit of celebration, where joy is multiplied and shared.

Sermon #96: Are Men and Women Equal?

A thought-provoking question has sparked discussions and debates throughout history: "Are men and women equal?" We should explore the unique characteristics and roles of men and women, considering their physical and functional differences and their similarities in complementarity and ontological value. Let us turn to the Scriptures to gain wisdom and understanding.

In Genesis 1:27, we find the foundational truth about human creation. It states, "So God created mankind in his own image, in the image of God he created them; male and female he created them." From this verse, we understand that both men and women are created in the image of God. This affirms the equal value and worth that God places on every individual, regardless of gender.

First, physical and functional differences. In contrast, men and women share equal worth and value but possess distinct physical and functional differences. Biologically, men and women have different physical characteristics, such as hormonal makeup, reproductive systems, and body structures. These differences serve functional purposes, enabling each gender to fulfill unique roles and responsibilities assigned by God.

Second, similarities in complementarity. Despite their differences, men and women share an inherent complementarity. Just as puzzle pieces fit together to form a complete picture, men and women are designed to complement one another. God's intention for this complementary relationship can be seen in various aspects of life, including marriage, family, and the broader community. Each gender brings unique strengths, perspectives, and gifts that, when combined, create a more holistic and balanced whole.

Third, ontological equality and value. When discussing the equality of men and women, it is essential to recognize their ontological equality—the equality of being. Both genders share the same fundamental dignity and worth as bearers of the divine image. Their equality does not diminish or negate their differences; rather, it affirms that both men and women are equally valued and loved by God, deserving of respect, honor, and equal opportunities to fulfill their God-given purpose.

Fourth, respect God's design. As followers of Christ, we are called to embrace God's design for men and women. This involves recognizing and appreciating the unique characteristics, strengths, and roles assigned to each gender. Rather than viewing differences as sources of division or superiority, we should celebrate them as part of God's beautiful plan for humanity.

"Are men and women equal?" must be approached with a holistic understanding encompassing differences and similarities. Physically and functionally, men and women possess unique characteristics and roles. However, they also share similarities in their complementarity and ontological value, being equally created in the image of God. Rather than seeking to assert superiority or dominance, we are called to embrace and celebrate the diverse contributions that both genders bring to relationships, families, and society.

As we navigate the complexities of gender in our world today, let us foster an environment of mutual respect, love, and appreciation for one another. Let us reject any form of discrimination or prejudice, recognizing that our unity as the body of Christ transcends gender. Together, as men and women, we can exemplify God's love and reflect His image in all areas of life.

Remember, equality does not mean sameness. God created us with purpose, intention, and diversity. In His wisdom, He designed men and women to unite in unity, complementing and supporting one another in fulfilling His plan for our lives. The differences between genders should not be a source of division, competition, or inequality but a cause for celebration and collaboration. God's design for men and women is unique; we must resist the temptation to conform to societal expectations or cultural norms that devalue or diminish either gender. We should challenge stereotypes and prejudices that limit the full expression of each person's unique gifts and calling. Instead, let us affirm and encourage one another to flourish in the roles and responsibilities God has entrusted to us, recognizing that our differences contribute to the richness and diversity of the body of Christ.

We must extend grace, compassion, and understanding to one another in our journey of understanding and embracing gender differences. Regardless of our gender, we are all equally loved, forgiven, and redeemed by the sacrifice of our Savior. We find true freedom and purpose through His grace, transcending societal expectations and cultural constructs.

Sermon #97: Legacies of Motherhood

Today, we gather to honor and celebrate the incredible influence of godly mothers. A godly mother leaves a lasting legacy that extends far beyond her lifetime, shaping her children's lives and impacting future generations. In this sermon, we will explore the sevenfold legacies that emerge from the lives of godly mothers, drawing inspiration from the text and key points.

First, it is the legacy of faith. A godly mother leaves the legacy of faith, just as Hannah did. She nurtures a deep trust in God, demonstrating unwavering faith through life's trials and challenges. Her children witness her reliance on God's provision, her fervent prayers, and her unwavering commitment to follow His ways. This legacy of faith becomes an anchor for her children, guiding them in their own journey of faith. Second, it is the legacy of prayer. Like Hannah, a godly mother leaves the legacy of prayer. She intercedes on behalf of her children, lifting them to God and seeking His guidance, protection, and blessing. Through her prayers, she invites God's presence and power into their lives, shaping their destinies and covering them with His grace. The legacy of prayer becomes a source of strength and comfort for her children throughout their lives.

Third, it is the legacy of sacrifice: A godly mother exemplifies the legacy of sacrifice, just as Jochebed did. She selflessly gives of herself for the well-being and future of her children. Her sacrificial love knows no bounds as she puts her children's needs above hers, making personal sacrifices to provide for them, protect them, and nurture their growth. This legacy of sacrifice instills in her children a deep appreciation for selflessness and compels them to live lives of generosity.

Fourth, it is the legacy of teaching. Lois and Eunice embody the legacy of teaching. A godly mother invests time and effort in instructing her children in the ways of God. She imparts wisdom, knowledge, and understanding of the Scriptures, equipping her children to navigate life's challenges with godly discernment. Her teaching becomes a foundation upon which her children build their lives, shaping their character, values, and decisions.

Fifth, it is the legacy of encouragement. A godly mother leaves a legacy of encouragement, just as Elizabeth did. She uplifts and affirms her children, instilling a sense of worth, purpose, and confidence within them. Her words and actions inspire her children to embrace their God-given potential, overcome obstacles, and pursue their dreams. This legacy of encouragement empowers her children to face life's challenges with resilience and determination.

Sixth, it is the legacy of example. A godly mother leads by example, demonstrating a life of integrity, humility, and ion. Her actions align with her words, and her acter shines forth as a beacon of light. Her children observe her walk with God, witnessing her love for others, forgiveness, and servant-heartedness. This legacy of example inspires her children to emulate her virtues and to live lives that honor God and bless others.

Seventh, it is a legacy of love. Above all, a godly mother leaves a legacy of love. Her love is unconditional, sacrificial, and steadfast. It permeates every aspect of her relationship with her children, nurturing their emotional well-being, fostering security, and creating a sense of belonging. Her love reflects the love of God, pointing her children to the ultimate source of love and shaping their understanding of God's love for them.

Reflect on the sevenfold legacies of a godly mother, honor and cherish their incredible influence in our lives. Recognize the profound impact of their faith, prayers, sacrifice, teaching, encouragement, example, and love. Express gratitude for the godly mothers who have shaped us and continue to inspire us with their unwavering devotion. Remember our responsibility to carry them forward. Eemulate her virtues and pass on her legacy to the next generation. The sevenfold legacies of a godly mother remind us of mothers' incredible impact on the world.

Sermon #98: A Godly Heritage

A godly heritage encompasses several key elements. First and foremost, it is built upon a strong foundation of faith in a higher power or religious beliefs passed down through generations. Morality and ethics play a significant role in instilling virtues such as honesty, integrity, compassion, justice, forgiveness, and respect for others. Prayer and devotion are central to fostering a deeper connection with the divine. Sacred texts and scriptures are studied and passed down, providing guidance and wisdom. Active involvement in a religious community or fellowship provides support, accountability, and opportunities for spiritual growth. Acts of service and compassion towards others reflect selflessness and empathy, while love and forgiveness form the bedrock of harmonious relationships and healing.

Out text captures King David's goodly heritage: "The lines have fallen to me in pleasant places; indeed, my heritage is beautiful to me." (Psalm 16:6). First, it is a heritage of divine provision. The psalmist acknowledges that the "lines have fallen to me in pleasant places." This statement implies that God has provided for them, assigning a favorable portion or inheritance. Therefore, one element of a godly heritage is recognizing and appreciating God's provisions and blessings.

.s a heritage of contentment and gratitude.
almist expresses that their heritage is "beautiful"
them, indicating contentment and gratitude. A godly
heritage involves cultivating a thankful heart and
finding beauty and fulfillment in what God has provided
rather than seeking worldly possessions or pursuits.

Third, it is a heritage of trust in God's guidance. The
psalm conveys the psalmist's trust in God's guidance
and protection. This underlying theme suggests that an
element of a godly heritage is placing trust in God's
leading, relying on His wisdom and guidance in every
aspect of life.

Fourth, it is a heritage that relies on God's presence. The
psalmist seeks refuge in God, saying, "I have set the
Lord always before me" (Psalm 16:8). A godly heritage
involves acknowledging and depending on God's
presence, seeking Him as a constant companion, and
finding solace and strength in His nearness.

Fifth, it is a heritage that rejects idolatry. Within the
broader context of the psalm, the psalmist renounces
the worship of other gods and expresses loyalty to the
one true God. Therefore, an element of a godly heritage
includes steadfast devotion to God and rejecting
idolatry and false gods.

While Psalm 16:6 doesn't explicitly outline a
comprehensive list of elements for a godly heritage,
these insights help us understand the themes and
attitudes that contribute to a godly life and heritage
within the context of the psalm. What is your heritage
like?

Sermon #99: The Enlightened Elites

Enlightened elites refer to individuals or groups with a higher level of knowledge, understanding, wisdom, or enlightenment in a particular domain. These individuals are often seen as leaders or influencers who have gained deep insights into social, cultural, philosophical, or spiritual matters and are driven by a sense of purpose to contribute positively to society. They exhibit critical thinking, open-mindedness, empathy, and a strong ethical compass. Enlightened elites are not solely focused on personal gain but strive to use their knowledge and influence to bring about positive change, inspire others, and promote the well-being of individuals and communities. They may contribute through intellectual pursuits, innovative ideas, social activism, philanthropy, or spiritual teachings, among other avenues. Moses of the Old Testament and Gen as a generation are enlightened elites.

Moses is an example of an enlightened elite in the Bible (Exodus 9:1). First, he led the Israelites through the Red Sea. One of Moses' most famous acts was parting the waters of the Red Sea, allowing the Israelites to escape from the pursuing Egyptian army. This miraculous event demonstrated God's power and marked a significant moment in the liberation of the Israelites.
Second, he received the Ten Commandments. Moses ascended Mount Sinai and received the Ten Commandments directly from God. These commandments, encompassing principles of moral and

ıct, formed the foundation of religious and
ıws for the Israelites and profoundly influenced
ʊ-Christian traditions.

Third, he guided the Israelites in the wilderness. Moses served as a leader and guide during the Israelites' journey through the wilderness. He provided direction, settled disputes, and conveyed God's instructions to the people, ensuring their physical and spiritual well-being during their 40 years of wandering. Fourth, he established the Tabernacle: Moses played a pivotal role in constructing and establishing the Tabernacle, a portable sanctuary where the Israelites worshipped and offered sacrifices to God. He received detailed instructions from God on its design and function, solidifying a central place of worship for the Israelite community.

Fifth, he interceded for the Israelites. On multiple occasions, Moses interceded with God on behalf of the Israelites, seeking forgiveness and mercy. His role as a mediator and advocate demonstrated his deep care and concern for his people, highlighting his compassion and desire for their well-being. Sixth, he confronted Pharaoh and advocated for liberation: Moses confronted Pharaoh, the Egyptian ruler and demanded the release of the Israelites from slavery. Through a series of plagues and demonstrations of God's power, Moses stood as a voice for justice and freedom, ultimately leading to the Israelites' liberation from Egyptian bondage.

Seventh, he instituted a system of governance: Moses established a system of governance among the Israelites, appointing leaders and judges to help administer justice and resolve disputes. This organizational structure provided a framework for maintaining order and ensuring fairness within the community.

Gen Z and the Enlightened Elites

As the current generation, Gen Z has the potential to be agents of change and influence society in numerous ways. First, they are enlightened elites in their activism and advocacy, and Gen Z has shown a strong inclination towards activism and advocating for social and environmental justice. They can use their voices and platforms to raise awareness, mobilize communities, and push for meaningful changes in climate change, racial equality, LGBTQ+ rights, gun control, and more. Second, they use technological Innovations effectively. Gen Z is often called "digital natives" due to their fluency in technology. They can harness their technical skills and knowledge to drive Innovation, create disruptive solutions, and address pressing societal challenges in healthcare, education, sustainability, and accessibility.

Third, they are social entrepreneurs. Gen Z has a growing interest in social entrepreneurship, combining business acumen with a focus on social and environmental impact. They can start businesses or nonprofit organizations prioritizing ethical practices, sustainability, and initiatives addressing societal issues. Fourth, they are mental health advocates. Gen Z has experienced increased awareness and discussions around mental health issues. They can actively promote mental health awareness, advocate for accessible and affordable

.hcare, combat stigma, and foster supportive .uties prioritizing well-being.

Fifth, they are political engagement. Gen Z has shown a heightened interest in politics and civic engagement. They can actively participate in democratic processes, exercise their voting rights, engage in political campaigns, and use their voices to shape policies and advocate for changes in areas that align with their values. Sixth, they use cultural and Interfaith dialogue. Gen Z embraces diversity and values inclusivity. They can foster cultural understanding, promote dialogue among different communities, and work towards building bridges of understanding and empathy across cultures, religions, and backgrounds.

Seventh, they understand sustainable Living. Gen Z has a deep concern for the environment and sustainability. They can drive change by adopting and promoting sustainable lifestyles, advocating for renewable energy, reducing waste, supporting eco-friendly initiatives, and raising awareness about the importance of environmental conservation.

God elevated one deliverer in Moses; now he raises many deliverers in Gen Z. With Gen Z activated, it's time to let my people go!

Sermon #100: A Time for Growth

Luke 2:52 is a powerful statement about the growth and development of Jesus Christ Himself. It reads, "And Jesus increased in wisdom and stature, and in favor with God and man." From these words, we can extract seven imperatives that provide profound insights into our personal growth and development as followers of Christ. Join me as we embark on a journey through the Seven Imperatives of Growth.

First, there is the imperative of wisdom. As Jesus grew, He increased in wisdom. Wisdom encompasses knowledge and the ability to discern and apply that knowledge in a righteous and meaningful way. Just as Jesus sought wisdom, we, too, must pursue wisdom diligently. This imperative urges us to be lifelong learners, to immerse ourselves in God's Word, and to seek guidance from the Holy Spirit in all our decisions.

Second, there is the imperative of stature. Jesus also increased in stature, referring to physical growth and his overall development. People should nurture their physical bodies, recognizing they are temples of the Holy Spirit. This imperative challenges us to prioritize self-care, exercise, healthy habits, and the responsible stewardship of our bodies.

Third, there is the imperative of favor with God. Luke tells us that Jesus increased in favor with God. As

'hrist, our ultimate goal is to please and
ʰ our lives. It is an imperative that
.ℯ importance of cultivating a deep, intimate
.ɪship with our Heavenly Father through prayer,
ʋrship, obedience, and a heart that longs to align with
His will.

Fourth, there is the imperative of Favor with Man: Jesus also grew in favor with man. While our primary focus is on our relationship with God, we must not neglect our interactions with others. This imperative reminds us of the significance of demonstrating Christ-like love, compassion, forgiveness, and humility toward our fellow human beings. By doing so, we can build bridges and be agents of reconciliation and unity in a divided world.

Fifth, there is the imperative of emotional growth. Although not explicitly mentioned in the verse, we can infer that Jesus experienced emotional growth during His earthly journey and encountered various emotions, including joy, sorrow, anger, and compassion. This imperative challenges us to develop emotional intelligence, acknowledge and process our feelings, and allow the Holy Spirit to transform our hearts and attitudes.

Sixth, there is the imperative of spiritual maturity. Jesus, being fully God and fully man, demonstrated remarkable spiritual maturity. This imperative calls us to deepen our spiritual lives by developing spiritual disciplines such as meditation, fasting, and solitude. It prompts us to seek spiritual mentors and fellowship with other believers, providing opportunities for accountability, discipleship, and growth in our faith.

Seventh, there is the imperative of impactful living. Lastly, Jesus' growth was not just for personal development but also for impacting the world around Him, and he came to bring salvation, healing, and transformation to humanity. This imperative reminds us that our growth is not meant to be self-centered but rather to equip us to fulfill our God-given purpose. We are called to be salt and light, serving others, sharing the good news, and making a positive difference in our communities and beyond.

The journey of growth is a lifelong process. As we reflect on the Seven Imperatives of Growth derived from Luke 2:52, let us commit ourselves to cultivate wisdom, nurturing our physical bodies, seeking favor with God and man, embracing emotional growth, pursuing spiritual maturity, and living impactfully. May the example of Jesus Christ inspire us to strive for growth in all areas of our lives, knowing that through our growth, we can bring glory to God and bless those around us.

Spiritual death occurs due to stagnation, where individuals fail to grow spiritually, remaining stagnant in their faith and unable to deepen their understanding of God. It also includes a lack of purpose, where individuals may struggle to discern their spiritual calling, resulting in a lack of direction. Moreover, spiritual death involves a sense of disconnection from God, oneself, and others, leading to isolation, loneliness, and despair. Ultimately, failing to grow spiritually can result in negative outcomes such as physical limitations, increased vulnerability to disease, reduced life expectancy, a sense of purposelessness, disconnection, and an inability to overcome life's trials. Prioritizing both physical and spiritual growth is crucial for a healthy and fulfilling life.

References

Asimov, I. (1980, January 21). A Cult of Ignorance. Newsweek, 19.

Backley, S. (Year). The Champion in All of Us: 12 Rules for Success. Publisher.

Hedegard, D., & Taylor, S. (2013). WHEN God INTERVENES: An extraordinary story of faith, hope, and the power of prayer. Tyndale House Publishers, Inc.